THE NEW INVITATION TO ANTHROPOLOGY

Fifth Edition

Luke Eric Lassiter
Eric I. Karchmer
Dana E. Powell

ROWMAN & LITTLEFIELD
Lanham • Boulder • New York • London

Senior Acquisitions Editor: Alyssa Palazzo
Assistant Acquisitions Editor: Samantha Delwarte
Sales and Marketing Inquiries: textbooks@rowman.com

Credits and acknowledgments for material borrowed from other sources, and reproduced with permission, appear on the appropriate pages within the text.

Published by Rowman & Littlefield
An imprint of The Rowman & Littlefield Publishing Group, Inc.
4501 Forbes Boulevard, Suite 200, Lanham, Maryland 20706
www.rowman.com

86-90 Paul Street, London EC2A 4NE

British Library Cataloguing in Publication Information Available

Library of Congress Cataloging-in-Publication Data
Names: Lassiter, Luke E., author. | Karchmer, Eric I., author. | Powell, Dana E., 1973– author.
Title: The new invitation to anthropology / Luke Eric Lassiter, Eric I. Karchmer, Dana E. Powell.
Other titles: Invitation to anthropology
Description: Fifth edition. | Lanham, Maryland : Rowman & Littlefield, 2024. | Revised editon of: Invitation to anthropology. Fourth edition. 2014. | Includes bibliographical references and index.
Identifiers: LCCN 2023030280 (print) | LCCN 2023030281 (ebook) | ISBN 9781442277144 (cloth) | ISBN 9781442277151 (paperback) | ISBN 9781442277168 (epub)
Subjects: LCSH: Anthropology.
Classification: LCC GN25 .L37 2024 (print) | LCC GN25 (ebook) | DDC 301—dc23/ eng/20230710
LC record available at https://lccn.loc.gov/2023030280
LC ebook record available at https://lccn.loc.gov/2023030281

∞™ The paper used in this publication meets the minimum requirements of American National Standard for Information Sciences—Permanence of Paper for Printed Library Materials, ANSI/NISO Z39.48-1992.

Cover Image: Dragon at Wat Huay Pla Kang, located in Chiang Rai, Thailand

Contents

Preface

It has been ten years since the publication of the last edition of *Invitation to Anthropology*. To say that a lot has happened in the world in this intervening period feels like an understatement. Our goal with this fifth edition, titled *The New Invitation to Anthropology*, was to better link the key concepts and principles of anthropology to recent social and political events as well as to other changes in media, technology, and society that students know best. At the same time, our intent was to maintain the accessible style of the book that made earlier editions popular and pedagogically useful. Professors and others familiar with earlier editions will notice that the overall structure of the book remains the same, but within each chapter there are significant revisions and updates, which we outline for you below.

The first major change in this edition is the authorship. The original author, Luke Eric Lassiter, has been joined by Eric I. Karchmer and Dana E. Powell. Both Karchmer and Powell had been using *Invitation* in their introductory anthropology courses at Appalachian State University for many years. When Lassiter approached them about collaborating on the fifth edition, they were delighted to bring their classroom experience with the text to the new edition. As part of their efforts, Karchmer and Powell also recruited a select group of undergraduate students—majors and recent graduates of the anthropology department at Appalachian State University—to intensively review the fourth-edition text and offer suggestions on updates, with an eye toward issues of inclusivity, diversity, and contemporaneity. We would like to thank our former students Hannah Bennett, Will Riedlinger, Gabrielle

Timbrook, Rachelle Trouten, Edgar Villeda, and Leah Wilson for their valuable contributions to the fifth edition. Karchmer and Powell of course also brought their own respective expertise to this project. Karchmer is a medical anthropologist, specialist in China and East Asia, and a scholar and practitioner of Chinese medicine; Powell is an environmental anthropologist, specialist in Native American / Indigenous Studies and political ecology, and an advocate of collaborative and experimental ethnography.

Before detailing some of the important changes in the book, we feel it is vital to be clear about what remains the same. We know that continuity will be important for instructors who have already adopted earlier editions for their courses. First, we kept the chapter order and themes the same as the fourth edition; many of the specific chapter sections also remain, although new ones have also been added and a few have been removed. Second, we also retained most key concepts and definitions from the fourth edition. We were a little less conservative with key terms (signified by bolded text), trimming away some terms that felt extraneous while adding new ones that seemed important for anthropology in the 2020s. Finally, we tried to keep the clear, accessible writing style of Lassiter's early editions; this last point has proven year after year to be one reason that professors and students alike supported the adoption of this book. With that said, Lassiter's folksy tone may be diminished in this edition, as Karchmer and Powell brought their own voices and perspectives to the text. Nonetheless, we all worked hard to keep the text approachable, to stay true to the goal of "inviting" students into this dynamic discipline.

With regard to specific changes, some of the most significant new additions will be found in part II, but the more comprehensive revisions are contained in part I. As with earlier editions, part I, "Anthropology, Culture, and Ethnography," focuses on the key concepts and methodologies of cultural anthropology, but we felt it was important to better situate these chapters within their historical context, while also relating them to current events.

Chapter 1 has been renamed "The Origins of North American Anthropology: Colonialism, Change, and the Critique of Race." We begin with a more in-depth look at how modern anthropology emerges out of nineteenth-century theories of race and social evolutionism. This historical context helps to better highlight Franz Boas's critique of race and his contributions to anthropology's definition of culture. Chapter 2, "Anthropology and Culture," does not depart radically from the fourth edition. We still focus on the concept of culture and its implications. At the same time, however, we feel our definitions are clarified by the contextualizing work of chapter 1 and further refined by our examples. In chapter 3, "Ethnography," we also try to better situate the methodological innovations of Bronislaw Malinowski within his historical circumstances. Inspired by the suggestions of our student reviewers, we also gave greater attention to ethnography as written genre and its more contemporary innovations.

Some of the most exciting new material can be found in part II, which has been renamed "Key Themes in Cultural Anthropology." Chapter 4 remains the most sweeping of all the chapters, tracing the origins of the contemporary world system from the agricultural revolution, ten thousand years ago. We have renamed it "Cultural Adaption and Globalization: The Roots of Our World System," and we have added new material on social class and globalization. The chapter concludes with a discussion of how contemporary anthropologists are exploring the problems of climate change and environmental destruction.

In recent years, we have all witnessed remarkable cultural changes in the realm of gender and sexuality. As a result, we gave careful attention to the revisions of chapter 5, now named "Sex, Gender, and Inequality: Cross-Cultural Perspectives." We updated and refined the discussion on sex and gender as foundational concepts for this field. We also expanded our discussion of gender-based inequality by including an introduction to the concept of intersectionality. Given the significant changes to the previous two chapters, we decided to leave chapter 6 on kinship, "Works, Success, and Kids: On Marriage, Family, and Kinship," more or less unchanged in the fifth edition. Chapter 7, "Beyond Universal Truth: Anthropological Approaches to Religion, Healing, and Knowledge," on knowledge and belief, had been the shortest chapter. For the fifth edition, we extended the analysis of these key terms by first providing a historical examination of the anthropological contributions of E. E. Evans-Pritchard. Then we broadened the application of these concepts beyond the original topic of religion to also explore the anthropological study of medicine, healing, and knowledge.

Lastly, the visual layout of the book will also be somewhat different. We continue to be grateful to the photographic contributions of Danny Gawlowski, award-winning photojournalist and assistant managing editor for the

Seattle Times. We have also incorporated images from our own fieldwork, as well as those of other anthropologists. We have also given special attention to the text boxes that were called "Anthropology Here and Now" in the fourth edition. In this edition, we have tried to revise and reposition these narrative breaks as more than mere supplementary updates on the discipline. Rather, we hope that instructors and students will use them as stepping-off points for the exploration of themes in the main text through specific case studies. Each text box now has its own title and sometimes accompanying images to help draw the reader in.

In all of these revisions, we have tried to remain true to the original vision of *Invitation to Anthropology*, as a story about the complicated but hopeful emergence of a new academic discipline. Although born within and against the violence of European colonial conquest, anthropology has aspired to understand the diversity of the human experience in ethical and transformative ways, even if it has not always lived up to these ideals. Through the combined voices of three authors, we hope that this new edition will provide a richer and more nuanced story about anthropology, one that will better guide its readers in their own explorations of human diversity.

I

ANTHROPOLOGY, CULTURE, AND ETHNOGRAPHY

The Origins of North American Anthropology

Colonialism, Change, and the Critique of Race

STORYTELLING

Simply put, **anthropology** is the study of human beings in all of their biological and cultural complexities, both past and present. But what exactly does this mean? What do anthropologists actually know, and what do they do? Who are anthropologists, what is their philosophy or outlook, and why do they choose this particular area of study? We plan to address all of these topics in this book, but think it best to begin with a story: a narrative about why and how anthropology as a field of study emerged in the first place, in a certain place and time. And, like all good stories, this one has numerous plot twists, complex characters, and many important lessons worthy of our attention.

We begin with a story because stories are a powerful way to get our attention, but also because we believe that anthropologists, at their best, are storytellers. Anthropologists tell powerful stories about the nature of the human experience. Walter Benjamin, a German literary scholar of the early twentieth century, instructed us that storytelling is not passing along "information," but is a creative practice of poetic engagement, with every story shaped by the teller themselves and thus transformed through the telling.[1] Anthropologists strive to do just that: tell stories that are both our own and not our own, that emerge from relationships we have with persons, communities, landscapes, texts, images, and artifacts over long periods of time.

The story we wish to tell here is about the origin of the discipline of anthropology itself. We recognize that this story, like all stories, will bear the imprint of its tellers, as Benjamin reminded us. That's not because our story will be deceptive in any obvious way; rather, it will reflect each of our own engagements with the complex origins of our profession. We hope that the multiplicity of authors in this edition of the book will create a polyphonic mode of storytelling, drawing on our similar but also very different experiences as anthropologists trained in North America, with alliances and influences that range across the globe. Through this story of American anthropology that we share below, we hope to draw you into the field—to "invite" you into the world of anthropology—to experience its richness, and perhaps to make your own contributions to this ongoing and unfinished narrative.[2]

This is a truly exciting time for anthropology, but that does not mean scholars agree about the significance of anthropology's origin story—or even that there is a singular "origin." As we will see, the founding and early development of the discipline was led predominantly by White men conducting research in colonial contexts. Some scholars have argued that the power inequalities of these beginnings led to biased perspectives that the discipline has never overcome. One scholar has even made the "case for letting anthropology burn," so to speak.[3] We share a hopeful interpretation of anthropology's complex and imperfect origin story and are inspired by development in the late twentieth and early twenty-first centuries. Anthropology is now practiced by scholars all over the world, from increasingly diverse backgrounds. Although the discipline emerged out of European imperialism, anthropology today is bringing exciting insights to the many social, political, health, and environmental crises that confront people all around the globe.

THE SETTING: EUROPEAN CONQUEST OF THE AMERICAS AND THE WORLD

Anthropology is a relatively young field that emerged as an academic discipline in the late nineteenth and early twentieth centuries. But its roots go back to the beginnings of European imperialism, to the colonizing "voyages of conquest" from the fifteenth through seventeenth centuries. These events set in motion a cascade of global transformations, leading to the subjugations of Indigenous peoples, the destruction of preexisting political structures, the transformation of local communities and lifeways, the seizure of land, a transoceanic trade of enslaved humans, and the creation of vast global networks of trade. By the late nineteenth century, it had culminated in the colonization of the vast majority of the peoples of the world. There is no way to capture in a few sentences how radically the world was altered by these centuries of domination by a small

ANTHROPOLOGY HERE AND NOW

Types of Colonialization

Colonialism is not only the central historical backdrop for the emergence of the discipline of anthropology, but the consequences of this multi-century event remain with us today. Scholars of colonialism make a useful distinction about two basic forms of colonial regimes that can help us better understand the conditions under which anthropologists work. One type of colonialism, known as **settler colonialism**, has been described perhaps most famously by the Australian scholar Patrick Wolfe, whose work has been influential for anthropologists. This form of colonialism refers to the colonial processes in regions, such as the Americas, Australia, New Zealand, and a few areas in Africa. A driving principle of settler colonialism is that Europeans sought to seize land from Indigenous peoples and invariably adopted a "logic of elimination," driving Native peoples off the desired land and often killing them in the process. By the turn of the twentieth century, when Franz Boas and other early anthropologists were encountering the Indigenous populations of North America, they were working with the historical descendants and survivors of the violent, sometimes genocidal, practices of settler colonialist regimes.

Other parts of the world, in particular, Africa and Asia, became entangled in another type of colonial domination, often called **extractive colonialism**. These colonies were generally part of the nineteenth-century acceleration of European imperialism. But unlike settler colonies, new colonies in Africa and Asia were integrated into the rapid growth of the market-based, capitalist economies of Europe. The colonial regimes in these areas were not oriented toward seizing land from Indigenous peoples but instead toward "extracting" natural resources from these areas. These regimes were not genocidal like settler colonies, but they could be ruthless and brutal in other ways that had enormous consequences for the Native people of these colonies. There is a large and growing body of literature on the ongoing impacts of extractive colonialism and how it inexorably pulled far-flung regions of the world into the metropolitan concerns of their European masters.

One early pioneer in this field of research was the scholar and activist Walter Rodney. Born to a working-class, African-Caribbean family in British Guyana, Rodney earned a PhD from the School of Oriental and African Studies in London when he was just twenty-four years old. He later wrote a groundbreaking book, *How Europe Underdeveloped Africa*, on the devastating consequences of European imperialism in Africa, arguing that colonial policies undermined the social, economic, and political development of African societies. Even women's status and the general health of African peoples, he argued, had been impoverished by colonization. Rodney traveled widely in Africa and the Caribbean and was also known as a great orator and political organizer. Tragically, he was assassinated in British Guyana at the age of thirty-eight for his political views. His work and activism continue to inspire contemporary research on colonialism and its ongoing effects.

For more on these two scholars, check out these sources:

Walter Rodney, *How Europe Underdeveloped Africa* (Brooklyn, NY: Verso, 2018 [1972]).

Patrick Wolfe, "Settler Colonialism and the Elimination of the Native," *Journal of Genocide Research* 8.4 (2006): 387–409.

number of Western European nations—Britain, France, Belgium, Portugal, Spain, the Netherlands, Italy, and Germany (and joined by Japan in the late nineteenth century)—so we want to focus on what these historical facts meant for European thinkers and, ultimately, for the new field of anthropology.

One of the most striking dimensions revealed by these expanding European empires was the vast human and environmental diversity of the world. These discoveries raised questions for Europeans, such as how other peoples and places are related—or unrelated—to the world that Europeans had previously taken for granted. Such questions did not alter the dynamics of imperialism. The expansion of empires was driven by economic and political ambitions to acquire wealth and power by monopolizing "natural resources" from faraway lands (from camphor to quinine, from humans to timber), a process driven by "God, Gold, and Glory" and reliant upon the dehumanization and objectification of non-European places and peoples. Nonetheless, these questions ultimately led scholars by the mid-nineteenth century to begin seriously exploring the relations of Europeans to a world that was far more complex than previously thought. For the emerging field of anthropology, these investigations proceeded in two basic directions: One was the exploration of race, the supposed biological diversity of human beings; and the other was culture, the wide range of ways in which humans lived and associated with one another. In this chapter, we focus on the question of race, and take up the question of culture in chapter 2.

STASIS AND CHANGE IN EUROPEAN THOUGHT

The issue of human biological diversity was not new in the nineteenth century, when the field of anthropology began to take shape. European colonizers had been interacting with the Indigenous peoples of the Americas—through trade, conquest, enslavement, land theft, and mass killings—since the arrival of Columbus in 1492. By 1517, Europeans were bringing enslaved Africans with them to the Americas, creating an involuntary diaspora of global magnitude.

European ways of thinking about human difference were radically altered in the mid-nineteenth century by naturalist Charles Darwin and his interest in the problem of evolutionary change. With his groundbreaking book, *The Origin of Species*, in 1859, Darwin's theory of evolution would reverberate throughout the scientific community, impacting nearly all aspects of European thought, including the emerging field of anthropology.

Darwin argued that we live in a world of constant change. This may appear obvious to modern observers, who can easily see, for example, technology and pop culture change right before our very eyes.

While we may take the idea of change for granted today, this was not so in the past. Well into the eighteenth and nineteenth centuries, people in the Western world (Europe and North America) generally tended to see the Earth as unchanged since creation. They understood their world through a fixed order created by God, called the **Great Chain of Being**.[4]

The Great Chain of Being was an assumption on the part of Europeans about stasis or stability rather than change or evolution. This theory assumed

The process of change is all around us. The small islands that make up the Outer Banks of North Carolina, for example, are slowly shifting westward, like many so-called barrier island systems along North America's Atlantic coast. Although North Carolina's famed Cape Hatteras Lighthouse (the tallest lighthouse in the United States) was originally built over a quarter of a mile away from the ocean in 1870, by the late twentieth century the ocean had reached and begun to erode the building's founda-tion. It faced imminent destruction. In 1999, the lighthouse was moved on a large plat-form (center) one-half mile inland. It will need to be moved still farther inland in about a hundred years. Photo courtesy of the North Carolina Department of Transportation

that the world was only a few thousand years old, that its fundamental design had always existed as God had created it, and that it had changed little since creation. Furthermore, God had created everything on the planet within an eternal hierarchy. Thus, all things abided somewhere on a scale of perfec-tion, from minerals and plants on the bottom to insects, reptiles, and lower mammals, respectively, to human beings, who were just below the angels, who were, in turn, under (one) God—who was, of course, at the very top, for Europeans. In the Western world, many early scientists sought to elaborate God's plan as they collected plants and animals from around the world.

To better understand what the Great Chain of Being meant for European thinkers, and its assumptions about human biological diversity, we can con-sider the work of the famous naturalist, Carolus Linnaeus, who developed

The Great Chain of Being was a classical conception of the metaphysical order that portrayed the universe according to a gradient of existence, from lower forms like minerals all the way up to God, the most divine form of being. This image is a reproduction from Didacus Valades's Rhetorica Christiana, published in 1579. Pictorial Press Ltd. / Alamy Stock Photo the classification system we today call **taxonomy,** or **Linnaean hierarchy** (kingdom, phylum, class, order, family, genus, and species). His most lasting achievement was the creation of the binomial system of scientific nomenclature, which is still in use today. In addition to classifying plants and animals according to his binomial system, Linnaeus applied it to humans in the 1758 edition of *System of Nature*. Here is how Linnaeus defined the four human "races" and their characteristics:

Homo sapiens europaeus (aka, "white Europeans")
White, serious, strong. Hair blond, flowing. Eyes blue. Active, very smart, inventive. Covered by tight clothing. Ruled by laws.

Homo sapiens asiaticus (aka, "yellow Asians")
Yellow, melancholy, greedy. Hair black. Eyes dark. Severe, haughty, desirous. Covered by loose garments. Ruled by opinion.

Homo sapiens americanus (aka, "red Americans")
Red, ill-tempered, subjugated. Hair black, straight, thick. Nostrils wide; face harsh, beard scanty. Obstinate, contented, free. Paints himself with red lines. Ruled by custom.

Homo sapiens afer (aka, "black Africans")
Black, impassive, lazy. Hair kinked. Skin silky. Nose flat. Lips thick. Women with genital flap; breasts large. Crafty, slow, foolish. Anoints himself with grease. Ruled by caprice.[5]

Linnaeus was among the first to define race for the scientific community, and he did so squarely in the historical context of colonialism. European colonization of the Americas was already into its third century at that point and starting to become more entrenched in other parts of the world. The kind of assumptions expressed by Linnaeus, in which White Europeans were depicted as "serious and strong" and all other races were "melancholy and greedy" or "ill-tempered and subjugated" or "impassive and lazy," clearly reflect an assumption of European superiority. Moreover, this system of ranking also reflects an assumption about the fixed order of life, much like the gradations found in the Great Chain of Being. What's significant for our story is that these so-called classifications became even more pernicious and dangerous in the aftermath of Darwin's theory of evolution.

ANTHROPOLOGY HERE AND NOW

Discussion Question

Linnaeus's categorization of four human races clearly goes well beyond what we would consider today to be "biological" distinctions. Look closely at how Linnaeus distinguishes between the supposed four human races. What characteristics would you consider biological, psychological, behavioral, social, and so on by today's standards? How does Linnaeus's description of the four races seem to relate to the Great Chain of Being? In what ways are our contemporary ideas about race different or similar?

DARWIN AND THE QUESTION OF CHANGE

The Great Chain of Being was a philosophy rooted in deeply held religious beliefs about the biblical account of the origins of life. It obviously left little room for thinking about change in the world. It would take the work of many great scientists to dislodge it. One of the most prominent challengers to this previous interpretation of planetary history was a Scottish geologist by the name of Sir Charles Lyell, who wrote *Principles of Geology* (which he revised eleven times between 1830 and 1872). He advanced a geological theory that the Earth's physical features resulted from steady, gradual processes of change. Basing his conclusions on close observation of geological forms, he argued that the Earth was much older than Europeans had previously thought—not thousands but millions of years old. Slow, steady change was a constant process on planet Earth; geological forms had not existed unchanged for thousands of years just as God had created them. Geological forms (say, the Grand Canyon) were created by years and years of natural wear and tear. One geological form, Lyell suggested, is constantly giving way to another.

Lyell really rocked his world. It may not seem like much today, but at the midpoint of the nineteenth century—during the height of the Atlantic slave trade, the US policy of "Manifest Destiny," and the seizure of Native American lands by settlers—the debate about stasis and change was among the hottest going (with Western intellectuals, that is). And for good reason. Among Lyell's most important ideas was that geological change, although continuous, is nondirectional and nonprogressive. Lyell's close observations revealed that there seemed neither rhyme nor reason to the changes in geological forms. To suggest that change was random and directionless and that perhaps God had little interest in it was serious, indeed.

Charles Lyell's work had a major influence on British naturalist Charles Darwin and his own theory about *biological* change. Long before Darwin, many philosophers, writers, and scientists (including Charles Darwin's grandfather, Erasmus Darwin) had begun to think about what made biological change—or **evolution**—work. But it was not until Charles Darwin wrote *On the Origin of Species* in 1859 that a theory of evolution gained acceptance—that is, Darwin's observations did more than anyone else's to explain what made change work for living organisms. His theory of evolution became part of the historical context for our story, when new fields of study were emerging at what Comanche critic Paul Chaat Smith has called "the most profound encounter in human history."[6]

It is also important to recognize that the global sea voyages of "discovery" also created the conditions for Darwin to develop his theory of evolutionary change. Wind-powered seafaring vessels were the key technology granting Europeans military and scientific access to antipodal locations and populations. It was also the very technology that enabled Darwin's profoundly influential, five-year voyage on the HMS *Beagle* during the 1830s, which took him to the Galapagos Islands in South America, where he observed a surprising diversity of species and began formulating his theory of biological evolution. Ultimately, Darwin suggested that changes in the environment wielded a pressure on all living things to change so that they might survive to reproduce. Much like a breeder who wields pressure on farm or domestic animals by intentionally selecting for desired traits, Darwin argued that the natural environment exerted a similar pressure on all organisms. In a changing environment, traits that enabled reproduction would be passed on to the next generation; traits that impeded reproduction would not.

Darwin called this pressure to survive and reproduce **natural selection**. "As many more individuals of each species are born than can possibly survive," wrote Darwin, "and as, consequently, there is a frequently recurring struggle for existence, it follows that any being, if it vary however slightly in any manner profitable to itself, under the complex and sometimes varying conditions of life, will have a better chance of surviving, and thus be *naturally selected*. From the strong principle of inheritance, any selected variety will tend to propagate its new and modified form" [emphasis in original].[7]

Darwin observed how farmers and animal breeders selected certain traits to create new breeds of plants and animals. The breeding of dogs is a classic example of what Darwin called "artificial selection." Dogs have been bred to serve many purposes, from hunting, to sheep herding, to home protection, and much more. Darwin reasoned that the natural world operated in a similar manner on all organisms. mart_m / iStock

NATURAL SELECTION: THE STORY OF THE PEPPERED MOTHS

A central element of Darwin's theory of evolution is that, like Lyell's geological change, there is no endpoint or goal of evolution. Organisms adapt to their environments, but there is no moral judgment attached to this process. Unlike the Great Chain of Being, there is no such thing as higher or lower forms of evolution according to Darwin. Unfortunately, this point was misunderstood by countless followers of Darwin with tragic implications for the question of race. But before we turn to this more distressing part of our story, it is important to explore Darwin's theory of natural selection.

Take this classic example. In Manchester, England, the lives of peppered moths have been heavily documented. Prior to 1900, within the population of peppered moths, the vast majority were lightly peppered, but a very few were heavily peppered in their pigmentation. After 1900, however, the population changed. The more heavily peppered moths—that is, the darker-shaded ones— were now in the majority, and a very few lightly peppered moths occurred in the population (only about 5 percent). In the 1960s, the peppered moth population began to change back to the pigmentation ratio seen prior to 1900.

The peppered moth can have varying degrees of darker and lighter coloration.
Nature Photographers Ltd / Alamy Stock Photo

What is going on here? Obviously, the population's makeup is changing. But what is *causing* the population to change? Well, natural selection is what is going on here: A change in the environment wielded a pressure that forced a change.

Here's the big picture. Prior to 1900, all peppered moths produced both lightly and heavily peppered moths as offspring, but the lightly peppered moths were in the majority—in other words, "parent peppered moths" could expect to have several lightly peppered "baby moths" develop from their larvae, but only a few heavily peppered moths. And here's why: The heavily peppered moths (after emerging as adults) usually did not live very long. Because of their heavily peppered bodies, birds could easily detect them and pick them off as food. The lighter-shaded moths, in contrast, could easily escape detection, especially against lichen-covered trees that resembled their body color. And, because these lightly peppered moths could escape detection, they could mature and produce the next generation of moths with greater success than the heavily peppered moths.

After 1900, something happened in the cities of Britain. Industrialization was going full speed ahead. With no antipollution or clean air laws, Manchester was a dirty place indeed. Within a very short period of time the trees turned gray and black. This was a change in the environment, and it reversed the situation for peppered moths. Now birds could easily detect lightly peppered moths. The heavily peppered moths were more concealed, especially against the now-dirty, lichen-covered trees that resembled their body color.

As a result, very few light-colored moths reached maturity to produce the next generation of larvae.[8] After the 1960s, however, clean air and antipollution laws led to a cleaner Manchester, and once again, the population changed back to the form observed prior to 1900.[9]

This peppered moth story is a terribly oversimplified description of the process of natural selection, but suffice it to say that this phenotypical change in the population of peppered moths was driven by, first, a shift in the surrounding environment, and second, the ability of some individuals to reproduce and pass their adaptive success to the next generation. The process of evolution, importantly, must have something with which to work if it is to promote survival, reproduction, and change. In the case of the peppered moths, without their genetic diversity—that is, if they had had no heavily peppered moths in the population in the first place—they probably wouldn't have been able to survive after 1900 when the environment changed. This is important. The *need* for heavily peppered moths did not drive the change in the population; natural selection could work only with the available variability. This is what Darwin had in mind when he wrote that "unless profitable variations do occur, natural selection can do nothing."[10] For Darwin, then, variability and reproductive success (the ability to produce the next generation) is what ultimately made natural selection work in environments where survivability of all individuals is always limited. Importantly, without the ability to adapt to changing environments through reproductive success, every living organism faces extinction. Considering that 98 to 99 percent of all the species that have ever lived on the planet are now extinct, all living things must struggle to keep changing. Without that ability, we will quite literally cease to be.

Darwin's overarching question concerned the origin of species—how and why one species would develop into another over time. Although Darwin understood that the agent for variability and reproduction was heredity, he did not fully understand how the actual interaction of heredity with the local environment worked through the process of reproduction to create biological change. Especially since the emergence of modern genetics, the complexities of biological change are today known to be much more complicated than Darwin could have imagined. Yet at the base of our current understanding of biological change is Darwin's original idea of adaptation through natural selection. It is among the mechanisms that allow insects, for example, to adapt so successfully to insecticides—like some fruit flies that have developed over a thousandfold resistance to insecticides, some mosquitoes that have adapted insecticides as food, or the diamondback moth (a pest that threatens cotton crops), which has developed an adaptation whereby its legs actually detach when it lands on crops that have been treated with insecticides (untainted, the moth flies safely away and new legs replace the old). It is among the mechanisms that permit the flu virus—and currently the COVID-19 virus— to adapt and change as it moves through human bodies around the world.[11] It is among the mechanisms that explain why changes in the human body continue to unfold.

To be sure, this is the stuff of biological change, or, in Darwin's terms, evolution, and it has been demonstrated in the laboratory as well as observed in the natural world innumerable times.[12] While human evolution can only be observed with painstaking research that requires close examination of the fossil record, because of our long cycles of reproduction, it is much easier to track in rapidly reproducing organisms.[13] We are getting a powerful lesson in the mechanism of evolutionary change as we watch each new variant of COVID-19 emerge and sweep across the globe.

ANTHROPOLOGY HERE AND NOW

Resources on the Theory of Evolution

You can learn more about the complexities of evolution and how anthropologists and other scientists are continually expanding our understanding of life on planet Earth by accessing *Evolution: A Journey into Where We're From and Where We're Going* at www.pbs.org/wgbh/evolution. The site includes numerous resources and links to original source materials, videos, articles, and interactive pages.

This may strike you as a lot of talk about geology, biology, and evolution for a chapter meant to introduce anthropology, but ideas about change and difference are central to our story of "discovery," conquest, colonialism, and the emergence of anthropology. With the stage now set, we can turn to our story about the emergence of anthropology and one of its bleaker chapters.

SOCIAL EVOLUTION AND THE INTERPRETATION OF "RACE"

Ever since Darwin first proposed natural selection as the mechanism of change in living things, people have misunderstood it and, in some cases, abused this idea to advance social or political agendas. For most English speakers, in everyday speech, the word *evolution* often implies progress, the purposeful movement from a less advanced state to a more advanced one, from a state of imperfection to one of perfection. But for Darwin, evolution was not about "progress," and this remains the case for biologists and anthropologists today.

But where do we get the idea that evolution necessarily *implies* progress—or the unfolding movement toward "better" forms of life? This is a complex question that we cannot fully answer in this chapter, but we can show that the conflation of evolution and progress was a problem from the very beginning and led to some of the most tragic abuses of Darwin's claims.[14] British social philosopher Herbert Spencer, who was a key figure in helping to spread Darwin's theory of evolution in the late nineteenth century, summarized its main proposition as the so-called "survival of the fittest." That's right—Darwin himself did not invent the term *survival of the fittest*.[15] Although Darwin would eventually use the phrase to describe an individual's biological ability to reproduce within a breeding population, Spencer coined "survival of the fittest" to advance his own ideas about the so-called favored "races" of humanity. Significantly, Spencer used Darwin's natural selection to advance his own ideas about human social progress and white superiority, which he argued resulted from "more fit" or favored human societies and groups prevailing over less fit and less favored societies (such as Indigenous peoples of the Americas, peoples of African descent, and others from the Global South).[16]

SOCIAL EVOLUTIONISM AND SOCIAL DARWINISM

For the new field of anthropology, we can trace two important intellectual trajectories that emerged, within Euro-American thought, from the idea of evolution. The first is related to the historical development of societies and is known as **social evolution** (also called *evolutionism* or *unilineal evolution*). This theory held that all human societies passed through similar sequences or stages of development.

A powerful contributor to this new concept of social evolutionism was the early anthropologist Louis Henry Morgan, who lived in Upstate New York and was fascinated with the lives of Iroquoian peoples, whose homelands were in that region, especially their kinship relations. Based on his observations of the Iroquois and his extensive collection of writings about other Native peoples that had been observed by European colonizers, Morgan made a sweeping universalist argument, claiming that all human societies develop through distinct stages. In his 1877 book, *Ancient Society,* he argued that all human groups must progress through three basic stages: from "savagery" to "barbarianism" to "civilization." He believed that the current diversity of human life across the globe captured all the various stages of human social development, but each society was capable of changing over time, of moving up Morgan's putative ladder of evolutionary development, and toward what he and his peers saw as the pinnacle of social life: White Euro-American society.

Morgan's schema was linear, moving in one direction, which is why it is sometimes called "unilineal evolution." His ideas were modestly progressive for his day despite the obvious racism we can read into them now: He was arguing that humans were all one species, with a similar origin, traveling shared pathways ("savagery," "barbarism," and "civilization") toward increasingly "higher" levels of development. This was a departure from other nineteenth-century thinkers who argued that some non-Western / non-European peoples might in fact not be human at all, possessing a different evolutionary origin. Although Morgan was not explicitly drawing on Darwin's work, we can see how the powerful mixture of ideas about evolutionary change and progress would have lent credence to his proposition that all societies "climb" the same developmental ladder.

This is where our story takes a more ominous turn and concerns the second intellectual trajectory that emerged within Euro-American thought from the idea of evolution. Morgan's ideas about the development of societies lent a veneer of quasi-scientific justification for viewing European societies as more advanced and others as backward. But other followers of Darwin reworked his ideas in ways that had even more dangerous implications for the concept of race. Spencer's vulgarization of Darwin with his concept of "survival of the fittest" helped to create a new theory about supposed human biological differences, known as **social Darwinism**—the idea that certain races of humanity were naturally superior to others. Adherents to this idea held that the technological or material advantages of certain peoples was a mark of their evolutionary "fitness," while the disadvantages of other people indicated their lack of evolutionary fitness. For social Darwinians, government programs that offered assistance to the poor or other disadvantaged groups

When social evolutionists encountered the ruins of ancient civilizations, they often presumed that they must have been built by early European explorers and traders. That they had been built by the ancestors of local groups of so-called savages was unthinkable. Pictured here is the exterior wall and an interior passage (insert) of Great Zimbabwe, the ruins of an ancient city built in southern Africa (in the modern-day country of Zimbabwe) by Shona-speaking peoples between a thousand and seven hundred years ago. Photos by Luke Eric Lassiter

were interrupting a natural process that would lead to the ultimate elimination of the "unfit." Whereas Morgan's social evolutionism seemed to hold the possibility of social advancement, however difficult it might be, Spencer and the social Darwinists saw human social differences as an arena of biological struggle, where the weakest were doomed to die off. Social Darwinism would ultimately have an enormous effect on how people thought about "race" as a category of biological difference. Although social Darwinism has long since been debunked, its effects are still with us today in our ongoing misperceptions about the category of race.[17]

Before the eighteenth century, the term **race** was used infrequently to describe differences among human groups, but by the early 1800s the word "race" became a regular part of English speech to denote presumed biologically inferior and superior groups of people. While Europeans and Americans (and many other societies, for that matter) had indeed differentiated people based on observable phenotypical characteristics like skin color, never before had the word *race* been linked with survival of the fittest and carried such powerful social meanings. Europeans and, by extension, Euro-Americans, had come to believe that they were more advanced than their neighbors. In the historical context of colonization, European domination of other races was given a false scientific legitimacy by supposedly linking it to one of the most important scientific theories of the late nineteenth century—Darwin's theory of evolution.[18]

The problematic "logic" of social Darwinism helped to set into motion the consequences of racial thinking for the next century, and we feel its impacts even today. By the early 1900s, many people—scientists and laypersons alike—accepted that biology, behavior, mental capacity, and individual ability could be explained by a person's race, which itself could be "observed" or known by "reading" a person's phenotype. In the United States, for example, it was widely believed in the early 1900s that White Americans who had ancestry in Northern or Western Europe (except for peasant, Catholic Ireland) inherently had better genes for intellect and for disciplined, civilized behavior. It was believed that this group was *"naturally"* civilized. By contrast, African or Native Americans were inherently inferior and were *naturally* predisposed to undisciplined, uncivilized behavior. Black men and women, for instance, were widely believed to harbor in their biology an irresistible sexual urge, common—social Darwinists argued—to the "lower, inferior races." Similar racialized thinking extended to Asian populations and was tested in several high-profile cases in the US Supreme Court, where Japanese and South Asian immigrants argued unsuccessfully for their "whiteness" in order to obtain US citizenship. As far back as 1790, US Congress passed the US Nationality Act, which limited the eligibility for citizenship through naturalization to "free white persons." Immigrants who could not meet whiteness standards lost their land and were deported. Being socially and legally understood as "White" was thus required to be a US citizen—whiteness equaled citizenship—until racial restrictions to citizenship were formally removed in 1952.

Yet while some struggled to obtain citizenship, others resisted it. When citizenship was extended to Native Americans in 1924 with the US Indian Citizenship Act, many Native leaders criticized this move as part of the settler government's ongoing efforts to culturally and politically assimilate Indigenous nations and persons. Free people of color during slavery and after emancipation in 1863, and well into the "Jim Crow Era" in the early twentieth century, mounted campaigns of resistance to racialized citizenship codes. Frederick Douglass and Sojourner Truth, among many others, made this struggle for the extension of citizenship and enfranchisement across "racial lines" a central component of early movements for civil and human rights. This struggle continues to the present day as questions about racism haunt political struggles over voting rights and immigration policy.

Such racialized, biologized thinking in the nineteenth and early-twentieth centuries helped to justify a growing conviction among White supremacists that people of color were biologically and socially inferior. These beliefs were also used to justify violence. For instance, some argued that the sexual "impulses" of "inferior" races could be curtailed only by public torture and killings known as lynching, which reached an all-time high in the United States around the turn of the twentieth century. In the eight-year period between 1888 and 1896 alone, there were well over 1,500 documented lynchings.[19]

Among many repulsive and troubling things about these targeted lynchings was how they were part of a public spectacle. The pioneering Black sociologist, W. E. B. Du Bois, gave us a graphic description of one such event in 1916, when thousands came to see the lynching of a young boy, Jesse Washington, in Waco, Texas.

> While a fire was being prepared of boxes, the naked boy was stabbed and the chain put over the tree. He tried to get away, but could not. He reached up to grab the chain and they cut off his fingers. The big man struck the boy on the back of the neck with a knife just as they were pulling him up on the tree. . . . He was [then] lowered into the fire several times by means of the chain around his neck.[20]

Horrific events such as these offer potent testimony as to how widely White Americans believed in the racial inferiority of Black Americans and other people "of color," but also how White supremacists used violence as a tactic to "keep people in their place." While such events may appall us today, they were not at all unusual in the decades prior to and after the turn of the twentieth century. This was a time when newspapers, popular magazines, and movies like *Birth of a Nation* fueled growing and popular ideas about the superiority and inferiority of the so-called races. And "science," under the guise of social Darwinism, explained, rationalized, and justified these ideas.[21]

ANTHROPOLOGY HERE AND NOW

Violence against Black Americans, Past and Present

In the summer of 2020, George Floyd, a Black man, was accused of using a counterfeit twenty-dollar bill in a Minneapolis convenience store. He was detained by police officers outside the store and died as one officer, Derek Chauvin, kneeled on his neck. This scene was captured on video and ignited an outpouring of grief and protest. In the aftermath of this event, public debates about racial justice and police violence against Black people in the United States have become particularly intense. Should we see George Floyd's death as a continuation of the horrible "logic" of social Darwinism that fueled such grotesque violence against Black Americans and other people of color more than a century ago?

As we edited this book in the wake of this turmoil, we have tried to be particularly conscious of how this book can advance meaningful discussions about racial justice. We struggled for many months over whether to include the photograph below of an early-twentieth-century lynching of two Black men. This image had been used in previous editions of this book, but some students urged us to remove it because they found it too traumatic. Initially, we decided it should be removed to make the text more appropriate for an inclusive learning environment. But in the fall of 2021, authors Powell and Karchmer were both in Taiwan, where they met with Taiwanese anthropologists who have been using earlier editions of *Invitation to Anthropology* in their classrooms for years. They told us that without this image, their students could not have comprehended the violent history of racism in the United States or believed that these gruesome events actually took place. They were concerned that removing the picture would contribute to lessening, or even erasing, some of this tragic history.

These conversations were very influential for us. Given how diverse the readership of this book has become, we thought the best way to proceed was to keep the lynching image, but to juxtapose it against one of the famous murals dedicated to George Floyd. There is clearly no single way to present the violent history of racism in the United States. We hope that the tragic death of George Floyd can help us move forward with the difficult conversations about race that are clearly still very much needed.

Lynchings were very public events in America before and after the turn of the twentieth century. This famous 1930 photograph of a lynching in Marion, Indiana—witnessed by thousands—was sold and distributed as a souvenir, even finding its way onto postcards. Courtesy of Archives and Special Collections, Ball State University

Following the violent and tragic death of George Floyd while being detained by police in the summer of 2020, protesters expressed their outrage through vigils and artwork, such as the mural above. According to the George Floyd and Anti-Racist Street Art Database, Floyd's death has been commemorated by 2,700 pieces of public art, a testament to the social impact of the event. munshots / Unsplash

There was more. If superior and inferior races existed as biological facts, it followed, with this logic, that the races should not mix. If they did, the inferior races would "taint" the superior ones. The United States had already implemented miscegenation laws prohibiting the marriage of White people and people of color that dated back to the early nineteenth century. But after 1900, many White Americans became increasingly worried that the "lower races" and immigrant groups from Eastern and Southern Europe were contaminating American society, diminishing its competitive fitness. Was there a way, they wondered, that America could weed out "unfit" people from the gene pool? The answer was called **eugenics**, a popular movement that focused on the selective breeding of the "fittest" people and the weeding out of "unfit" people.[22]

In the United States, both state and federal governments implemented policies to forcibly sterilize those deemed "unfit" or of "inferior stock." People of color were not the only targets of these policies. In the early twentieth century, the state of Virginia sterilized thousands of individuals who were mostly poor, White people from Appalachia, based on the false claims of eugenics.[23] They did so in accordance with the popular science of the day in both the United States and Europe.

In 1929, Indiana University professor Thurman Rice wrote,

We formerly received practically all our immigrants from northern Europe. They were for the most part of an excellent type and would blend well together. . . . The situation is very different to-day; most of the recent immigrants who are coming to-day . . . have come from eastern and southern Europe, and from other lands even less closely related; they do not mix with our stock in the "melting pot," and if they do cross with us their dominant traits submerge our native recessive traits; they are often radicals and anarchists causing no end to trouble; they have very low standards of living; they disturb the labor problems of the day; they are tremendously prolific.[24]

In Europe, a popular biology textbook written in the 1920s read,

If we continue to squander [our] biological mental heritage as we have been squandering it during the last few decades, it will not be many generations before we cease to be the superiors of the Mongols. Our ethnological studies must lead us, not to arrogance, but to action—to eugenics.[25]

Adolf Hitler apparently read these very words in German. While in prison, he used this biology textbook and others like it to support the ideas he set forth in *Mein Kampf*. Not surprisingly, they formed the basis for his emerging racist ideology. Hitler did not just dream up the idea of producing a superior Aryan race through selective breeding, nor did he dream up the idea of eliminating other groups from the gene pool.[26] Unlike other eugenicists of the day, however, Hitler and the Nazis took these ideas to an unprecedented extreme. It was only after Hitler orchestrated the murder of six million Jews and millions of other "unfit" persons, including people with disabilities, Catholics, Romany, homosexuals, and others, that the ideological foundations of eugenics and social Darwinism finally lost any veneer of scientific or academic credibility.[27]

And yet, eugenics thinking is not at all in the distant past. As recently as the 1970s, Native American women in the United States were forcibly sterilized, without their consent, in great numbers; stories abound of women as young as fifteen years old going into hospitals for tonsillectomies and coming out with tubal ligations. This forced sterilization was carried out by the US government's Indian Health Service, the unit responsible (under treaty obligations and US law) for providing health care to federally recognized American Indians. These effects are still felt within Native Nations today, impacting perceptions of biomedical health care as well as the health outcomes of individuals.[28]

THE STORY OF FRANZ BOAS AND THE EMERGENCE OF THE CONCEPT OF CULTURE

Recall for a moment the setting and the opening scene of our story: A debate concerning the idea of observable change and difference in eighteenth- and nineteenth-century science sets into motion a chain of events linking Lyell's *Principles of Geology* with the emergence of Darwin's *Origin of Species*, which, in turn, becomes the raw material for misinterpretations of evolution ranging from social evolutionism to Spencer's survival of the fittest, social Darwinism, and eugenics. When debated within the larger global context of European imperial domination of most regions of the Earth, the claims about which races and societies were superior or inferior seemed to be justified by the political realities of the era.

Now we come to the point in the story when modern anthropology comes into play. We say *modern anthropology* because, in actuality, *anthropology* was the label often given to studies of human beings in the eighteenth and nineteenth centuries; the label was frequently applied to contemplations of so-called primitives and, by extension, to musings about social evolution. But *anthropology* was a generally ambiguous label in these early days. It did not begin to emerge as a distinct discipline until the mid-nineteenth century. And the ideas and concepts that set the foundation for *modern* anthropology (at least in the United States) did not emerge until after the turn of the twentieth century.

As we have already seen with Lewis Henry Morgan and his theory of unilinear social evolution, early anthropology had a complex relationship with colonialism, often advancing concepts that reinforced the political status quo. In fact, some critics have called anthropology the "handmaiden of colonialism." But the discipline that began to emerge in the early twentieth century started to turn away from associations with colonialism and became extremely critical of the racism of the times.

In North America, this was set into motion mainly by the German immigrant and scholar Franz Boas, one of the most important and influential figures in the founding of American anthropology.[29] Ultimately, Boas would help give the modern discipline of anthropology a foundation in the critique of both race and social evolutionism. Boas was a German-trained physicist and geographer. Of Jewish descent, he left Germany at the age of twenty-eight, immigrating to the United States in 1886—partly because of the anti-Semitism he had experienced in his young life. After arriving in the United States, Boas's interests shifted to the emerging new field of anthropology. He eventually founded the department of anthropology at Columbia University in New York City, where his dynamic research and teaching attracted a diverse group of graduate students, including many women who would become important figures in the field, such as (but not limited to) Ella Cara Deloria, Zora Neale Hurston, Ruth Benedict, Gladys Reichard, Frederica de Laguna, and Margaret Mead.

In the response to the intertwining debates about social evolution, social Darwinism, and race in the late nineteenth and early twentieth centuries, Boas began to espouse an idea that was profoundly radical for the early-twentieth-century United States (and elsewhere): that **society** or **"culture"** was a complex set of meanings, not things or technology, and that any one culture or society could not be understood solely in comparison to European or American society. In fact, he shifted the analysis away from the social evolutionists' emphasis on progress toward "civilization" (some evolutionists also used the term "culture," but merely as a synonym for "civilization"), replacing it with a newer idea of **culture**—which all people possess, equally. That is, he upended the notion that some societies were civilized or "cultured" while others were not, arguing instead for what he called "the relativity of all human cultivation." His students took up this perspective and reformulated it as the central idea of **cultural relativity**: that each society or culture must be understood on its own terms, as a product of its unique history, and not on the terms of outsiders. He argued that words like *savage, barbarian,* and *civilized* (advanced by the social evolutionists) were relative terms, terms that were used by Euro-Americans to judge other peoples from the outside. He argued that in order to understand others unlike yourself, you must understand their world from their point of view. To do this, he developed a method for living with other people, learning their languages, studying their diverse expressions of culture (artifacts, songs, performances, modes of relationship to one another), and experiencing other societies firsthand.

Franz Boas came to this conclusion not through conjecture but by living and studying geographic landscapes with the Inuit (formerly called "Eskimo") on Baffin Island in the Arctic Circle, in the 1880s. Many social evolutionists (e.g., social Darwinists) assumed that people like the Inuit were "savages" and had simpler minds than Europeans. But Boas found that the Inuit had incredibly complex ways of knowing and relating to the landscape—a knowledge much more detailed and precise than maps made of the Arctic region by his own contemporaries in Europe. His Inuit teachers tracked distance through time (in the language of "nights of sleep"), were expert hunters of Arctic wildlife, and keen navigators of an environment that most outside of the polar region would consider inhospitable to human life. Based on his work alongside Inuit men (skilled as he was, Boas had little access to women's knowledge as a male researcher), Boas thus reasoned that different environments created different kinds of needs, which led different groups of people to create different technologies in response. And yet, people did things in spite of restrictions placed by the environment, performing ceremonies and other activities that defied the harsh climate and were as praiseworthy as any aspects of European "culture" revered in his homeland. This was, in his words, "the relativity of all human cultivation."

Franz Boas and the Hunt family in 1894. George Hunt (back row, second from left) was an important research collaborator for Boas (back row, far right). American Philosophical Society

Boas also recognized that Inuit people faced many of the same problems as so-called "civilized" societies: the food quest, marriage and family, birth and death, conflict—but they went about solving these problems in very different ways. For Boas, this could be explained by differences in culture rather than differences in biology or different stages in social development. For example, complex knowledge of the landscape had little to do with the biology of the Inuit and certainly did not reflect a lesser stage in social development. Instead, he argued that Inuit culture had created, over the generations, a practical guide to living in the extreme cold and physical conditions of the Arctic. Boas realized that, although the environment created certain needs, possibilities, and limitations, many Inuit cultural practices had little to do with their surroundings. In truth, language, economics, politics, religion, marriage, family composition, and conflict resolution had more complex foundations. The most important thing to understand about why a particular society is different from another, Boas said, rested in a particular people's history.

Boas's approach to understanding a particular society would eventually be called **historical particularism**, which postulates that each society or culture was the outgrowth of its unique past. Boas argued that a particular society or culture was much like an individual: If you want to get to know someone, it helps to know where they come from. An individual, like a society, is essentially the amalgamation of unique experiences that have transpired in that individual's past and continue to shape them in the present. Simply put, for Boas, you are the outgrowth of your unique past. And by extension, Boas suggested, a society is an outgrowth of its unique past. This idea boldly departed from the earlier unilinear notion that all societies traveled upon the same "road to progress," epitomized by European civilization at the top.

Boas thus maintained that any culture or society, like any individual, is too complex in its uniqueness to be compared to another. He argued that comparing individual societies to each other (as the social evolutionists did in their sequence of development from savage to barbarian to civilized) was more an exercise in value judgment than an exercise in science. Comparison is relative to those doing the comparing, he said. From an Inuit point of view, for instance, Europeans—who, unlike the Inuit, had standing armies, warfare, widespread poverty, and dirty cities—were the "savages."

Boas's unique contributions to the concept of culture not only enabled a critique of social evolution but also of social Darwinism as well. Social Darwinists presumed the consequences of successful war exploits, imperialism, and colonialism to be a fact of nature—a product of the more fit ("the civilized") surpassing the less fit ("the savage"). They did not consider that "exploitation," "domination," or "colonialism" were social and historical constructions of their own making, designed to serve their own political ends. Social Darwinists, in turn, assumed that those who "have" and excel, do so because of their inherent or biological constitution. Failure or success was seen as innate, prescribed, and predestined.

Boas understood that differences between peoples could be explained by culture, by the "particular histories" of individual communities and not by biology (what people would later call "genes"). Boas certainly was not alone in his critique of race. Many other critics, like W. E. B. Du Bois, railed against the racist theories of social Darwinism and eugenics in the years before and after the turn of the twentieth century and up to World War II (1939–1945). But Boas was surely one of the most vocal. He was not afraid to take a strong ethical stance on a wide range of social issues, such as boldly calling out anthropologists working as spies for the US government in a 1919 article for *The Nation*, angering many of his colleagues.[30]

Boas's critique of race was not just based on his study of culture. He also spent years collecting data from diverse populations all over the world, as well as collecting his own physical measurement data from immigrants passing through Ellis Island, New York. Boas could find absolutely no evidence supporting the idea that one race was superior to another or that one race was inherently more intelligent than another. Importantly, he took a scientific approach to debunking theories of racial superiority. It was not that the idea of racial equity was politically correct or socially sanctioned at that time; certainly, his position emphasizing human diversity and equality was definitely against the grain. It was, more significantly, that Boas could find no evidence for claims of racial superiority/inferiority. His work began to expose race as an ideology held by some at the expense of others, not a biological fact. In 1928, Boas wrote that "anatomists cannot with certainty differentiate between the brains of a Swede and of a Negro. The brains of individuals of each group vary so much in form that it is often difficult to say . . . whether a certain brain belongs to a Swede or to a Negro."[31] Boas's critique went much deeper than this, however. The idea of superior and inferior races was ultimately flawed because the very *concept* of race was flawed.

With this in mind, consider the following.[32]

The concept of race presumes that there are more biological similarities *within* a particular race than between them. According to this logic, European Americans, for instance, have more in common with each other than with African Americans, and vice versa. It follows, therefore, that clear differences demarcate these racial categories, making them separate from one another. But what Boas and subsequent anthropologists found was that there were, first, more *differences* between those within a so-called race, and, second, more *similarities* between those individuals of supposed different so-called racial categories. So, contrary to the logic of race, people are just as likely to share similarities across racial lines as they are within themselves, depending on what traits we examine. "From a purely biological point of view," wrote Boas, "the concept of race unity breaks down. The multitude of genealogical lines, the diversity of individual and family types contained in each race is so great that no race can be considered as a unit. Furthermore, similarities between neighboring races and, in regard to function, even between distinct races are so great that individuals cannot be assigned with certainty to one group or another."[33] Indeed, contemporary biologists have not identified any genetic or other biological markers of race, even though these problematic categories continue to be used in everyday life and even in scientific studies.

Let's consider Boas's claim, focusing solely on the categories of "White" and "Black." Boas is saying essentially that the differences *within* a so-called race are much more profound than the differences *between* the so-called races. What exactly does this mean? Well, let's look at skin pigmentation. Among human beings, skin tone varies from very light to very dark. Among Europeans, for instance, skin color varies from very light in the northern latitudes to medium in the Mediterranean region. Many Americans might decide to place these Europeans in the racial category of "White" if they lived in the United States, based on the fact that they have ancestry in Europe.

Among Africans, skin color varies from medium in the north to very dark in parts of central and southern Africa. People in parts of northern Africa have skin tones very similar to their European neighbors in the Mediterranean, and in some cases, they are lighter; yet many Americans might decide to place some of these northern Africans in the racial category of "Black" and others in the racial category of "White," despite the fact that there may be little to no difference in color between these Europeans and Africans, these so-called White and Black people. Conversely, many Africans might decide to place these individuals in completely different categories of "White" and "Black." In these cases, the comparisons of differing pigmentation cannot be separated from cultural associations and interpretations of what we (think we) see.

To put this conundrum in more technical terms, we could say that the categories of "White" and "Black"—and "race" itself—are socially constructed. That's because if you were to line up all the people in the world based solely on skin pigmentation, from light to dark, the place where you would draw the line between "White" and "Black" or between "White" and "yellow" or between "yellow" and "red," is completely arbitrary—that is, any given individual might place the line anywhere.

This was Boas's point: Race, he demonstrated, was not based on empirically sound evidence. It was an arbitrary, human-made creation, a social construction. Furthermore, Boas argued, when speaking of biology, human beings as a whole had more similarities than differences, mainly because we have all been interbreeding since the emergence of *Homo sapiens*. "The history of the human races . . . ," wrote Boas, "shows us a mankind constantly on the move; people from eastern Asia migrating to Europe; those of western and central Asia invading southern Asia; North Europeans sweeping over Mediterranean countries; Central Africans extending their territories over almost the whole of South Africa; people from Alaska spreading to northern Mexico or vice versa; South Americans settling almost over the whole eastern part of the continent here and there; the Malay extending their migrations westward to Madagascar and eastward far over the Pacific Ocean—in short, from earliest times on we have a picture of continued movements, and with it, of mixtures of diverse peoples."[34]

Archaeological and genetic evidence has only reinforced Boas's point: No one group of human beings has ever stayed put or been isolated long enough to create a separate breeding population that would buttress a separate biological subspecies, or "race." Contemporary human biology concurs: When examining human DNA, the racial divisions of humans break down. To be sure, we are generally the same on a biological level. The differences we think that we see—in hair texture, eye color, skin tone—are purely superficial, and only a fraction of the complex **human genome**.

It is important to clarify that Boas was *not* arguing that biological differences are illusionary. Things like skin pigmentation, body stature, hair type, or eye color obviously exist and are reproduced over and over again within populations. But the problem with the concept of race, Boas argued, had to do with the presumed *relationship* between observable characteristics like skin pigmentation, body stature, hair type, or eye color. Boas found quite the opposite, actually. For example, while many East Africans have dark skin, they are generally tall, like many Native Americans from the northern plains. While many Native Americans from the northern plains are tall, they generally have dark eyes, like many southeastern Europeans. While many southeastern Europeans have dark eyes, they generally have wavy hair, like some Australian aborigines. While some Native Australians have wavy hair, they generally have dark skin, like many East Africans—and so on, and so on, and so on.

Once again, Boas argued that the problem concerns the category of race. Depending on which observable biological characteristic we focus on, we end up with different racial categories. If we decided to focus solely on populations that generally have tall body stature—in the same way that we often focus solely on skin color—we would put East Africans, Native Americans from the northern plains, and Scandinavians in a same racial grouping. Even more importantly, the superficial traits that are easily observable with the naked eye have no direct connection to more complex human behaviors.[35] If we recall the racial classifications of Carolus Linnaeus from his 1758 edition of *System of Nature,* he attributed intelligence, psychological tendencies, and social practices to each racial subgroup. In a similar way, our folk notions of race are rarely about mere physical appearance.[36] In subtle ways, assumptions about race almost always imply other attributes. When we speak of so-called racial groups, we may be suggesting that one group is more or less intelligent, musically talented, athletically gifted, artistically inclined, and so on.

Boas's insights about the biological fallacy of race, made in the early twentieth century, have been consistently upheld by contemporary human biological research. When scientists have looked for other biological markers of race, they have failed to find them. Take blood types, where we find that the distribution of A, B, O gene frequencies also does not correspond with our folk concept of race. In East Africa, some populations have an A, B, O gene frequency distribution that is almost identical to some European populations.

ANTHROPOLOGY HERE AND NOW

Race: The Power of an Illusion

It can be hard to understand how entrenched notions of race are in US society. Even those individuals most committed to the equality of the races tend to assume that race exists as a biological fact. The Public Broadcasting Service (PBS) has produced an excellent three-part series that looks at biological, historical, and social dimensions of race in the United States. Each episode reveals unexpected dimensions about the problem of race in America, from its biologically fallacy ("Difference between Us"), to its surprisingly short history ("The Story We Tell"), to its perpetuation through certain institutional arrangements ("The House We Live In"). Each one is well worth watching. For more information, visit https://www.pbs.org/race/000_General/000_00-Home.htm.

But, in this regard, these Europeans and East Africans are very different from West Africans, many of whom tend to have a much higher distribution of the B blood type in their population (which is similar, by the way, to some Asian populations). Simply put, when considering A, B, O blood distribution alone, some Europeans and East Africans can have more in common than East Africans have with West Africans.[37] This kind of overlap is not the exception; in fact, it is often the rule. As anthropologist Jonathan Marks writes, "A large sample of Germans, for example, turns out to have virtually the same [A, B, O blood distribution] as a large sample of New Guineans. . . . A study of Estonians in eastern Europe . . . finds them nearly identical to Japanese in eastern Asia."[38]

Let's take another example: sickle-cell anemia, a disease of the blood cells that ultimately affects blood circulation. Sickle-cell anemia is a condition often associated with Black Americans. That is because many have ancestry in particular African populations who also have the condition, even today. But sickle-cell anemia is not limited to Africa. It can be found in the Mediterranean region and in parts of southern Asia and the Middle East.

This raises an important point in understanding how human biology works. From a biological point of view, biological variations like sickle-cell anemia are associated with **populations**, not races. The recurring presence of sickle-cell anemia in Africa, the Mediterranean, southern Asia, and the Middle East corresponds closely with the presence of malaria in these regions. People in these populations who are born heterozygous for sickle-cell anemia (i.e., they have inherited a sickle-cell allele from one parent, not both) have an adaptive advantage over those who are homozygous for sickle-cell anemia (i.e., they have inherited a sickle-cell allele from both parents, which can be deadly if left untreated). Because the heterozygous genetic arrangement protects against malaria, these individuals can and often do live to reproduce within a population plagued by both sickle-cell anemia and malaria. (It is, of course, an imperfect evolutionary trade-off, but as you now know, natural selection does not work toward perfection; it works with what it has to advance survivability in a changing environment.)[39] Today, biological anthropologists offer the term **clines** for us to use, as we reimagine the distribution of human difference across space and time. Moving away from the old, false notion of fixed and distinct "races" living in certain places/locations, thinking in terms of clines allows us to see gradations across space; movement, migration, and diaspora; and the relationships between and among populations across planet Earth.

All of this is to say that biological characteristics like sickle-cell anemia—or the distribution of blood types, skin pigmentation, body stature, hair type, or eye color—work in concert with natural selection (and several other mechanisms, like sexual, directional, or stabilizing selection) to produce and reproduce a range of biological characteristics that advance the survival of a particular population within a particular region. Native southern Africans conventionally have dark skin, may be tall, have a near absence of sickle-cell anemia, have dark-colored eyes, have a high distribution of the O blood type, and so on because of where they live and with whom they marry and have children, not because they fall within a racial category that many would call "Black."

We are, of course, glossing over what's sometimes called **cultural selection**: the impact of society or culture on biology. More Americans, for instance, will marry within their so-called race, reproducing over and over again certain observable characteristics that they can see, like skin color. But this brings us back to Boas. Boas, his students, and succeeding generations of anthropologists argued that race is created by society or culture, not biology. Indeed, they said, it is a social construction, collapsing biology, behavior, and intelligence. Instead of being an empirical fact, race emerged in European and American history as a folk concept that has since had enormous power to shape how people think about human similarities and differences and, consequently, how people live and experience their own lives and interpret those of others.[40]

Having said this, it is important to clarify the two points we are making. First, Boas was a key figure in revealing that there is no biological basis for the concept of race. Subsequent generations of anthropologists and biologists have confirmed his conclusion. There are no biological means to classify humans into racial subgroups in the way that Linnaeus did in the eighteenth century. Biologically, we are truly all one. Second, this point—as radical as it is—only applies to the realm of biology in our world. Culturally and socially, we continue to group *Homo sapiens* into our folk categories of race. We live as if we belong to different racial subgroups.

Even more concerning, too many of us still think that these folk categories of race indicate differences in the intelligence, athleticism, or other behaviors of these groups. As contemporary anthropologist Audrey Smedley says: "Race has no intrinsic relationship to human biological diversity. . . . [S]uch diversity is a natural product of primarily evolutionary forces, whereas race is a social invention."[41] In other words, we continue to live in a world shaped by folk categories of race and, even worse, divided by racism and animosity to certain groups.

When we view race through the lens of history, it becomes absolutely clear that the concept of race emerged to give credence to institutions like slavery and to ideas such as social Darwinism and eugenics. Slaves, primitives, or barbarians were called slaves, primitives, and barbarians because of a racial category to which they were assigned. And so-called slaves and primitives and barbarians *had* to be dominated, as the logic went, because of their presumed inferior status; they were, as social Darwinists argued, like children. To be sure, the concept of race emerged among people who, within the context of power relations between and among groups, thought themselves to be superior. Today, we still live with the pernicious remnants of this social invention. Whether we realize it or not, race continues to be, as Audrey Smedley writes, "about who should have access to privilege, power, status and wealth, and who should not."[42]

ANTHROPOLOGY HERE AND NOW

Contemporary Critiques of Boas

Franz Boas clearly was an enormous, foundational influence on the development of anthropology in the United States, but his work has not been beyond reproach or criticism by contemporary anthropologists. Lee Baker argues that Boas's research on the physical differences of immigrants "dealt a blow to scientific racism because he demonstrated the plasticity and instability of racial types," but Boas also supported policies of assimilation, which by today's standards could be considered racist.[1]

Likewise, Margaret Bruchac has argued that Boas's work with George Hunt, his research collaborator of Tlingit (maternal) and British (paternal) descent, was critically dependent on Hunt's female relatives, including his mother, sister, and two Kwakwaka'wakw (Kwakiutl) wives, for ethnographic data/information. Unfortunately, the voices, identities, and recognition of the contributions of these women are absent from Boas's publications.[2]

For further reading, see:

L. D. Baker, "The Racist Anti-Racism of American Anthropology," *Transforming Anthropology*, 29 (2021): 127–42, https://doi.org/10.1111/traa.12222.

M. Bruchac, "My Sisters Will Not Speak: Boas, Hunt, and the Ethnographic Silencing of First Nations Women," *Curator: The Museum Journal* 57 (2) (2014): 153–71, https://doi.org/10.1111/cura.12058.

Notes

1. Baker, "The Racist Anti-Racism of American Anthropology."
2. Bruchac, "My Sisters Will Not Speak."

So it was through Boas that modern American anthropology began to solidify around the critique of race and a more rigorous study of human biology and human culture. In addition to framing American anthropology within systematic methodologies and theoretical structures, Boas was very active in the public arena. His anthropological work provoked him to extend his critique of race and racist policies into the public realm. He practiced what he preached. A close friend of W. E. B. Du Bois, Boas publicly supported the formation of the National Association for the Advancement of Colored People, spoke at its first organizational meeting, and publicly denounced racism.[43] Taking such public stands, not surprisingly, led to attacks, some even from within the field of anthropology. He was even sanctioned by the American Anthropological Association during World War I, when he published his powerful essay in *The Nation* criticizing anthropologists who used their knowledge of other cultures to become "spies" for the US government during wartime.

Teaching at Columbia University, Boas took on students that other emerging anthropology programs often denied—namely, women, Black, and Indigenous students.[44] Boas's students included Zora Neale Hurston, whose works in African American literature and folklore were way ahead of her time, experimenting with ethnographic writing and theory in a genre that transgressed social science and drew upon her own background in the US South; Ella Cara Deloria, a Dakota Sioux scholar whose ethnographic novel, *Waterlily*, and other works on the Sioux engaged questions of gender, labor, and everyday life, in a manner that Boas himself could not access as an

ANTHROPOLOGY HERE AND NOW

Museum Exhibition on Race

Anthropologists are still actively involved in educating the public on the problems of race. The American Anthropological Association developed a traveling exhibit called "Race: Are We So Different?" as part of its public outreach. The exhibit was on a US national tour from 2007 to 2018. It now is on long-term display in select museums around the country. Get more information on this invaluable exhibition and access a rich selection of related resources available online at www.understandingrace.org.

outsider; and Margaret Mead, whose pioneering work on women, children, sex, and sexuality changed the way America thought about gender and adolescence. Importantly, these and a number of other students would carry on Boas's tradition of establishing an analytic of behavior in culture, critiquing race, and engaging wider (nonacademic) audiences in these discussions, continuing a public-facing tradition in anthropology that persists to this day and, some argue, is increasingly urgent in a time of climate crisis, racial injustice, and a global pandemic.

THE STORY'S LESSON: A CALL FOR CRITICAL ENGAGEMENT

Every story has a purpose for its telling, whether that purpose is explicitly or implicitly expressed. In the realm of our everyday experience, we choose among a multitude of encounters to evoke as memory and, in turn, to shape as story. Our story of the origins of the discipline of anthropology is the same. What we do with that story is what is at stake today. And the experience and history of the discipline is complicated, polyphonic, and diverse—far more so than what our space allows in this short chapter. Lots of others besides Boas helped to set American anthropology's central tenets, including Anténor Firmin, Lewis Henry Morgan, and James Mooney, among others.[45] As anthropologist Lee D. Baker reminds us, "Boas's contributions were significant, but he did not work alone."[46]

Thus, we could have chosen to tell a different story about the origins of anthropology. But we focused on Boas in part because his work continues to enlighten us about the problems of race. Unfortunately, we still live in a society that continues dangerously to equate biology with behavior. Although we are living at a time when attitudes about race are in the midst of significant flux, as recently as the 1990s, marginal social scientists—legitimized by extensive media coverage—were claiming in widely read books like *The Bell Curve* that people of color are intellectually inferior to White people. These studies carried authority and power because they were passed off as "science" and legitimized as reasonable voices in a discussion about race. As such, they are still, even today, being used to justify racist thinking and practices in much the same way that social Darwinism was used to justify Euro-American domination of non-Western peoples. To paraphrase Cornell West, and as we all know, "Race still matters."[47]

As anthropologists primarily located in North America, working in the tradition of Boas while also seeking to transform anthropology, we are compelled to challenge continuing reverberations of such studies and their implications. The story about Boas and the emergence of North American anthropology is not just a story about the maturation of a discipline. It presents us with a powerful metaphor for engagement: It is about critically analyzing and challenging mainstream and "taken for granted" ideas about human difference, writing and speaking against inequalities to create more inclusive and equitable societies. One way in which anthropologists today strive to do this is through critical **reflexivity** (which we will return to in chapter 3) on our own positions and by carefully considering the ethical implications of their research for the communities with whom they work.

This story of anthropology's complex origins should illustrate to us that knowledge is a powerful tool, having direct and material consequences on people's lives. Anthropologists today work on a wide range of topics, many of them very different than the issues that animated Boas's research, but they may all see themselves carrying forward the spirit of his work, moving the needle of the discipline toward more emancipatory horizons.

NOTES

1. Walter Benjamin, *Illuminations*, ed. Hannah Arendt (New York: Schocken Books, 1968).

2. See Edward M. Bruner, "Experience and Its Expressions," in *The Anthropology of Experience*, ed. Victor W. Turner and Edward M. Bruner (Chicago: University of Illinois Press, 1986), 3–30.

3. Ryan Cecil Jobson, "The Case for Letting Anthropology Burn," *American Anthropologist* 122 (2) (2020): 259–71.

4. For deeper coverage of the following discussion, see Peter J. Bowler, *Evolution: The History of an Idea*, 3rd ed. (Berkeley: University of California Press, 2003).

5. Excerpted from Jonathan Marks, *Human Biodiversity: Genes, Race, and History* (New York: Aldine de Gruyter, 1995), 50.

6. Paul Chaat Smith, *Everything You Know about Indians Is Wrong* (Minneapolis: University of Minnesota Press, 2009).

7. Charles Darwin, *On the Origin of Species* (New York: Avenel Books, 1979 [1859]), 68.

8. For a much more thorough and nuanced discussion, see H. B. D. Kettlewell, "Selection Experiments on Industrial Melanism in the Lepidoptera," *Heredity* 9 (1955): 323–49; "A Survey of the Frequencies of *Bison betularia* (L.) (Lep.) and Its

Melanic Forms in Great Britain," *Heredity* 12 (1958): 51–72; and *The Evolution of Melanism* (Oxford: Clarendon Press, 1973).

9. See, for example, J. A. Bishop and Laurence M. Cook, "Moths, Melanism and Clean Air," *Scientific American* 232 (January 1975): 90–99.

10. Darwin, *Origin of Species*, 132.

11. See, for example, Randolph M. Nesse and George C. Williams, "Evolution and the Origins of Disease," *Scientific American* 279, no. 5 (1998): 86–93.

12. See Jonathan Weiner, *The Beak of the Finch* (New York: Vintage Books, 1995), for numerous detailed descriptions of this evidence.

13. See, for example, Peter R. Grant, *Ecology and Evolution of Darwin's Finches* (Princeton, NJ: Princeton University Press, 1986).

14. Even Darwin, in fact, recast many of his original ideas through the lens of progress, such as in *The Descent of Man* and in later editions of *Origin of Species*.

15. Spencer, however, convinced Darwin to use "survival of the fittest" as a synonym for natural selection, which Darwin did in later editions of *Origin of Species* (Jonathan Marks, personal communication).

16. See Lee D. Baker, *From Savage to Negro: Anthropology and the Construction of Race, 1896–1954* (Berkeley: University of California Press, 1998), 26–53.

17. Ibid.

18. Audrey Smedley, *Race in North America: Origin and Evolution of a Worldview* (Boulder, CO: Westview Press, 1993), 36ff.; Alden T. Vaughan, *Roots of American Racism: Essays on the Colonial Encounter* (Oxford: Oxford University Press, 1995).

19. Baker, *From Savage to Negro*, 26–53, 248.

20. Excerpted from ibid., 131.

21. Ibid., 54–80, 127–42.

22. Marks, *Human Biodiversity*, 77–97.

23. See Samuel R. Cook, *Monacans and Miners: Native American and Coal Mining Communities in Appalachia* (Lincoln: University of Nebraska Press, 2000), 84–134. See also J. David Smith, *The Eugenic Assault on America: Scenes in Red, White, and Black* (Fairfax, VA: George Mason University Press, 1993).

24. Excerpted from Marks, *Human Biodiversity*, 85.

25. Excerpted from ibid., 88.

26. Ibid., 88–89.

27. Ibid., 89–95.

28. See, for example, Jane Lawrence, "Indian Health Service and the Sterilization of Native American Women," *American Indian Quarterly*, vol. 24, no. 3 (2000): 400–419; and Sally J. Torpy, "Native American Women and Coerced Sterilization," *American Indian Culture and Research Journal*, vol. 24, no. 2 (2000): 1–22.

29. The following discussion is eclectically based on, first, Franz Boas's writings, especially Franz Boas, "The Limitations of the Comparative Method in Anthropology," *Science* 4 (1896): 901–8; *The Central Eskimo* (Lincoln: University of Nebraska Press, 1964 [1898]); *Anthropology and Modern Life* (New York: Norton, 1928); and *Race, Language, and Culture* (New York: Free Press, 1940); and, second, more general descriptions of Boas's role within the overall emergence of anthropology—see, for example, Douglas Cole, *Franz Boas: The Early Years, 1858–1906* (Seattle: University of Washington Press, 1999); Melville Jean Herskovits, *Franz Boas: The Science of Man in the Making* (New York: Scribner, 1953); George W. Stocking, *Race, Culture, and Evolution: Essays in the History of Anthropology* (New York: Free Press, 1968); and *The Ethnographer's Magic and Other Essays in the History of Anthropology* (Madison: University of Wisconsin Press, 1992).

30. David Price, "Anthropologists as Spies," *The Nation* (November 2, 2000).

31. Boas, *Anthropology and Modern Life*, 20.

32. The following discussion on race relies heavily on Boas, *Anthropology and Modern Life*; Marks, *Human Biodiversity*; and Ashley Montagu, *Man's Most Dangerous Myth: The Fallacy of Race*, 6th ed. (Walnut Creek, CA: AltaMira Press, 1998).

33. Boas, *Anthropology and Modern Life*, 63.

34. Ibid., 30.

35. J. L. Graves Jr. and A. H. Goodman, *Racism, Not Race: Answers to Frequently Asked Questions* (New York: Columbia University Press, 2021).

36. Jonathan Marks, *What It Means to Be 98% Chimpanzee: Apes, People, and Their Genes* (Berkeley: University of California Press, 2003).

37. For a comparative survey of blood-type frequency distribution around the world, see A. E. Mourant, Ada C. Kopec, and Kazimiera Domaniewska-Sobczak,

The Distribution of the Human Blood Groups and Other Polymorphisms, 2nd ed. (London: Oxford University Press, 1976).

38. Marks, *Human Biodiversity*, 130.

39. Our discussion of sickle-cell anemia here is a bit oversimplified, especially in regard to changes in these populations (and their diaspora) due to the introduction of modern medicine. For an easy-to-read and broadly based discussion of how sickle-cell anemia and a host of other diseases can be understood within an evolutionary and biomedical framework, see Randolph M. Nesse and George C. Williams, *Why We Get Sick: The New Science of Darwinian Medicine* (New York: Times Books, 1994).

40. See, for example, Montagu, *Man's Most Dangerous Myth: The Fallacy of Race*, 6th ed.

41. Audrey Smedley, "The Origin of Race," *Anthropology Newsletter* 38 (September 1997): 50, 52.

42. Ibid.

43. See Baker, *From Savage to Negro*, 119.

44. See, for example, ibid., 150–63.

45. See Carolyn Fluehr-Lobban, "Anténor Firmin: Haitian Pioneer of Anthropology," *American Anthropologist* 102, no. 3 (2000): 449–66; Elisabeth Tooker, "Lewis H. Morgan and His Contemporaries," *American Anthropologist* 94, no. 2 (1992): 357–75; L. G. Moses, *The Indian Man: A Biography of James Mooney* (Urbana: University of Illinois Press, 1984), especially 222ff.; and Baker, *From Savage to Negro*.

46. Baker, *From Savage to Negro*, 100.

47. See Cornell West, *Race Matters* (Boston: Beacon Press, 1993).

2

Anthropology and Culture

Much has happened in American anthropology since Boas, his students, and his contemporaries established anthropology as a professional discipline in its own right. They helped to place questions of human biology and culture at the center of the discipline. They also helped to establish the general institutional framework and disciplinary specializations that continue to shape the way anthropologists work, teach, and conduct their research. Anthropologists are today broadly concerned with human differences and similarities—past and present, biological and cultural, local and international.

The four major subfields of anthropology.

As anthropology became part of the academic mainstream in the early twentieth century, it developed four main subdisciplines: **biological** or **physical anthropology**, **archaeology**, **linguistic anthropology**, and **cultural anthropology**. Although these subfields are now split into sub-subfields and sub-sub-subfields, these four subfields are still the main way anthropologists organize themselves today. Biological or physical anthropology focuses on human biology, archaeology centers on human technology and material culture, linguistic anthropology concentrates on language, and cultural anthropology addresses culture. Although we focus primarily on culture and cultural anthropology throughout this book, we make forays into the other subfields of anthropology. As we have already seen in chapter 1, the historical relationship between culture and biology was crucial to the emergence of anthropology as a whole. Likewise, we find it necessary to refer to the other subfields of anthropology as we continue to refine the concept of culture and explore its related subfield of cultural anthropology.

THE SUBFIELDS OF ANTHROPOLOGY

Let's start with physical or biological anthropology. This field is concerned primarily with human biology, but biological anthropologists conceptualize human biology in very broad terms. From the social problem of race to the actual biological complexity of populations, from disease to health, from heredity to genetics, from bone structure to cell structure—biological anthropology does many different things. A unifying concept in biological anthropology, however, is biological change, or evolution. Through this lens, biological anthropologists seek to understand biological changes over the long and short terms. Biological anthropologists take up subjects ranging from the evolution of the human species to the evolution of SARS-CoV-2, the virus that causes COVID-19. Moreover, they seek to understand human biological variation within the larger framework of the biological variation found among all animals. Just where humans fit into the overall scheme of biological evolution remains an important question for deciphering how we are both similar to and different from other animals, including our closest living relatives, chimpanzees, gorillas, and other primates.

Archaeology shares an interest in the human past—as well as many of its research methods—with biological anthropology, such as the "archaeological dig." But it diverges from the study of human biology to focus on human technology or **material culture** (i.e., materials that human beings purposefully create either as tools to adapt to their environments or as meaningful expressions of their experience). To put it simply, the key concept in archaeology is the **artifact**, an object created by humans. But the point is not about collecting artifacts, like a treasure hunter might do. Archaeologists place these artifacts within larger social contexts to *infer* and *understand* human behavior. Thus, from religion to economics, from small villages to large cities, from weapons of war to arts and crafts, from the development of agriculture to the fall of civilizations, from human exploitation of the environment to human adaptation to the environment—archaeologists use artifacts situated in their larger social context to uncover the secrets of human society in both the past and the present.

Linguistic anthropology focuses exclusively on **language** because of its central role in defining who we are as humans. In a general sense, we depend on language like no other animal to survive. And as we use it to communicate complex ideas and concepts, language is, to be sure, at the very heart of culture. As such, it is a rich source for expressing the diversity of human experience. In a more particular sense, the whole range of an individual society's

Language involves much more than the spoken word. We use a variety of symbols— sounds, gestures, and body language, for example—to impart meaning when we communicate with others. Many linguistic anthropologists thus seek to understand language as a process of communication inextricably bound to social contexts. Photo by Danny Gawlowski

collective experience is contained in language. For instance, the word for *love* in English is translated as "respect" in another language. Knowing this helps linguistic anthropologists understand that not everyone sees the world in the same way, and our diversity of languages reflects and, many linguists say, *shapes* our uniqueness.

The idea that language not only reflects but can also shape how we think and how we act—sometimes called the *Sapir-Whorf hypothesis*—is an important concept for understanding differences across cultural groups. Named after two influential anthropologists, this hypothesis suggests that language is such a powerful medium through which we engage with the world, that different language groups will have radically different ways of understanding and living in the world. Ideas about "love" or "respect"—to continue with the same example—may index similar human feelings, but their historical use and development within particular cultural contexts also indicates the very different emotional registers in which human beings relate to each other. Very interesting stuff indeed.

Because language can mean both spoken and nonspoken discourse, a central concept in linguistics is **communication**. In anthropological terms, communication is the use of arbitrary symbols to impart meaning. This means that certain sounds or gestures have no inherent meaning in and of themselves; we assign meaning to them, and through them, to impart meaning to others. While a belch at the dinner table is considered a rude gesture among polite company in the United States, apparently it communicates a compliment in some other countries. Or consider how a slight nod of the head may mean yes among most Americans; the same gesture might be meaningless among non–English speakers who use other gestures to communicate an affirmative response nonverbally. It's not the gesture of nodding or the sound of belching itself but rather the meaning *behind* the gesture or sound. Thus, from sounds and gestures to the composition of language families, from the history of words to their ongoing evolution, from the different ways men and women communicate to how power structures are transmitted through spoken language, linguistic anthropologists seek to understand the intricacies of human communication within larger social contexts (both past and present).

Finally, let's turn to cultural anthropology. Cultural anthropology—often called **sociocultural anthropology**—shares with anthropological linguistics a focus on human communication. But its central, driving concept—culture—

is much broader in scope. Although culture is a term that we may use frequently in our everyday conversations, in an anthropological sense, **culture** is an academic concept that is not used casually. For our purposes, we will define it as *a shared and negotiated system of meaning informed by knowledge that people learn and put into practice by interpreting experience and generating behavior.*[1] This is a mouthful—and based on several different anthropological definitions and understandings of culture (see note 1 at the end of the chapter)—but don't worry about apprehending exactly what we mean by this just yet. We will go into more depth later. For now, let's say simply that culture is the lens through which we all view the world; at the same time, culture is that which produces the social differences found in our world. What makes American society different from, say, French society is culture; what makes the feel of one town different from another is culture; what makes my family different from yours is culture. In the same sense, we all share similarities within a cultural group, like the questions surrounding the meanings of birth, marriage, inheritance, or death. This is the stuff of cultural anthropology.

From gender roles to the cultural construction of race, from music to the social construction of violence, from politics to economics, from law to the concept of freedom—cultural anthropologists study culture to understand the powerful role it has in our lives.

While biological anthropology, archaeology, linguistic anthropology, and cultural anthropology now constitute the four so-called subfields, anthropologists also recognize a wide range of sub-subfields and specializations. Biological anthropologists might specialize in primatology, paleoanthropology, bioarchaeology, molecular anthropology, or forensic anthropology. Archaeologists can choose to focus on zooarchaeology, paleobotany, geoarchaeology, historical archaeology, or other concentrations. Linguistic anthropologists might focus on descriptive linguistics, ethnolinguistics, historical linguistics, or sociolinguists. Lastly, cultural anthropologists branch off into an even greater tangle of expertise. They may identify as specialists in cognition, development, economics, environment, gender, law, media, medicine, politics, religion, and so on. You do not need to remember any of these sub-subfields now. You should just be aware that they are part of the dynamism of the discipline and that they keep it moving forward in interesting ways.

In spite of this trend toward ever greater specialization, anthropologists are also attentive to the real-world implications of their expertise. This pragmatic orientation is sometimes recognized as another subdiscipline called **applied anthropology**—the application of anthropology to contemporary social problems. But applied anthropology can also be a perspective, an approach that can permeate all areas of anthropology, from biological anthropology and archaeology to linguistic and cultural anthropology. From forensic anthropologists (who apply biological anthropology to solve, for example, murder cases) to cultural resource-management archaeologists (who apply archaeological research to federal and state mandates to preserve the archaeological and historical record for the future) to medical anthropologists (who apply biological, linguistic, and cultural anthropology to address health problems), the work of anthropology in the public realm is multifaceted. Sometimes this approach is also called **public anthropology**.

ANTHROPOLOGY HERE AND NOW

Applied Anthropology: Supporting Indigenous People's Rights

Many anthropologists apply anthropological perspectives, critiques, and methods to professional or volunteer work with social movements and nongovernmental organizations. This inclination is not new; in 1972, inspired by his work as an anthropologist with Indigenous peoples in Brazil, David Maybury-Lewis co-founded the organization Cultural Survival to advance the United Nations Declaration on the Rights of Indigenous Peoples and support Indigenous movements for self-determination and human rights. In her essay on Maybury-Lewis's impact, fellow public anthropologist Louise Lamphere notes this as innovative work for a time when many anthropologists were dedicated only to "objective social science research, publication, and teaching" (Louise Lamphere, "David Maybury-Lewis and Cultural Survival: Providing a Model for Public Anthropology, Advocacy, and Collaboration," *Anthropological Quarterly* 82 [2009], 1049–54). Cultural Survival's website highlights a range of projects taking place from Brazil to Southeast Asia (https://www.culturalsurvival.org/).

DEFINING CULTURE

So what is culture, anthropologically speaking? Among anthropologists, culture has a different meaning from the way that "culture" is used in everyday English. We may think the meaning of this term is pretty straightforward; don't we use it all the time in our everyday discourse? But it turns out to be a slippery concept. We lay out the basic definition in this chapter, but you should not expect to fully grasp the implications of the concept immediately. That will take some time. But we hope that by the end of this book, you will have a good working grasp of the concept and its transformative implications. We believe that a mastery of the anthropological definition of culture has the power to change the way you look at the world, perhaps even the way you live your life. But before we get into this heady stuff, we need to set the stage.

Culture also turns out to be a relatively new word, an important new term in the English language (as well as other languages) that does not come into popular use until the twentieth century. Understanding the history of this term can help us better appreciate just how radical a concept it was and continues to be. In order to begin unpacking its various connotations, we invite you to first try a little experiment, either on your own or preferably with some friends or classmates, to try to define how you actually use the term "culture" in everyday language. Please take a look at the exercise below.

ANTHROPOLOGY HERE AND NOW

Speaking Culture

How do we use the term "culture" in everyday English? Work with some of your classmates or friends and think about everyday uses of the term. Can you write down a basic definition? (Hint: Your definition should not be the technical one we have already given you. Everyday use is not so complex.) How many different definitions of the term can you come up with? In English, there may be more than you think. If you speak another language, reflect on the uses of "culture" in that language. How do they differ from English uses?

Perhaps one way you might have defined the word "culture" in the exercise above is something akin to "the traditions, customs, beliefs, ceremonies, foods, or dress of a particular group of people." If so, your definition actually comes quite close to one of the first definitions used by anthropologists. In 1871, an early British anthropologist named Edward Burnett Tylor wrote in a book called *Primitive Culture* that "culture . . . taken in its wide ethnographic sense is that complex whole which includes knowledge, belief, art, morals, law, custom, and any other capabilities and habits acquired by man as a member of society."[2] This seems like a pretty reasonable definition and far more digestible than the one we use for this book, but it turns out to be very unsatisfactory.

To understand why anthropologists moved away from this definition, we need to recall some of the history of anthropology that we discussed in chapter 1. Tylor was a contemporary of Lewis Henry Morgan (whose book *Ancient Societies* was published in 1877), and both scholars believed in the notion of "social evolution." In other words, both Tylor and Morgan assumed that human societies could be classified by their differences in customs, morals, or beliefs, together with their various forms of technological expertise, along a developmental scale. As reasonable as it might have seemed at first glance, Tylor's definition was a tool for ranking the development of society. It did not differ significantly from Morgan's concept of "civilization," which was assumed to describe only European and North American society.[3] Although anthropologists have moved on from Tylor's use of "culture," it is still very much a part of our everyday language. Whenever we speak about culture as something that is refined, acquired, cultivated, and possessed by only a few, then we are invoking this older, social evolutionist use of the term. We may think about going to an art museum, the performance of a symphony orchestra, or a Broadway play as a chance to acquire a little "culture." There is nothing linguistically incorrect about this use of the term, but it completely misses the more complex and interesting way that modern anthropologists use the term.

As problematic as Tylor's definition was, it stuck around for a while; in fact, it was common in introductory textbooks until the 1950s and 1960s. But the use of the term culture and the context in which it was used shifted dramatically. That's because a new generation of anthropologists led by Franz Boas and others, at the turn of the twentieth century, began to question the "social evolution" framework behind it. These anthropologists were not interested in ranking societies, judging the merits of their everyday customs, or measuring their relative technological distance from European "civilization." Although it took some time to completely shift away from Tylor's definition of culture, these anthropologists did not want to merely compile a list of things and practices, such as the burial customs, marriage rituals, and spiritual beliefs of a group of people. Eventually they recognized that these entities are the by-products or *artifacts* of culture, not culture itself. Culture provided the larger context in which expressions, practices, artifacts, etc. acquired meaning. This is where things get a little more complicated.

An old Buddhist saying reminds us, "The finger that points at the moon is not the moon." That saying is relevant here. It means that we should not be fooled into thinking that the messenger is the message, or that the means that point us to an end are the end itself. In the same way, we should not be fooled into thinking that the by-products or artifacts of culture are culture itself. Instead, they point us to deeper human meanings. For many anthropologists, then, culture is the *meaning behind* that which humans produce. Morals, beliefs, customs, or laws are things; the significance that humans *give* these things is meaning. For example, the American flag is not American culture, but its negotiated meanings are—that is, the American flag can be said to point us to a deeper national conversation about what it means to be Ameri-can. Of course, this is something people discuss, debate, and argue. And this is the point: American culture is not static; it is not a thing or a group of things. It is a complex system of meaning created and maintained by people. And the same can be said for all systems or networks of interacting people who inscribe meaning on experience.

At this point, we are ready to dive back into our contemporary definition of culture and start breaking down its implications. As we said before, in an anthropological sense, culture *is a shared and negotiated system of meaning informed by knowledge that people learn and put into practice by interpreting experience and generating behavior.* In order to better understand what this complicated definition means, let's take it apart.

Culture as a Shared and Negotiated System of Meaning

To begin with, a system refers to a group of interacting or interrelated parts that operate in relation to one another. In reference to culture, those parts are (of course) people. For these *human* parts to interrelate as a meaningful system, however, there must be a broad base of shared (but not necessarily equally agreed-on) meanings. At any point where people can communicate and negotiate these shared meanings, culture is at work. When we speak of American culture, for instance, we reference a system of interacting people who share, within certain limits, a common experience. But that experience, of course, can be widely diverse. In the context of American society (read, "system"), diverse people thus interact with each other on many different levels and in many different contexts, where they communicate and negotiate to varying degrees an American experience, and, in turn, engender American culture. We can say the same for the workings of Japanese culture, New York City culture, or even "university culture." Conversely, we can say that the interrelated parts—the people—are not the culture. The interrelated parts are, in broad terms, human societies, which, as a necessary condition for culture, give rise to various "systems of meaning."

This is not to say, however, that these various systems of meaning that we call "culture" are necessarily circumscribed by clear boundaries, like geographical or political borders. To be sure, they overlap, intersect with, and compete with one another. In fact, the boundaries of where one society begins and another ends, where one culture starts and another fades, are themselves being renegotiated all the time. Thus, culture is better understood as a process. The parts that make up the system—people—are not puppets or stick figures. People like you and me constantly negotiate meaning with others, redefining what it means to belong to one group or another. The Internet provides a good example of this process. We can speak of an ever-changing culture of the Internet—something that has emerged with the technological innovations of the last few decades—but we can also observe subgroups and their subcultures that have taken shape within various forums, such as Facebook, Instagram, TikTok, or other apps.

So, just as we can talk about Japanese culture or Mexican culture or American culture or university culture or Facebook culture, we can also talk about something as particular—and indeed, peculiar—as family culture. Although clear cultural differences between families emerge between those living in, say, Brazil and Korea, different families *within* a society also have their own systems of meaning that make them unique and different from one another. Remembering this **internal differentiation** within all cultures is critical, lest we slip into generalizations or **essentialisms**—perspectives that treat culture as monolithic, static, and where everyone acts/thinks/lives the same.

Although a symbol like the American flag (seen here in a Hispanic nightclub in Evansville, Indiana) represents the United States, it in no way captures the full range of diversity within American culture. Indeed, this symbol means different things for different people. Photo by Danny Gawlowski

In Lassiter's family, for instance, telling stories was always an important part of dinnertime conversation, which often lasted for hours. His parents were farmers as children, and because this kind of dinnertime conversation was so important in their childhood, they carried the tradition with them when they left the farm. Telling stories is, of course, not unusual, but the particular stories that were told related to a particular experience that his family shared, a system of meaning that they constructed and reconstructed each time they had dinner (especially when they argued about the details or meaning of a story). Today, these stories make them who they are; they are the collective memory, or, in an anthropological sense, the collective (and negotiated, debated, and contested) system of meaning—in a word, their family culture.

Culture Is Learned and Informed by Knowledge

We are not born with an innate understanding of a particular system of meaning. It must be learned, and to learn something literally means to acquire knowledge. Cultural knowledge is not inherited or inscribed in our biology. This is important: We are not *born* with culture. We learn it. Although all humans have the biological capacity for language, the many different languages we all speak are learned through experience, study, practice, and trial and error. So while all people may not share the same language, we all share the language-learning process. Likewise, we all share the biological ability to learn culture.

Learning culture is not merely an interesting capability of human beings, secondary to biological instincts or drives. Rather, it is at the heart of what it means to be human. As we showed in the last chapter, even human biology, or our experience and understanding of human biology, can be seemingly shaped by cultural knowledge. As we discussed, race is a powerful example of the way cultural concepts shape biological experience. In America, we tend to marry within so-called racial groups, thus reproducing certain observable characteristics, like skin color, which in turn are assumed to biologically divide us into racial groups. We also learn to see ourselves as part of a racial group with associated behaviors; we learn to recognize and reproduce the boundaries between these racial groups; and we learn perceptions that define our interpretation of our own and other racial groups' behavior.

Another powerful example of how we learn to impose cultural knowledge on biology is eating. All humans face the biological need to nourish their bodies with food. But *when* to eat (such as after sundown during Ramadan) or *how* we eat (such as the custom of talking during dinner in much of the United States, or remaining silent during a meal, which is the custom in some Native American communities) or *what* we eat (whether it is curdled milk [cheese] or insects) is each intimately tied to what we learn through a limited range of experience. Even the idea that a particular food or drink tastes good or bad is acquired. Although tasting involves a biological reaction, our minds learn to cast that biological reaction in a certain way, associating pleasant or unpleasant sensations with certain foods or drinks.

In the same way that we learn to mold basic biological needs, we also learn to forge our vision of the world around us. Morality, or that which we consider to be right and wrong, is an example. We *learn* that burying our dead to dispose of them is right and correct, or we learn, as was the custom in some ancient cultures, that eating our dead to reintegrate them into our own living bodies is the right and proper thing to do. We *learn* that it is morally right to have one spouse, or we *learn*, as is also the custom in some groups, that it is right and responsible to take your spouse's unmarried siblings as spouses. We *learn* that it is morally wrong to kill another human being, or we *learn* that it is acceptable to kill another human being during war.

All of this learning—whatever its form—must take place within a system of meaning. Because we learn from others, learning is an active social process that people put into practice all the time. Anthropologists often call this process of learning culture **enculturation**. Enculturation often refers to the passing of cultural knowledge to children, but enculturation is a constant and ongoing process that goes on throughout our lives. Very recently, both children and adults have learned how to use computers; our society now takes them so much for granted that we can barely imagine our lives without them. When learning what's cool and what's not, we are being enculturated. When we learn the grammar, syntax, and meanings of a new language, we are

Enculturation is an incredibly powerful process through which one learns the system of meaning related to a particular set of behaviors. Children are continually assimilating the values, norms, and practices of the society around them, but all individuals will undergo this process when they live or work in new social circumstances. Enculturation is a lifelong process. Photo by Danny Gawlowski

being enculturated. In fact, you are being enculturated—at least to a certain extent—into the world of anthropology as we share the language, concepts, and perspectives of anthropology with you.

Culture as Practice

In order to serve the workings of "culture"—that is, as a shared and negotiated system of meaning—people must put this learned knowledge into practice. We put this knowledge into practice by *interpreting our own and others' experience* in everyday social interaction, which in turn we use to shape our actions (i.e., *generate behavior*). Still a tall order? Let's begin with the experience part of this equation.

Every human life is composed of experience; constant encounters with the world around us carry us from birth to death. These encounters with the natural and cultural environment are what we call experiences. These experiences are not completely raw encounters—they don't happen in a vacuum. From the time we are born, all new experiences are viewed through the lens of previous experiences. And those previous experiences help to determine how the new experience will be shaped, interpreted, and understood.[4]

ANTHROPOLOGY HERE AND NOW

YouTube and the Negotiation of Meaning

YouTube, of course, is a repository of audiovisual experiences where people the world over share and negotiate meaning on a daily basis. It has even become a noun in the English language to describe a digital livelihood of "a YouTuber" (as a profession). Such a platform, now so taken for granted, was unimaginable just one generation ago. It continues to change as other platforms, such as Instagram and TikTok, compete with it. The ever-evolving culture of YouTube is one of the topics of study for anthropologist Michael Wesch (Kansas State University), whom *Wired* magazine has called "the explainer." He has several well-known and award-winning YouTube videos himself. Check out his webpage at www.michaelwesch.com.

But these new experiences are framed not only by our own previous experiences but also by the larger, collective experiences—or, simply put, culture—of the particular groups in which we interact. Think about it. In this vast system of meaning we share, our personal experiences intermingle with the personal experiences of others in a much larger system of meaning that transpires in everyday social interaction, which, of course, occurs on a number of levels.[5]

Furthermore, in the context of this culture definition, "interpreting experience" refers to both the way we interpret the experience of self within a particular culture and how we encounter and experience others. When we decide that eating insects is gross or that marrying more than one spouse is wrong, we are viewing these cultural practices through the lens of our experiences, through our own enculturation into particular groups. And this is exactly how culture works: We learn and share knowledge that we use to interpret our own experiences as well as the experiences of others.

Now, on to the behavior part. In the context of our culture definition, *behavior* means to act or conduct oneself in a specified way. Of course, knowledge shapes those actions, but beyond this, our systems of meaning become enacted, embodied, and practiced through behavior, which we in turn negotiate with others in the context of society. When we answer our phone and say hello, we are putting a particular system of meaning into action—that is, we are acting out knowledge that exists in our minds. When someone dies and we follow a prescribed way of disposing of the body, we (the living, that is) are enacting systems of meaning—extending that which is in our minds into the actions of our very bodies, over and over again, shaping and reshaping the process from generation to generation. We are, of course, using behavior in a much wider sense than a simple reaction to a stimulus. When talking about the anthropological concept of culture, behavior implies a far broader range of actions and practices. Indeed, behavior is what makes experience real; it forges culture into the diversity of human activities found in the world.

An important consequence of our definition of culture is that particular human actions do not carry meaning in and of themselves. This can be a difficult point to grasp, but it is essential to understanding our definition of culture. Behavior always arises in a specific context, always exists within a larger system of meaning. Anthropologists James P. Spradley and David McCurdy put it this way: "Culture is . . . the system of knowledge by which people design their own actions and interpret the behaviors of others. It tells an American that eating with one's mouth closed is proper, while an Indian, from south Asia, knows that to be polite one must chew with one's mouth open. There is nothing preordained about cultural categories; they are arbitrary. The same act can have different meanings in various cultures. For example, when adolescent Hindu boys walk holding hands, it signifies friendship, while to Americans the same act may suggest homosexuality."[6]

Reading Spradley and McCurdy's words, other examples come to mind. When we cross our fingers and hold them next to our head in the United States, we are often expressing hope. Yet the same action in parts of highland New Guinea can imply something altogether different: It is an insult having sexual connotations.[7] For many Americans, when we look straight into the eyes of someone while we are talking to them, it means that we are listening; it is the polite thing to do. To look away while you are talking might suggest you are trying to hide something. But in some Native American communities, looking straight into the eyes of someone while talking to them would be considered rude.

These brief examples illustrate how actions and practices can have different connotations in different social contexts, that is, different systems of meaning. It is not the action itself that has meaning; it is the context—the system of meaning—within which that action occurs. This is what is meant by *arbitrary*. And, to reiterate the point one last time, *human behavior does not carry meaning in and of itself*. Any human action exists within larger systems of meaning, and we call those systems of meaning "culture."

Now you should more fully understand what culture, in an anthropological sense, is. It does include the things that humans produce (as in Tylor's definition), but ultimately these things or artifacts are always couched in a *shared and negotiated system of meaning informed by knowledge that people learn and put into practice by interpreting experience and generating behavior*. This definition of culture should make more sense at this point. Are you still having a hard time putting your finger on just what culture is? Are you getting that uncomfortable feeling that culture may be messy and unwieldy? Congratulations! You have arrived. Culture is nebulous rather than absolute, chaotic rather than harmonious, dynamic rather than idle, ubiquitous rather than esoteric, complex rather than simple. It is, because people are.

Human behavior does not carry meaning in and of itself. Any particular human action exists within larger systems of meaning that we call culture. All three authors remember their American parents demanding proper "table manners" at mealtimes when they were young. In the picture above, a Sikh family enjoys a meal at a Baisakhi celebration, eating in a manner that is completely appropriate to the cultural context, but would have been unacceptable in a traditional American home. zixia / Alamy Stock Photo

IMPLICATIONS OF THE CONCEPT OF CULTURE

In order to help you go deeper with your understanding of culture, we believe it is helpful to tease out some of the implications of our culture definition. In this section, we want to share five ways that the anthropological definition of "culture" will differ from the folk understanding of the term that you probably had before. If you feel overwhelmed by the new definition, you may find it helpful to keep these five implications in mind to help work through any confusion you may have.

1. Culture is multiple.

Because culture is always being renegotiated, it can never be an unchanging set of behaviors. If we assume that culture is a monolithic, unchanging, single list of traits—like Tylor's original definition—then we always risk slipping into stereotypes, or worse. That does not mean that there are no discernible trends. Anthropologists are often trying to identify general patterns of behaviors within a society. But it is essential to remember that these trends are always being renegotiated, often in subtle ways. Being sensitive to this process is essential for avoiding assumptions that may strike people as prejudicial and offensive and may lead to serious consequences for the group being misjudged.

One fairly innocent example can help clarify our point. While working on the revisions for this edition, Karchmer and Powell were living in Taiwan. Their children were attending a local Taiwanese school, where they were the only students from the United States. Although the three children felt very welcomed at the school, they found themselves having to navigate some surprising assumptions about Americans.

> One day, our eldest son came home from his local elementary school and exclaimed that his sixth-grade classmates wanted to know why Americans eat McDonald's hamburgers every day. Despite our son's protests, some of his classmates insisted that they were sure this was exactly what Americans did. There were lots of laughs around the family dinner table that night, which happened to feature Chinese-style cuisine. Although our son loves hamburgers, he dislikes eating at McDonald's and vehemently opposes any attempt to go there. Our son immediately saw the claims of his classmates as an absurd characterization of American cuisine. He was also struck by the irony that a number of his classmates would occasionally forego the school lunch, which he thought was both delicious and healthy, so that they could eat a McDonald's lunch, hand-delivered by their parents. This misconception about American culture seemed quite innocuous, particularly in the supportive environment of our son's well-run school. But it invites deeper reflection on how misconceptions of other cultures originate and what their impacts might be in a more charged environment.

We share this lighthearted vignette as a reminder that sweeping assumptions about the behaviors of any large group of people will almost always miss the mark. In large-scale, contemporary society, culture is always multiple, layered, and contradictory, even when there seem to be perceptible trends.

2. Culture is taken for granted and embodied.

When we state that culture is "learned," we are talking about a process that is deeper and more enduring than classroom learning, where we cram for a test and then promptly forget in a few weeks everything that we regurgitated for the exam. Anthropologists like to claim that the process of enculturation happens on a physical level. Cultural knowledge is "embodied," so to speak, to the point that much of our actions do not require thought. An American extends a hand in greeting, and it is grabbed and shaken in return. A European woman leans her head toward an acquaintance and receives a kiss on both cheeks. In the mid-twentieth century, anthropologists documented that standard greetings in areas of highland Papua New Guinea involved vigorous rubbing of the thighs and sometimes genitalia.[8] Two Japanese businessmen encounter each other and bend at the waist, back straight, hands at the side; the greater the angle of their upper bodies, the more they show respect. As these quick examples show, we have deeply internalized forms of greetings. We know automatically how to respond to a greeting in the cultural context in which we were raised. But we might feel completely out of place, or worse, if we were suddenly required to greet someone whose culturally appropriate form of greeting was unfamiliar to us.

We are often rather poor observers of our own cultural practices because we are so deeply enmeshed in them. Powell and Karchmer were reminded of this phenomenon in striking fashion several years ago, when their young son's caregiver, a middle-aged woman who had recently immigrated from rural China to North Carolina, gave their eighteen-month-old toddler his first haircut while they were at work.

> We arrived home in the late afternoon after a long day at work. Before the babysitter left, she proudly showed us the haircut she had just given our son. We stared at our son; we were in shock. The babysitter was perplexed by our crestfallen expressions, which we could not hide despite our best efforts. She had expected admiration and gratitude for a job very well done. When the confusing emotions subsided, we realized that we were so dismayed because we both considered a child's first haircut to be a rite of passage, an event that all parents would want to witness, if not bestow themselves. Prior to this moment, we had never spoken about and probably could not have even

articulated our attachment to a child's first haircut. A few days later, when we had regained our composure, the babysitter, whom we considered a dear friend, apologetically explained that nothing could be more mundane than cutting a child's hair where she grew up in rural, northern China. In fact, parents often shaved the child's head on a regular basis, and almost always on the child's first birthday. The hope was that frequent shaving would help the child's hair grow back more robustly. She explained that she had noticed our son's hair was getting in his eyes and after mentioning it to us several times, she figured we were too busy to cut it ourselves and decided to do us a favor. She never could have imagined our response. Perhaps more surprisingly, we could not have imagined it either.

In retrospect, this misunderstanding seems silly, even comical. But at the time, Powell and Karchmer were shocked, hurt, and felt a deep sense of loss that they were not present for their son's first haircut. To return to our larger point about culture, they were totally unaware of how highly they valued a child's first haircut. The sense of disappointment they felt on that day was real and not something they could rationalize away with their anthropological training. Fortunately, over time, everyone was able to laugh about this misunderstanding. Powell and Karchmer frequently asked the babysitter, who was quite skilled with a pair of scissors, to assist with future haircuts for their children.

3. Culture is normative.

Part of the process of enculturation is learning what is right and wrong within a particular society. We are rewarded for doing what is culturally accepted and punished for going against conventions. Cultural practices establish the "norms" of behavior. When we enforce those norms, we can say that culture has a normative effect. These processes are often deeply engrained and so well established that we rarely notice them until an offense is registered. For example, waiting in lines is considered polite public behavior in certain societies. When people try to "cut" to the front of the line, they may be yelled at, scolded, or perhaps even physically attacked. In other societies, however, there may be no such norm, and elbowing your way to the front is fully expected. We should not underestimate the power of these norms or imagine that we might flout them. As many scholars have shown, the most fundamental aspects of our life experiences are molded through these forces. What it means to be male or female, a member of a social class, ethnic group, religious sect, and so on, all entail powerful norms that shape one's life.

4. Culture is related to power.

Through enculturation, we may also learn the skills, behaviors, and actions that give us differential access to resources in a society. We often like to imagine that the successful members of society are its most talented. The cream rises to the top, as the expression goes. Anthropologists have a different perspective on how certain individuals or groups of individuals achieve access to certain resources while others do not. They argue that becoming successful in a particular society, which in turn gives one access to specific resources and power, is something that must be learned through the acquisition of a certain set of mannerisms, skills, certifications, knowledge, and so on. For example, a college degree is an increasingly important requirement for accessing well-paying employment opportunities in many societies. But getting into college in the first place often requires certain kinds of family structures, access to well-functioning schools, teachers and parents that teach children how to comport themselves in academic settings, etc. Once the college degree is in hand, it may open the door to certain work opportunities that give an individual the training, skills, and cultural competency to advance further in a career trajectory.

5. Culture is all-encompassing.

Lastly, anthropologists see cultural processes woven into all aspects of our daily lives. This perspective challenges our everyday assumptions about the concept of culture. Because culture, in its older meaning, is historically associated with the arts and humanities, we often think of the sciences as having little to do with culture. The anthropological definition of culture rejects any such divide. The systems of meanings in which daily activities are carried out do not pertain to particular areas of social life and not others. Thus, even the scientist working at her lab bench in the quest for new knowledge operates within certain cultural assumptions. She may believe in a certain definition of objectivity and modern forms of knowledge-making, while rejecting other, empirical ways of knowing the world that have sustained traditional communities around the world for generations. Her rigorous training may make her an expert in her area of scientific exploration, but it does not liberate her from the systems of meaning into which she has been enculturated. The all-encompassing quality of culture is one of the radical implications of the anthropological definition of this term, and it will take some time to digest and assimilate its consequences.

An important methodological corollary to the all-encompassing quality of culture is that it requires anthropologists to take a **holistic** approach to their research. Anthropologists cannot limit their study of a community to certain aspects of social life, while totally ignoring other features. This *holistic perspective* pushes anthropologists to try to understand the big picture and not get lost by focusing solely on details. Thus, in anthropology, holism encourages us to understand humans as both biological and cultural beings, as living in both the past and the present. Elucidating the relationships in all that is human is especially important to holism. Holism reminds us that regardless of whether we are biological, archaeological, linguistic, or cultural anthropologists, anthropology is ultimately concerned with understanding the human condition in *all of* its complexities. As such, anthropologists realize that there are a number of ways to understand the human condition, from literature and art to science and mathematics. Indeed, literature, art, science, and mathematics are each a distinct area of study that leads us to understand human beings in a unique way. Taken together, they give us a greater understanding of the whole.

We recognize that the anthropological definition of culture can feel unwieldly to new students of the discipline. Even if that is not the case for you, we encourage you to reflect on the five points above as a practical means for incorporating the culture concept into your studies and your everyday life. As you do, you will find yourself thinking more and more like an anthropologist.

STUDYING CULTURE: HOLISM AND COMPARATIVISM

Given that culture is nebulous, chaotic, dynamic, ubiquitous, and complex, how do anthropologists actually know what they know about culture? What are the conceptual tools they use to go about *understanding* the culture concept in all of its dimensions? More importantly, what are the conceptual tools that we need to appreciate the power of culture in human life?

First and foremost, the holistic perspective of anthropology emphasizes understanding how the parts of culture work together to create a larger system of meaning. The interrelations among a society's history, politics, and economics are examples. We can't really understand one part—history—without understanding the other parts, politics and economics. This is holism, plain and simple. In the study of culture, to focus only on economics, for example, is to miss larger patterns. Anthropologist James L. Peacock puts it this way: "To think holistically is to see parts as wholes, to try to grasp the broader contexts and frameworks within which people behave and experience. One such framework is culture. Anthropology is concerned not only with holistically analyzing the place of humans in society and in nature but also, and especially, with the way humans construct cultural frameworks in order to render their lives meaningful."[9]

Take the study of American culture. To understand such a complex system, we would want to take into account the history and development of this individual nation-state, its economics and politics, as well as its individual traditions, values, or customs, *and* how they interact with one another as a system, which of course includes the American people themselves. If we wanted to understand a smaller part of American culture, like religion, we would want to take into account all the components of religious belief in America—from Catholicism to Protestantism, from Islam to Judaism, from **fundamentalism** to atheism. We would also want to take into account how religious belief is negotiated in this country, its deeper meanings to American identity, and how it spills over into other realms of American experience, like politics. Still further, if we wanted to focus on the culture of one particular religion in the United States, or even the culture of a particular church, once again we would want to take into account its every part and *how it interacts* with other parts as a system.

Here's another example. **Ethnomusicology** is an area of study that combines aspects of both musicology and anthropology to understand the role and meaning of music cross-culturally. Ethnomusicologists don't just study music, however. As a group, ethnomusicologists try to understand in a holistic way the larger human complexities of music, which is a cultural universal—that is, all human groups practice an expression that they separate from that which is spoken, an expression that we call, in English, "music." Ethnomusicologists (and other social scientists who study music) try to understand how musical expression in each case spills over into other areas of human activity and meaning. They do, because it always does.

Over and over again, music expresses and shapes deeper meanings about national, regional, or ethnic identity (think about the national anthems of modern nation-states); music expresses and shapes solidarity (think about the use of "We Shall Overcome" in the civil rights movement); music expresses and shapes political agendas (think about the use of pop songs in US election campaigns); music expresses and shapes protest and rebellion (think about punk music of the 1970s and 1980s); music expresses and shapes religious belief (think about the fact that people use music in almost every religious tradition); music expresses and shapes the buying and selling of commodities (think about advertising); music expresses and shapes human emotion (think about the use of music in the movie and television industry); and music even expresses and shapes how we think about ourselves (think of the radio stations you listen to or the music collections you own). In each case, if we focused only on the sound of music itself, we would miss its significance and power in other realms of human life and meaning. To understand music, at least as an ethnomusicologist, we must understand the larger contexts in which music expresses and shapes human activity.

To look for such connections between parts is holism. Yet, as might be apparent, holism is an insurmountable goal in many respects; it can seem completely overwhelming, especially when we consider that almost every human system is part of another larger system, which is in turn part of a still larger system. We could very well take the study of music or American culture to the point of infinity. With this in mind, you may very well ask: Can we ever grasp the wholeness of culture? Can we ever understand every component of a system as complex as American or world culture? When we consider that understanding all the subtle nuances of a single individual is nearly impossible, how can we presume to know as much about an entire group or society? Anthropologist James L. Peacock answers: "Holism is an important but impossible ideal. You cannot see everywhere or think everything. You must select and emphasize. To do this, you must categorize and make distinctions. Only in this way can you analyze and understand."[10]

Anthropologists thus approach culture with the philosophy of and struggle for holism but realize that ultimately one must focus on parts—parts that, when compared to other parts, point us in the direction of understanding larger human issues. Hence, anthropologists often study a particular church to make inferences about the role of religion in human life, or they study one kind of music to understand music's role within a particular society, or they study a small group of women in a rural village to understand larger issues of gender in human life. In each case, an individual study enters into conversation with other anthropological studies that, when taken together, have something to offer our understandings of religion, music, or gender, respectively.

Each of these studies, which focus on the particular, points us in the direction of holism, which in turn points us to a deeper understanding of culture. But just like the saying "The finger that points at the moon is not the moon," we realize its incompleteness—that we are always *in the process* of understanding culture.

ANTHROPOLOGY HERE AND NOW

From the Particular to the General

Anthropologists may study the particular to gain insight into larger human issues. Take, for example, the work of environmental anthropologist Laura Ogden (Dartmouth College), whose earlier work on alligators in the Florida Everglades and more recent work on beavers and lichen (among other things) in Tierra del Fuego, helps us gain a better grasp on how communities in seemingly out-of-the-way places experience environmental changes. Environmental anthropologists like Ogden often explore how human–environment relationships are affected by policies of the state, a set of farming practices, an infrastructure project, a site of industrial pollution, or other human activities to develop analytical insight on more general questions of what it means to be human. You can learn more about Ogden's research and environmental anthropology at http://www.laura-ogden.com/.

This does not mean that anthropologists, or anyone, for that matter, can *never* attain a clear understanding of culture. Rather, as James Peacock says: "Culture is not a physical thing but an attitude, a way of viewing the world. We can describe indications of a certain cultural pattern—people hurrying or loitering as clues to their assumptions about time, for example—but culture itself is an abstraction that we make based on such indications. There is nothing wrong with an abstraction so long as we recognize it for what it is."[11]

In this way, holism reminds us that the very concept of culture is an abstraction; it is *not a thing*, as we have already established. Yet Peacock implores us to remember that culture, although an abstraction, "can nonetheless have reality and power in experience."[12] This is why anthropologists often focus on the particular, on small communities, or on a few people—sites where culture is embodied, enacted, experienced, and in turn negotiated—on an intimate human level.[13] This focus on the intimate can provide one of the most effective ways to explore and reveal the power of the larger abstraction that is culture.

Anthropologist Philippe Bourgois, for example, lived and studied with over two dozen crack dealers in East Harlem for five years. By studying the particular among a very few in a small community, Bourgois was able to point us toward an understanding of the way worldwide economic patterns are articulated in the lives of drug users and dealers in an underground economy; how the use of violence becomes meaningful to success in the illegal drug trade; and how dealers respond to and shape larger drug markets. When reading Bourgois's work, we realize that the users and dealers he describes are a very small component of a much larger culture of illegal drug use and trade. Yet we also realize that Bourgois's study of a small number of drug dealers allows us to understand the larger culture of illegal drug use and trade in ways that broad generalizations about these issues never could.[14] Each anthropological study is like this. Although focusing on one particular *part*, it points us to broader discussions.

This means that in the study of culture, there is also a **comparative** perspective. The particular is always struggling against the general, and vice versa. On the one hand, while we may emphasize how culture is different from one group to the next, it is important to understand that all culture shares similarities (like the common problems presented by the food quest). On the other hand, while we may recognize that all culture has common elements, it is important to recognize that culture also has unique qualities (consider the ways people define "good" and "bad" food). Thus, in order to understand culture both particularly and generally, we must try to understand culture in all its complexities. We struggle to see parts in larger cultural contexts (holism), and we push for understanding the comprehensive role of culture in people's lives without losing sight of its particular expression in human experience (comparativism).

While holism and comparativism are important features of anthropology, they are not easily accomplished. People characteristically generalize and compare on the basis of their own experience. They often see the parts and connections they *want* to see. As the German philosopher Arthur Schopenhauer once said, "Every man takes the limits of his own field of vision for the limits of the world." Certainly, many people the world over believe their own religion to be the *right* religion, or they say that the music of other people all sounds alike, or they think that all people are essentially the same, or, at the other extreme, that nobody is like them. In order to pursue holism and comparativism in a more reliable way, we need to look at two more concepts that, when fully understood and properly balanced, make holism and comparativism possible: ethnocentrism and cultural relativity.

ETHNOCENTRISM AND CULTURAL RELATIVITY

These two concepts—ethnocentrism and cultural relativity—are among the most important terms related to newer anthropological definitions of culture. The former is a potential impediment to the study of culture; the latter represents an essential principle or orientation that enables the understanding of culture. Once you begin to feel comfortable with these concepts, you will be well on your way to thinking like an anthropologist.

Ethnocentrism is the tendency to evaluate the world from the basis of one's own experience. On a very fundamental human level, we cannot help but be ethnocentric. It is a fact of every human life. Our experience is limited, and what exists outside the limits of that experience is foreign and strange. But more than this, the cultural knowledge, customs, traditions, values, and ideas with which we are enculturated have enormous power in defining how we will continue to encounter, experience, and understand the world around us. Often, we are completely unconscious of the fact that the way we live and experience the world fashions our ethnocentrism. Indeed, ethnocentrism is so basic to our being that we may not even realize just how powerful it can be. Many Americans, for instance, are often unaware of how culturally specific "notions of beauty" shape their views of themselves and others. And those views can have powerful implications: Studies have illustrated that these notions of beauty can affect things like popularity, employment and hiring decisions, and even student evaluations of their professors. In one interesting study, researchers found that "attractive professors consistently outscore their less comely colleagues by a significant margin on student evaluations of teaching."[15] Of course, the physical qualities that make some professors "attractive" and others "less comely" are neither universal nor uniform; our attributions of attractiveness are rooted in ethnocentrism, shaped by very powerful cultural, often unconscious, ideas about what constitutes beauty.

Culturally specific, shared notions of beauty shape how we perceive and enact personal ideas of beauty. PeopleImages / iStock

Realizing the power of ethnocentrism is the first step toward understanding the bias that we carry in our studies of culture. No one can be completely bias-free. But everyone can, first, recognize that they are ethnocentric, and, second, seek ways to understand culture outside of their own view of the world. Put another way, we must shift ethnocentrism from the unconscious to the conscious realm of knowledge.

Within the narrow confines of our everyday lives, ethnocentrism guides us as to what behaviors are acceptable and proper. But in our ever-shrinking, globalizing world, ethnocentrism can get in the way of understanding other people and other cultural practices. It can prevent us from understanding the larger questions of culture. In fact, when ethnocentrism is taken to the extreme, it can turn into overt prejudice and racism, and even slip toward extreme forms of bigotry and hatred. If unchecked, ethnocentrism can cause us to not only miss the deeper intricacies of culture, but also the commonality of human experience. As a result, we ourselves become more set apart and less human.

Anthropologist Beth Conklin has taken on the topic of ethnocentrism in her excellent ethnography, *Consuming Grief.* She conducted research among the Wari, a small Indigenous group in the Brazilian Amazonian basin that was rumored to have once practiced cannibalism. In most societies, there are few human behaviors that are more taboo, more forbidden, than the consumption of human flesh. Recognizing the ethical risks of tackling such a topic, Conklin proceeded cautiously with her research. She was keenly aware that European colonizers had used charges of cannibalism as a rhetorical tool for justifying the conquest and subjugation of so-called "savage" peoples. Unsurprisingly, her Wari acquaintances were initially not receptive to her inquiries. Not only is cannibalism forbidden by the Brazilian government, but the Wari were also acutely aware of how outsiders viewed this topic. Conklin was even scolded by her Wari acquaintances for her insistent questioning on this issue over others that they considered much more important to their everyday lives.

Conklin took this admonition to heart. She expanded her inquiries, learning about the everyday life practices of the Wari, from family interactions to political arrangements with neighboring tribes, from healing practices to religious beliefs. Eventually she did learn that the consumption of human flesh had been part of the Wari rituals for mourning the deceased up until the 1950s, before the Brazilian government had established political dominion over the region. These acts were part of an elaborate set of rituals to grieve the passing of deceased relatives, and nothing like the colonial imaginings of "savages" lusting for human flesh. Conklin learned that the death of a relative was, and continues to be, an emotionally wrenching experience for the Wari. Family members respond to the loss of a loved one by eliminating all reminders of the deceased's physical presence, notably by destroying the loved one's former residence and belongings, as means to managing their pain. In early times, the body of the deceased itself was also destroyed—both physically and symbolically—through the practice of mortuary cannibalism. A burial would have been considered disrespectful to the deceased, since it meant abandoning the body to the "cold" and unwelcoming ground.

As Conklin came to understand, the act of consuming human flesh had been just a small part of an entire cosmology that linked humans to animals and other beings through a circulation of spirits between the worlds of the living and dead. It is this complex cosmology that becomes the ultimate focus of her ethnography. The above description is far too brief to do justice to Conklin's research and the fascinating cultural practices of the Wari. But this overview reminds us of the importance of consciously attending to our inevitable ethnocentrisms, of holding these emotions in check to allow for the possibility of other understandings. Anthropologists recognize our distaste for ways of living that seem to violate our own cultural norms as an obstacle to the study of culture in all its diversity and richness.

How do we overcome our own ethnocentrism, if ethnocentrism is so intrinsic to the human experience? Conklin's research shows us the way. When we consider human behavior from *others'* perspective, from the viewpoint of the people one is investigating, we are using the conceptual tool of **cultural relativity**. Cultural relativity is an important principle that derives from our newer definition of culture and an essential feature of modern anthropological research. It allows us to study culture through the frameworks of holism and comparativism.

Cultural relativity, you will recall from our discussion of Boas, is the idea that each society or culture must be understood on its own terms. It does not mean that we necessarily agree with every cultural practice that we come across; it means that if we really want to *understand* how culture works, we must look at culture from the viewpoints of those who create, maintain, and experience it, not from our own.

Take, for example, Bourgois's work with inner-city drug dealers. Bourgois did not condone the selling of drugs or the brute violence on which the culture of dealing illegal drugs often rests. Instead, Bourgois approached the drug dealers through the framework of cultural relativity rather than judgment so that he could understand how the culture of selling crack really works. After five years of living and studying on the street, Bourgois began to understand drug dealers as people struggling to survive on the margins of American society. He wrote that the drug dealers had "not passively accepted their structural victimization. On the contrary, by embroiling themselves in the underground economy and proudly embracing street culture, they are seeking an alternative to their social marginalization."[16]

While Bourgois came to these understandings through cultural relativity without succumbing to ethnocentrism, he also directly witnessed overt acts of violence. Understanding this "culture of terror" was critical to understanding how this component of street culture worked; it also reinforced Bourgois's conviction that the illegal drug trade and its accompanying attributes of violence were deeply detrimental to American society. While the drug dealers had found ways to survive in the inner city, they also had "become the actual agents administering their own destruction and their community's suffering."[17]

Bourgois's intimate five-year study would not have been possible without his determination to maintain a position of cultural relativity. Yet, like ethnocentrism, cultural relativity can also be taken to extremes. In fact, one common criticism of cultural relativity is that it absolves us from making judgments, from taking an ethical stand against acts of violence, intimidation, deception, or other forms of abuse. Consider violence against women. Women continue to suffer from rape, sexual assault, harassment, and international trafficking all around the world.[18] Does a stance of cultural relativism prevent us from raising our voices in protest against such acts? Does it instruct us to look away for the sake of understanding another society "on its own terms?"

This kind of extreme moral laxity would, of course, be very concerning, but it is not what anthropologists mean when they call for cultural relativism. To return to Bourgois's work, there are many points in his ethnography where he expresses dismay, even horror, at the capacity of his informants for all manner of violence, toward women, animals, and each other. He never excuses or condones this violence. But by staying true to the principle of cultural relativity, he helps his readers understand how these actions have become insidiously valorized by the marginalized conditions in which his informants live.

It is not uncommon to encounter attacks on cultural relativism. Partisans for a particular way of life might attack cultural relativism as enabling all kinds of horrific behavior, perhaps even genocide or ethnic cleansing, by a group of people because it is somehow part of "their culture." Certainly, this kind of moral nihilism would be chilling, but it is a distortion of the principle of cultural relativism that anthropologists advocate, and moreover, it is based on an impoverished definition of culture.

Let's explore the example of **genocide** a little further, since it is such an extreme example. Sadly, it turns out that genocide is a dark underside of many, many societies around the world. We may be most familiar with the Holocaust of Nazi Germany, but scholars have documented genocide and mass killing throughout human history.[19] The twentieth century alone has been particularly egregious for its acts of mass murder, including the Nazis' Holocaust (6 million), Stalin's Great Terror (1 million), and the Cambodian genocide of the Khmer Rouge (2.5 million). Estimates of those who have perished as a result of genocide in the twentieth century range as high as 28 million.

But consider the figures of genocides from just 1950 to 2000. From 1955 to 1972, the Sudanese army eradicated 500,000 Southern Sudanese people.

In 1971, in Bangladesh, the East Pakistan army murdered about 3 million people. In 1972, in Burundi, Tutsis killed around 200,000 Hutus, and in Rwanda, in the course of a few months in 1994 alone, Hutus exterminated well over 500,000 Tutsis. From North and South America to Eurasia to Africa, genocide is a phenomenon that all humans share in their collective past.[20] Unfortunately, the capacity for great violence seems to be shared by societies all over the world. It is likely that the political and military technologies of the twentieth century have only made this violence more extreme.

There are obviously some extremely dark sides to human societies, but that does not mean we have to abandon the principle of cultural relativism. Even human violence needs to be understood within its particular context. Moreover, the statement "Well, it's their culture" is actually just another example of the sweeping generalizations that the anthropological definition of culture rejects. Did the victims of genocide condone the violence against them? Do the victims of sexual abuse welcome such behavior? If we remember that culture is always multiple, that societies are always complex, we can realize that there can be extremely important anthropological research to be done in order to understand how some individuals are allowed to perpetuate violence while others are condemned to be victims. The real questions thus become: What are the social conditions that allowed this violence to flourish? How do community members respond to the violence and its terrible consequences? Can we work to change people's attitudes about each other? While recognizing the complexities of human differences, how can we build bridges of understanding between people?

Anthropologists have, in fact, been trying to answer just such questions, without endorsing the violence they study. In her book *Genocide Lives in Us*, Jennie Burnet explores how women in postgenocide Rwanda are renegotiating their roles in a society in which the violence of genocide continues to haunt the everyday fabric of life years after the event. Her analysis acknowledges the messy complexities of Rwandan society, where there are rarely clear lines between right and wrong, and many individuals have been both victim and perpetrator at different times.[21]

Ethnocentrism and cultural relativity are two essential concepts for cultural anthropology. While their definitions may seem straightforward, they can be difficult to grasp in practice. Both newcomers to the field and professional anthropologists alike must struggle to negotiate the complexities of these two concepts. We will continue to explore these challenges in the next chapter on ethnographic fieldwork. As we hope you will see, the reward for this struggle is a deeper and more nuanced understanding of the human condition.

SUMMING UP: ANTHROPOLOGICAL PERSPECTIVES ON CULTURE

Culture's role in human life is enormous. Yet popular ideas about culture are often limited to traditions, customs, or habits. Although these "things" are certainly part of culture, they are only a small part of a larger equation that can lead us to understanding human beings in all their complexities. And because human beings are complicated, so, too, is culture. Living in today's complex world thus means that we are increasingly called on to understand culture in much more complicated ways—from our daily interactions with others to the relationships between nation-states on the world stage. Not until

Cultural relativity is a tool for mutual understanding, but it should not be used uncritically in a way that may hinder our common efforts to address complex, multifaceted global problems. Indeed, all the world's citizens increasingly find themselves having to evaluate their cultural practices in light of our rapidly changing and ever more integrated world. Nelson Mandela (center), for example, argued that addressing Africa's AIDS epidemic required more than just educating the public. People must also change conventional cultural practices that augment the spread of this infectious disease. Photo by Luke Eric Lassiter

we understand culture in its broader framework can we approach complex human problems and reach for their complex solutions. Understanding the intricacies of culture can thus offer us a powerful tool for understanding and creating change in our own lives and in our own communities.

With this said, let's briefly review. First, we want to recall our basic definition of culture as *a shared and negotiated system of meaning informed by knowledge that people learn and put into practice by interpreting experience and generating behavior.* Breaking this down into its constituent parts, you will want to remember the following:

- Culture is a system of meaning (the system is made up of parts—that is, people).
- Culture is shared and negotiated among and between people.
- Culture is learned through enculturation and consists of knowledge.
- Culture frames and generates behavior (and vice versa).

Second, our definition of culture can sometimes seem abstract and hard to understand in practice. It will also be helpful if you can remember the key implications of the anthropological definition of culture.

1. Culture is multiple.
2. Culture is taken for granted and embodied.
3. Culture is normative.
4. Culture is related to power.
5. Culture is all-encompassing.

Given the complexity of the term, studying culture is a challenging task for anthropologists. They try to strike a balance between a holistic and comparative perspective. Two essential tools in their task are the concepts of ethnocentrism and cultural relativity. We believe that in our rapidly globalizing world, all readers, not just professional anthropologists, should be familiar with the challenge of ethnocentrism and the principle of cultural relativism. In order to understand what these two terms mean in practice, we must look specifically at the methodology of cultural anthropologists. This methodology is called ethnography, and it is the subject of the next chapter.

NOTES

1. This culture definition (and the following discussion of culture in the section "Defining Culture") is based on several sources. The focus on culture as a negotiated system of meaning is informed by Gregory Bateson, *Steps to an Ecology of Mind* (San Francisco: Chandler, 1972); James Clifford, *The Predicament of Culture* (Cambridge, MA: Harvard University Press, 1988); Clifford Geertz, *The Interpretation of Cultures* (New York: Basic Books, 1973); *Local Knowledge: Further Essays in Interpretive Anthropology* (New York: Basic Books, 1983); and Renato Rosaldo, *Culture and Truth: The Remaking of Social Analysis* (Boston: Beacon Press, 1993). The focus on cultural knowledge is revised from James P. Spradley, ed., in *Culture and Cognition: Rules, Maps, and Plans* (San Francisco: Chandler, 1972), 6–18, and especially *The Ethnographic Interview* (New York: Holt, Rinehart and Winston, 1979), in which Spradley states, "[C]ulture . . . [is the] acquired knowledge that people use to interpret experience and generate social behavior" (5). This perspective has precedence with Ward Goodenough's writings—see, for example, "Cultural Anthropology and Linguistics," in *Report of the Seventh Annual Round Table Meeting on Linguistics and Language Study*, ed. P. L. Garvin (Washington, DC: *Georgetown University Monograph Series on Language and Linguistics*, no. 9, 1957), and *Culture, Language, and Society* (Menlo Park, CA: Benjamin/Cummings, 1981). The departure from the rules of culture and elaboration of experience and practice of culture (especially in the discussion that follows) is informed primarily by Pierre Bourdieu, *Outline of a Theory of Practice*, trans. R. Nice (Cambridge: Cambridge University Press, 1977), which we pose here within the context of an introductory discussion. See also Michael Jackson, ed., *Things As They Are: New Directions in Phenomenological Anthropology* (Bloomington: Indiana University Press, 1996), and Victor W. Turner and Edward M. Bruner, *The Anthropology of Experience* (Chicago: University of Illinois Press, 1986).

2. Edward B. Tylor, *Primitive Culture*, vol. 1 (New York: Harper & Row, 1958 [1871]).

3. George Stocking, "Franz Boas and the Culture Concept in Historical Perspective," *American Anthropologist* 68, no. 4 (1966): 867–81.

4. See Edward M. Bruner, "Experience and Its Expressions," in Turner and Bruner, *The Anthropology of Experience*, 3–30.

5. Ibid.

6. James P. Spradley and David W. McCurdy, eds., *Culture and Conflict: Readings in Cultural Anthropology*, 8th ed. (New York: HarperCollins, 1994), 4–5.

7. Paul Wohlt, personal communication, 2000.

8. Kenneth Read, *The High Valley* (New York: Columbia University Press, 1965).

9. James L. Peacock, *The Anthropological Lens: Harsh Light, Soft Focus* (Cambridge: Cambridge University Press, 1986), 17.

10. Ibid., 19–20.

11. Ibid., 20.

12. Ibid., 23.

13. For a deeper discussion, see Peacock, *The Anthropological Lens*, 11ff.

14. See Philippe Bourgois, *In Search of Respect: Selling Crack in El Barrio* (Cambridge: Cambridge University Press, 1995).

15. Gabriela A. Montell, "Do Good Looks Equal Good Evaluations?" *Chronicle of Higher Education* (October 15, 2003).

16. Bourgois, *In Search of Respect*, 143.

17. Ibid.

18. See United Nations Population Fund, *The State of World Population 2000* (New York: United Nations Population Fund), especially chapter 3, "Violence against Women and Girls: A Human Rights and Health Priority."

19. Norman M. Naimark, *Genocide: A World History* (Oxford: Oxford University Press, 2017).

20. Michael N. Dobkowski and Isidor Wallimann, *Genocide in Our Time: An Annotated Bibliography with Analytical Introductions* (Ann Arbor, MI: Pierian Press, 1992); Israel W. Charny, ed., *Encyclopedia of Genocide*, 2 vols. (Santa Barbara, CA: ABC-CLIO, 1999); Isidor Wallimann and Michael N. Dobkowski, eds., *Genocide and the Modern Age: Etiology and Case Studies of Mass Death* (Syracuse, NY: Syracuse University Press, 2000).

21. Jennie Burnet, *Genocide Lives in Us: Women, Memory and Silence in Rwanda* (Madison: University of Wisconsin Press, 2011).

3

Ethnography

Because culture is a concept that is so central to the work of anthropologists, it is not surprising that anthropologists also have a unique methodology for studying culture and a special genre of writing to communicate their observations and experiences generated by such study. Perhaps it is also because methodology and communication are so intertwined that anthropologists have a single word that captures both activities—"ethnography." In this chapter, we will explore how anthropologists "do" ethnography (the methodology) and "write" ethnography (communicate their findings).

In order to explain the basics of ethnography, both as methodological practice and writing craft, we will need to return to the work of another founding figure in anthropology, Bronislaw Malinowski, a rough contemporary of Franz Boas. Before we do, we would like to begin with an excerpt from a recent ethnography. While ethnographic methods have not changed greatly since Malinowski, ethnographic writing continues to evolve in dynamic ways. We hope that this excerpt will give you some appreciation for the exciting developments in contemporary ethnographic writing, which in turn may help you think about the nitty-gritty of ethnographic method.

In *Running Out: In Search of Water on the High Plains*, anthropologist Lucas Bessire weaves storytelling with observation, creating a text that evokes a sense of place and urgency—two dimensions of powerful ethnography. The ethnographic writings of early anthropologists tended to be quite empirical, perhaps even dry by today's standards, as these scholars tried to demonstrate the "scientific" merit of their new discipline. Contemporary anthropologists are much more sensitive to the craft of writing itself, as this excerpt from Bessire clearly shows.

> On the high plains of western Kansas, there is no clear line between water and second chances. Although I didn't know it at the time, I was in search of both when I turned my Prius off a two-lane highway and onto the washboard gravel that led back to the farm.
>
> After fifteen years, the land matched my memories of it. I recalled precisely the vault of space, the circled sky the most dominant feature and the sun a physical weight. Grids of stubble that rotate every half-mile, from corn to wheat to sorghum to corn. Each field a parable about boys who become men by learning to plow every inch, by knowing what not to know, by never leaving or by never coming back . . .
>
> He answered the metal door in his preferred retirement getup, a SpongeBob bathrobe and a silverbelly Stetson. At that moment, I realized the only thing I could say for certain was that he was born to this gusty land. Before, he liked to keep his distance. By then, he had little choice. And sometimes distance is as close to caring for each other as a father and a son can get.
>
> I stayed one night. Like always, I slept in the fixed-up barn, not the house. When the irrigation motor woke me up, I knew I'd been gone too long. The unmuffled Case engine sits a mile-and-a-cornfield from the Little Rock House. The big motor pumps 1,400 gallons of crystalline groundwater per minute nearly every day from early spring to late fall straight into the desiccating wind. Its steady drone was the backdrop to my childhood summers on the farm, as ordinary as the heat and flies and storms. But that first night back, its ceaseless rhythm was distracting.[1]

In these opening lines, we observe the author doing something that would have been inconceivable in early ethnographic writings—returning home. In the early days of the discipline, the study of culture generally required traveling to a remote corner of the globe (at least from the perspective of the European and North American scholars). In addition, there was often still a subtle, quasi-colonial relationship between the anthropologists trained in the West and their research subjects, usually located somewhere within a European or American colony. Today these geopolitical relationships have changed, and anthropologists are far more attuned to potential power inequalities between researcher and community. At the same time, anthropologists have realized that their methods can be applied just as well in a local community as halfway around the world. Despite Bessire's very contemporary choice of research locale, he is doing something in these opening paragraphs that all ethnographies must do. He is setting the scene, before he introduces his main interest in the next section.

> Because it draws from the water sands under the former riverbed, this motor was one of the few wells in this corner of the Plains still pumping at full capacity. After eight decades of intensive irrigation, other wells in the county had dwindled. Many had gone dry. In 2014, the well at the Little Rock House hit bottom. My father redrilled and luckily hit water farther down. Since then he'd grown increasingly alarmed about the dropping water table. He asked around. Neighbors confirmed his suspicions. During my visit, my father told me about a nearly incredible scale of aquifer decline.
>
> His stories lingered after I left. Over the following weeks, I checked out my father's claims. The situation was worse than he suspected. I learned that southwest Kansas is a front line of the global water crisis. . . .
>
> Groundwater, in particular, is under threat. Worldwide, billions rely on it as their primary source of water. More than half of the water used in agriculture is mined from underground. . . . Far more groundwater is pumped than can be naturally replenished.
>
> The result is that most of the major aquifers in the world's arid or semiarid zones are rapidly declining. Groundwater extraction is draining aquifers across the globe, including those under the North China Plain, the Arabian peninsula, northern India, central Australia, California, parts of Chile, and many others. Most of this groundwater eventually makes its way to the sea. So much groundwater is pumped to the surface and drained into the oceans that it is now a major contributor to sea level rise, roughly on par with melting glaciers. Aquifers around the world are vanishing. Their disappearance often goes unnoticed or unmourned. Many will never return.[2]

In this second section, we observe Bessire shifting from the intimacy of his encounter with his father and memories of his childhood in Kansas to the water crisis that will be the central concern of his ethnography. We experience the rhythmic drone of the groundwater pump, imagine the gallons of water it sprays day after day, but also step back and learn that the disappearing aquifers of southwest Kansas are part of a water crisis affecting numerous areas of the globe. These two perspectives—what we can loosely call an insider's look at everyday life and an outsider's grasp of larger social, political, economic, or historic forces—are the linchpins of great ethnographic writing. At this point, you may already be hooked, ready to dive into Bessire's ethnography.

Storytelling like this helps anthropologists—and readers—"get at" culture, and is a departure from more scientifically driven narrative styles that aimed at a positivist description of a clearly demarcated world "out there." Instead, we see how ethnography, the focus of this chapter, can be a "sensibility," or a mode of knowing and relaying that carries the storyteller along with it.[3] Bessire's vivid description of the Kansas landscape, integrated with his own experiences and memories of it, and its emerging vulnerabilities due to climate change (aquifer depletion), takes us deep into a social realm, through the author's participation and observation, that we otherwise might not experience ourselves.

We started this chapter with this intriguing excerpt because we wanted to give you a sense of how the definition of culture is directly connected to how anthropologists study and write about culture. In the communities where anthropologists work, they follow the local practices, meanings, values, and creations as comprehensively as possible, and then they write about what they have observed, engaging in a form of storytelling about their community of research. The stories they construct are grounded on close, rigorous observation, but like any narrative, they also have transformative powers in and of themselves.

This chapter is dedicated to introducing readers to **ethnography**. To reiterate the key point above, anthropologists use this important term in two ways. First, ethnography refers to cultural anthropology's distinctive qualitative method for investigating and exploring the intricacies of culture as lived, such as when anthropologists state that they "do ethnography" in a particular locale. Second, it also refers to the product of that research, a form of writing that describes the cultural practices of a community.

In the previous chapter, we introduced an anthropological definition of culture, its driving concepts, and the philosophical constructs that orient anthropologists in their study of culture. This definition helped us start to address the deeper complexities of **ethnocentrism** (the belief that one's own cultural beliefs or practices are the "natural" and "right" way) and its counterposing concept of **cultural relativity** (which comes to us from Boas, as introduced in chapter 1). Ethnocentrism and cultural relativity form the essential guardrails for anthropologists as they "do" and "write" ethnography. We will see that the ethical principles at stake with ethnocentrism and cultural relativism are also at the heart of ethnography, both as methodology and writing practice.

ETHNOGRAPHY ACROSS THE ATLANTIC: BRITISH SOCIAL ANTHROPOLOGY AND BRONISLAW MALINOWSKI

Ethnography emerged in the early twentieth century partly in response to the nineteenth-century "armchair anthropology" of social evolutionists who rarely left their drawing rooms (offices), or who based their theories on written reports by travelers, military officials, or collectors, rather than their own empirical observations. Ethnography indexes "firsthand" or "direct" experience, however imperfect, incomplete, and unfinished. This is the kind of experience that comes from "being there" in a place, in a community, in a manner that is not that of the tourist, colonial official, or attendee at a special event, but that of an empathetic witness to everyday life.

The emergence of ethnography is a critical part of our anthropological story because it marks a serious departure from social evolutionary theories of human difference, by providing *empirical evidence through sustained engagement over time*. Today, ethnographic methods are used in fields outside of anthropology (for instance, in education studies), but it is important for our story that we understand why and how it first emerged *within* the then-young discipline of anthropology, as a novel approach to understanding culture that requires journeying "into the field"—whether that "field site" is down the street or on the other side of the planet.

Although most anthropologists working in North America associate the development of contemporary American anthropology with Franz Boas, many anthropologists associate the development of *ethnography* with Bronislaw Malinowski.[4] About the same time Franz Boas was molding American anthropology around cultural relativism and historical particularism (see chapter 1), Polish-born British social anthropologist Bronislaw Malinowski put forward a new, systematic way of observing and writing descriptions of culture. Malinowski influenced British social anthropology in ways that paralleled Boas's influence in the United States; both have had global impacts on anthropology's formations outside of the "West," although there are critical historical differences, and other anthropological genealogies in Asia, Africa, and Latin America, which are beyond the scope of this chapter. In the broadest sense, Boas and Malinowski offer two historical "anchors" for the emergence of the discipline as we know it today in North America and Western Europe.

Malinowski was, in many ways, embroiled in the same kinds of discussions as Boas, though on another continent. Like Boas, Malinowski advocated embedding oneself within the lives of a particular society for long periods of time; Malinowski's response to the social evolutionists who rarely left their offices was to cultivate what he called "the native's point of view." The goal of ethnography, wrote Malinowski, was "to grasp the native's point of view, his relation to life, to realize *his* vision of *his* world."[5] Like Boas, he believed that in order to understand another society, anthropologists ought to live with and among people, putting aside one's own judgments to understand others' culture from their point of view.

But unlike Boas, whose interests in race, language, and artifacts converged in an immersive experience to apprehend "the relative cultivation" of all humans, Malinowski set forth a highly *systematic* way of theorizing, practicing, and writing ethnography within an anthropological framework. This approach placed the search for the "native's point of view" squarely within a systematized methodology for studying culture. In his famous book *Argonauts of the Western Pacific* (based on two years of research with the Trobriand Islanders in the western Pacific between 1914 and 1918), Malinowski argued that doing ethnography should be based, at the very least, on three foundations. He summarized these three foundations as follows:

1. *The organisation of the tribe, and the anatomy of its culture,* must be recorded in firm, clear outline. The method of *concrete, statistical documentation* is the means through which such an outline has to be given.
2. Within this frame, the *imponderabilia of actual life,* and the *type of behaviour* have to be filled in. They have to be collected through minute, detailed observations in the form of some sort of ethnographic diary, made possible by close contact with native life.
3. A collection of ethnographic statements, characteristic narratives, typical utterances, items of folklore and magical formulae has to be given as a *corpus inscriptionum,* as documents of native mentality [emphasis in original].[6]

For Malinowski, then, doing ethnography should center, first, on the sound documentation of the social structure of a community; second, on documenting the everyday actions and behaviors of community members

Bronislaw Malinowski conducting fieldwork in the Trobriand Islands, ca. 1914–1918.
John Wiley & Sons Ltd / Alamy Stock Photo

through the use of **field notes**; and third, on capturing the cultural knowledge of the Native peoples from their point of view, information often gathered through the use of formal and informal interviews.

When Malinowski designed this systematic method, many British anthropologists, like their American counterparts, focused their ethnographic studies on regions that were seemingly remote from Western societies. This choice of field site was intended to challenge the prevailing ideas of social evolution and scientific racism, as we discussed in chapter 1, which held that humans could be hierarchically ranked from less civilized to most civilized. This focus on the so-called "exotic" is greatly and necessarily diminished in the twenty-first century, since the "exotic" nature of some societies was originally only determined by their geographic distance from European and North American societies. Anthropology is now a global discipline that attends to peoples both distant and close, both Western and non-Western. All cultural practices, for instance, are in some sense both "exotic" to outsiders and utterly familiar to insiders.

ANTHROPOLOGY HERE AND NOW

From Tribe to Nation: Critical Reflections

Anthropologists today critically reflect on the origins of their field, even as they carry forward its founding principles. Malinowski's use of the word *tribe* in his description of ethnographic method offers an example of this critical labor. The word *tribe* did not necessarily correspond with how Indigenous peoples or other societies perceived, governed, or socially organized themselves. In other words, the idea of a "tribe" was an analytic imposed by the anthropologist, to help make sense of social groupings of non-Western societies. But the connotations of this word suggest an "exotic," less "rational" form of political organization. Descendant communities of the original peoples in North America (as well as many places elsewhere) assert their political presence as Native and First Nations and Indigenous Peoples, not as "tribes." As anthropologist Audra Simpson recently wrote, it is high time for anthropology to "turn away from the ethnological [an older term for anthropology] shore" in its methodological and theoretical preoccupations with Native peoples as "objects" (that is, "tribes") to be studied (by anthropologists). Instead, she urges anthropologies to shift toward decolonial theory and a recognition of Indigenous Peoples and Nations as sites of theoretical knowledge production, critical analysis, and sovereignty practices that might even "refuse" anthropological inquiry altogether.[1]

Note

1. Audra Simpson, *Mohawk Interruptus: Political Life across the Borders of Settler States* (Durham, NC: Duke University Press, 2014).

Nevertheless, Malinowski's call for ethnographers to record culture's organization and structure through concrete documentation had an important impact on the development of ethnographic methodology. In developing this systematic method, Malinowski was implicitly responding to the norm for conducting a study of non-Western peoples that had been dominated by, on the one hand, missionaries, soldiers, or colonial authorities, and, on the other hand, by scholars who did "touch-and-go" surveys of local groups. Most social evolutionists spent little to no time living with local communities, and more often than not used broad-ranging reports from military exploits, missionary descriptions, or colonial records to interpret others' cultural practices and to construct their evolutionary models from a distance. For example, the famous British anthropologist James George Frazer wrote thirteen volumes on what he and others of that day called "the savage mind," and how those beliefs and customs represented an early developmental stage of social evolution. But when asked if he had ever seen or talked to any of these "savages," his answer was an emphatic "God forbid!"[7]

ANTHROPOLOGY HERE AND NOW

Beyond the Savage Mind

Even as the founding figures of anthropology, like Boas and Malinowski, were clearly rejecting the theoretical framework of their nineteenth-century predecessors, terms like "savage mind" continued to be used uncritically for many decades within anthropology. In fact, one of the most influential works of French anthropologist Claude Levi-Strauss, a leading intellectual of the mid-twentieth century, was translated into English as *The Savage Mind*. Despite this unfortunate and inaccurate translation of the title, the book celebrates the ingenuity and complexity of non-Western knowledge systems. Levi-Strauss's original analysis is still worthy of a close reading today. Fortunately, there is now a new English translation, published in 2021, in which the title is retranslated as *Wild Thought*. This new title is closer to the original French title, *La Pensée Sauvage*, avoids the derogatory implications of "savage" in English, and is a gesture toward a play on words in the French title. In French, Levi-Strauss's title also means "wild pansy," which perhaps captures his admiration for the beauty of the non-Western knowledge systems that he explored so passionately.

Like Boas, Malinowski argued that a true cultural description could be undertaken only through the medium of direct experience, or **fieldwork**. This was one of Malinowski's most impactful contributions: the explicit commitment to extended engagement over a long period of time by living in and with a particular community. From Malinowski's point of view, the **ethnographer**, the anthropologist who undertakes ethnography, could write an unbiased, objective description of another culture only through determined adherence to this model and its systematic approach.

Most if not all contemporary anthropologists contend that constructing a "scientific" or purely objective description of culture is impossible for at least two reasons: First, anthropologists do not operate outside our own cultural biases, or ethnocentrism, as we have already discussed. Second, our very presence in a society or community, as an outsider, will likely have impacts that change that society or community, at least in such a way as to affect one's perception of it. More contemporary social theory, such as postmodernist theory and science studies from the 1980s onward, have gone even further to show that pure objectivity—the ability to fully stand outside or above the phenomenon being observed—is itself a cultural construction of Western philosophy. We will return in this chapter, and others, to this complex issue of objectivity and representation.

Even if it was in the name of an unattainable objectivity, Malinowski's methodological innovations set anthropology on a radically new course. He reinforced the growing consensus among anthropologists in both Europe and the United States that a description of culture must be based on direct participation and observation and, further, that the ethnographer must, in Malinowski's words, "show clearly and concisely . . . which are his own direct observations, and which [are] the indirect information that form the bases of his account."[8] This imperative challenged the tendency of the earlier, nineteenth-century social evolutionists to not acknowledge their own limited or even nonexistent observations of an unfamiliar culture.

Malinowski was not only promoting a method for studying culture; he was also advocating a particular assumption, philosophy, or *theory of culture*, that still informs ethnography today. Malinowski argued that each part of culture had a purpose for its existence. This argument laid the groundwork for Malinowski's central theory: **functionalism**. Malinowski argued that the "stuff," or artifacts, of culture—actions, behaviors, beliefs, customs, or traditions—existed within the framework of cultural institutions like politics, economics, or family and kinship. For Malinowski, *culture ultimately fulfilled a function*: It somehow served basic human needs, needs that were universal to the human condition.

He argued, for instance, that the so-called "magical beliefs" of the Trobrianders were not a primitive religion, characteristic of an earlier stage of human development. Instead, Trobriand religious beliefs and practices had a function; among other things, they fulfilled the basic human need to address the uncertainty of life. He presented this theory of functionalism in a now-famous description of the "Kula," a lively form of social exchange in the Trobriand Islands, which formed the basis of Malinowski's book, *Argonauts of the Western Pacific* (1922).

In the Kula, Trobrianders traveled regularly from one Pacific island to another, trading goods in a western Pacific exchange network. Their travel, which took place in boats, was uncertain and dangerous. The Trobrianders, consequently, used magic rituals to ensure safe travel. And Malinowski argued that the Trobrianders' magic fulfilled a basic human need—that is, the psychological need to address the uncertain.

In Malinowski's analysis, the Trobriand practice was no different from the Christian use of prayer, which puts a particular uncertainty "in God's hands." For Malinowski, although the *expressions* of Trobriand belief and Christian belief differed markedly, their *function* was one and the same. They each fulfilled some purpose. And both institutions served a basic human psychological need by dealing with the uncertain. The Trobriand belief in magic, it turns out, is rather logical, as is the Christian belief in prayer. And in making this symmetry clear, Malinowski was placing Trobriand cultural practice on the same ethical and moral plane as European practice, revealing a commitment to understanding, as Boas had put it, the "relativity of all human cultivation," and working against earlier Eurocentric notions of hierarchical civilizations.

Today, anthropologists would argue that systems like religion are more complicated than this. Humans do not engage in certain activities only because those activities (religion, sex, marriage, playing music, growing food, creating governments, and so on) serve "a function." Anthropologists consider a wide range of complex and often contradictory motivations in human behavior and experience, considering the role of meaning and meaning-making as central to culture (as we discussed in chapter 2). Nevertheless, Malinowski's argument that culture is functional remains with us, to varying extents, in our concept of culture. When we discussed

For Bronislaw Malinowski, although particular cultural practices could differ markedly in their expressions, their function was one and the same. Each fulfilled some purpose. Practices like Trobriand magic or Christian prayer (pictured here), Malinowski suggested, thus served a basic psychological need to address the uncertain. Photo by Danny Gawlowski

the violence of the drug dealers in Philippe Bourgois's research (chapter 2), it could be argued that their behavior is being treated as a "function" of the underground drug trade. Moreover, the concept of functionality often remains intrinsic to the *practice* of ethnographic research. Contemporary ethnographers still approach culture, broadly and in various ways, with the assumption that cultural practices serve a purpose and engender meaning in some way or another.

The fundamental assumption that culture operates as a system (or with some degree of coherence for contemporary anthropologists) echoes our holistic perspective on culture as a shared system of meaning. In British social anthropology, this assumption first began to solidify around Malinowski and his contemporaries (e.g., A. R. Radcliffe-Brown). For example, Malinowski showed that the Trobrianders' belief in magic did not exist in a cultural vacuum. Such practices were connected to the Kula, as an extensive system of exchange among islands.

Here is how we can see Malinowski's theory of culture, as a functional whole, at work. The **Kula** was an extensive network of exchange, consisting of trading partners scattered throughout several western Pacific islands. The Kula centered on the exchange of two particular items, arm shells and shell necklaces, which traveled through the island villages in opposing directions at regular intervals. For Malinowski, the Kula system functioned to integrate the islands into a larger social and political system. While the arm shells and shell necklaces had no intrinsic value in and of themselves, they were highly desired because of the age of the objects and social prestige of their previous owners. Like an antique, famous painting, or the championship trophy of a sports competition, the Kula exchange items were made valuable by the hard work it required to obtain these special objects. The arm shells and shell necklaces also anchored a wider system of exchange, which included many other mundane items of trade. In this way, Malinowski inferred that Trobriand exchange was not "primitive" or "savage." Rather, it was like Western systems of exchange, also built around arbitrary meanings assigned to objects that have no inherent value in and of themselves, such as paper money.

ANTHROPOLOGY HERE AND NOW

Exchange Systems and Finance

The study of human systems of exchange and their relationship to other realms of life—like that of Malinowski's Kula—has long been a staple of anthropological study. In a recent ethnographic work on Wall Street, anthropologist Melissa Fisher (New York University) observes the first generation of highly successful women working on Wall Street. Fisher describes how individuals forge identities and successes within socioeconomic and political contexts, linking global markets and struggles for gender equity. You can learn more about her ethnography, *Wall Street Women*, at www.dukeupress.edu/Wall-Street-Women.

Malinowski's point was to illustrate that from religion to economics, people everywhere—from London to the Trobriand Islands—construct systems that have a function (i.e., a purpose for their existence) *and* that are intimately interconnected with other systems of meaning. In the Kula, magic was intimately tied to the exchange of goods; without it, moving from island to island, trading arm shells and shell necklaces, was just too dangerous. Malinowski wrote that the Kula "presents several aspects closely intertwined and influencing one another. To take only two, economic enterprise and magical ritual form the inseparable whole, the forces of magical belief and the efforts of man molding and influencing one another [in the trade of the arm shells and shell necklaces]."[9] Thus, while Malinowski argued that each cultural institution functioned to serve basic human needs (which he considered universal), he also argued that these institutions—like religion, economics, or politics—functioned as a whole, a whole called "culture."

Although you will almost surely never encounter the small archipelago of the Trobriand Islands and its Kula exchange in your lifetime (at least as Malinowski observed it), we should pause to appreciate the significance of what Malinowski achieved. He had the open-mindedness and intellectual clarity to move beyond the ethnocentrisms of his time. Instead of slipping into the social evolutionist model (or even more pernicious theories, such as social Darwinism) and assuming that Trobriand practices of magic, politics, trade, marriage, and so on, were indications of a lower level of social development, he developed a keen appreciation for the whole of Trobriand social life. In doing so, he advanced a methodological approach to the study of culture, which decisively moved anthropology away from the prejudices of the social evolutionist framework. His call to "grasp the native's point of view" is the foundation for the principle of "cultural relativism" and remains a guiding principle for all ethnographic fieldwork today. Although Malinowski's functionalist approach to the study of culture is now considered limited, for reasons discussed below, it was nonetheless extremely important for promoting a holistic approach to the study of culture in its day.

Today, ethnographers reject Malinowski's assumption that culture is a clearly bounded system. That assumption may have seemed plausible in the remote locations where anthropologists worked in the far less globalized world of the early twentieth century. It was not accurate then, but it is even less true for the highly interconnected world of the twenty-first century. Today contemporary anthropologists tend to focus on one aspect of culture, like religion or economics or politics. And they now assert (as we did in the previous chapter) that culture exists on multiple levels, and that boundaries between various cultural systems are murky at best. They generally do not claim that culture is a bounded, "functional" system like Malinowski once did. Nevertheless, the theoretical assumption that culture works as a system, as a set of interdependent meanings and practices, still remains intrinsic to the culture concept and to how anthropologists approach ethnography as both (a) *a qualitative method for fieldwork*; and (b) *a genre of writing.*

In sum, British "functional" ethnographies such as Malinowski's became archetypes for writing ethnography in the early twentieth century. The form would come to dominate the way anthropologists—not just in Britain, but all over the world—would write about culture as a meaningful system. Thus, while ethnography developed as a field method of embedded, sustained observation and engagement, it also developed as a very particular genre of literature, or storytelling. As a method of participating, observing, taking field notes, and interviewing, ethnography evolved as a challenge to social evolutionists, debunking the beliefs that the social life of so-called "savages" was less logical and less sophisticated than the social life of the so-called "civilized." For its day, the emergence of this kind of ethnography in Europe and North America was radical, challenging deep-seated colonial assumptions about other peoples and places.

As a particular genre of literature, ethnography has since become a diverse and distinctive literary approach for understanding culture. Today, ethnographic texts—and films, in more recent decades—take on a wide variety of topics and forms. Some are more humanistic and literary in style—in fact, often reading like creative fiction—while others are more social science–oriented, driven by clearly stated arguments and the mobilization of "ethnographic data" or authoritative voice. Ethnographers working in visual media, with still images or film, are also working in the realm of affect, creating what visual anthropologist Kerim Friedman calls "record, text, sense impression, and relational practice."[10] Whether written or visual, more literary or more social scientific, all ethnographies are forms of storytelling and all depend upon a situated, located storyteller: the anthropologist herself, in relation to a wider community or set of communities. Because the written ethnography, as well as ethnographic film, gives us insight into both the "native's point of view" as well as the storyteller's point of view, through varying approaches to description and analysis, ethnography also informs our larger theoretical understandings of human behavior and meaning-making.

Ultimately, then, ethnography is meant to inform the larger debate about the role of culture in people's lives everywhere and the radical diversity of the human experience. When done well, it has the potential to transform the way we understand the world, decentering the historical power and privilege of the West, which was built on centuries of colonialization, and suggesting new, more equitable foundations for relating to peoples all over the globe. Malinowski understood the potential of his new methodology for studying culture. In 1922, with fascist movements and racial prejudice on the rise in post–World War I Europe, Malinowski called for an embrace of human difference, much like Boas had. He wrote:

> In grasping the essential outlook of others, with reverence and real understanding . . . we cannot but help widening our own. We cannot possibly reach the final Socratic wisdom of knowing ourselves if we never leave the narrow confinement of the customs, beliefs and prejudices into which every man is born. Nothing can teach us a better lesson in this matter of ultimate importance than the habit of mind which allows us to treat the beliefs and values of another man from his point of view. Nor has civilised humanity ever needed such tolerance more than now, when prejudice, ill will and vindictiveness are driving each European nation from another, when all the ideals, cherished and proclaimed as the highest achievements of civilisation, science and religion, have been thrown to the winds. The Science of Man, in its most refined and deepest version, should lead us to such knowledge and to tolerance and generosity, based on the understanding of other men's point of view.[11]

ETHNOGRAPHY AS FIELD METHOD: ON PARTICIPANT OBSERVATION

Now that we have established the theoretical and disciplinary history that underpin ethnography as storytelling, let's look more deeply at how contemporary anthropologists go about studying culture through an ethnographic field method inherited from Malinowski, as well as Boas, and many others in subsequent decades that have refined this method. Anthropologists call this field methodology **participant observation**: the systematic and sustained engagement with a community that involves doing and being with that community in their everyday activities (the "participation" part), while also actively examining those activities through external perspectives that are generally unknown to the community members (the "observation" part). This approach—which many consider the core of ethnographic fieldwork—involves long-term participation, observing, taking field notes, interviewing local members of a community, and the attempt to analyze the significance of what has been observed.

Anthropologists contend that firsthand experience—gained by *participation*—is critical if you seek to understand culture from the viewpoint of those who live within and create it. Anthropologists contest the notion that we can understand culture thoroughly by touch-and-go surveys, interviews, or observation alone. For example, Philippe Bourgois points out that a good deal of wider scholarly knowledge about illegal drug use and dealing is generated by researchers doing brief interviews or surveys, many of which assume that users and dealers are honestly disclosing full information on the illegal drug trade. In addition, survey methodologies often target large numbers of study participants, in order to generate "data" that can be fed into large data sets and quantified. Ethnographic fieldwork, and the participant observation it is based upon, is attuned to stories, textures of everyday life, landscapes, and practices that may not appear statistically significant as "data" (though some ethnographic studies do indeed involve larger numbers and statistics) but carry weight as qualitative research for its depth and complexity. Just like Malinowski and Boas, Bourgois challenged the depth of conventional knowledge regarding the consumption and sale of illegal drugs by doing what other researchers almost never did—by living in a community dominated by active drug dealers, by participating in the everyday events of this community.[12]

Participation in another society, community, or group is often an arduous and demanding task, especially when the community or group is distant from one's own background and experience. Although participation—showing up, doing things, engaging—may sound straightforward, taking time to get to know another community in depth, and its accompanying cultural practices and relevant history, can be a complicated task. And this does not account for all the preparation that goes into beginning such an endeavor (we'll come back to this below). Anthropologist Melinda Bollar Wagner suggests that participant observation is not a "one and done" method, but a process that involves several interconnected phases of engagement and comprehension. She writes: "Participant observation proceeds through certain stages, whether it occurs in a faraway land with a culture very different from the ethnographers' own or whether it occurs in their native lands. The labels [anthropologists] use to identify these stages vary, but I think it is valid to say that [ethnographers] tend to experience the stages of *making entrée, culture shock, establishing rapport,* and *understanding the culture*" [emphasis in original].[13]

We find Wagner's four-phase scheme useful for seeing fieldwork as an unfolding and always unfinished process. We will add some of our own reflections on her schema after we have reviewed her four stages. *Making entrée,* the first stage, was clearly a challenge in Wagner's ethnography *God's Schools: Choice and Compromise in American Society.* Wagner outlines the way she approached the study of fundamentalist Christian schools through this experiential framework. Although she differed in her views about religion and education, she recognized that Christian schools must be understood from the viewpoint of the fundamentalist Christians who ran them in order to better grasp the diverse features of religion in the United States. But she wasn't a member of this community. How to get in? How to start?

Wagner explains that she made entrée into the group through a former student who had become a Christian schoolteacher. In fact, entrée is often made through an individual relationship like this, or set of relationships, and should involve invitation and consent (more on this below). After attending a secular teaching conference with her former student, Wagner began to ask her about Christian schools and her faith. After some time, Wagner was able to gain access to this world through her former student.[14]

Like many anthropologists, Wagner entered the group through what anthropologists call an informant or **consultant**—that is, someone who informs and regularly consults on the ethnographer's understanding of a particular community's culture. This person may even help set the direction for the ethnographer's research questions. Although ethnographers will often have many consultants, those who help the anthropologist enter a particular community often become "key consultants." Today scholars understand their relationships with key consultants in various ways, reflecting the changing dynamics of fieldwork, sometimes denoting these individuals as "partners," "colleagues," or simply "friends." This was certainly the case for the authors of this text. In Dana Powell's research, for instance, many of her more important relationships were established long before "the ethnography" began, so that using the old ethnographic terminology of "informants" for these former colleagues would have been a gross distortion of the collaborative nature of these relationships.

From Boas and Malinowski to Bourgois and Wagner, getting to know key consultants is critical to doing ethnography. In addition to allowing ethnographers to enter into their lives, ultimately, key consultants make possible the understanding of their community's culture. Should one embark on an ethnography of the culture of, say, Wall Street or the New York Stock Exchange, one would have to make entrée by getting to know the people who are part of it, determining an ethical and practical manner in which one could "join in" as a participant observer. One would have to get to know traders and bankers, and what they do every day—what they eat, laugh about, and worry about; how to read the daily numbers and global markets; and how to navigate Wall Street and the exchange floors, with all of the support staff and related infrastructure. One would have to get to know the food vendors on the street

Anthropologist James Todd (right) talks with NASCAR driver Mike Wallace. Although Todd spent countless hours doing participant observation at NASCAR racetracks, his research took him far afield to garages, campgrounds, church services, corporate offices, meetings with marketing executives, and even the memorial for legendary driver Dale Earnhardt. "My research," he says, "became about documenting the specific narrative forms and devices, as well as the political economies and organizational politics, through which this complex and fascinating entity—both corporation and community—reproduces both itself and a specific version of American regionalism." Photo by Don Coble

outside as well as the online, social media world of trading. If one wanted to understand this exotic system of meaning, one that many take for granted as "the economy," then one would have to gain access to it from its many different parts—that is, the people, places, and objects that generate this set of practices as a shared system of meaning.

Making entrée, however, can be even more involved than just meeting and getting to know consultants. One doesn't merely decide on a research topic or group to study and then just "show up" in the field. Many ethnographers spend a great deal of time reading prior ethnographies and other reports, surveying their study's feasibility, making preliminary trips to the field site, preparing their research design (i.e., how their ethnographic work will proceed in the field), crafting research questions (i.e., laying out what questions they will ask their consultants, as well as the larger theoretical questions in which their study fits), and seeking funding. And in addition to all of this, anthropologists must often gain permission to do their research from governments, organizations, local communities, and group leaders.

Making entrée into a community also raises ethical considerations, which contemporary anthropologists take very seriously. Anthropologists are obligated to tell their consultants *why* they are participating in their lives and *what* they are studying. Increasingly, anthropologists are doing collaborative work, co-designing research questions and projects with communities, so that the overall research design is informed by achieving outcomes (theory and action) of value to the participants themselves. Moreover, anthropologists must always put their consultants' physical safety, mental well-being, and overall welfare ahead of a study.[15] Making entrée into a particular society, community, or group, then, is always mediated by certain restrictions and constraints—both legal and ethical. Because of this, it follows that there are limits to gaining entrée, and in turn there are limits to the participation part of the ethnographic equation. There are some questions, some research projects, that are "off limits" to anthropology. Consider Powell's research within the Navajo Nation, where studies of ceremonial knowledge are no longer allowed. The Navajo Nation asserts sovereignty over this knowledge and marks the limits of what can be shared and published.

Making entrée, however, is only the beginning. It is often directly followed by **culture shock**—the meeting of two or more systems of meaning in the *body*, expressed as anxiety, inappropriate behavior, or physical illness. Simply put, once ethnographers enter a particular cultural scene, they often experience,

ANTHROPOLOGY HERE AND NOW

Research and Ethical Oversight

Today, almost all anthropologists will submit their research project designs for review by the Institutional Review Boards (IRBs) found at the universities and institutions where they work. Anthropology is by no means the only discipline to undergo IRB review. Scholars from any discipline that conduct research with human subjects must participate. These review processes can be cumbersome and time-consuming, but they do provide an important layer of protection for the communities where anthropologists work. Interestingly, many Indigenous nations have become increasingly proactive in establishing their own review processes for research in their territories. For example, many American Indian and First Nations in North America have their own research review boards and formal research permitting processes that all researchers (whether outsiders or tribal citizens) must go through. In New Zealand (Aotearoa), Maori scholars and activists have advanced a set of principles based on Kaupapa Maori philosophy, for research with or within Maori *iwi* (peoples/communities), as Linda Tuhiwai Smith discusses in the path-breaking book, *Decolonizing Methodologies: Research and Indigenous Peoples.*[1] For Maori and other Indigenous peoples, protocols such as these are also an exercise in sovereignty, the ability to assert self-determination in the context of settler society.

Note

1. Linda Tuhiwai Smith, *Decolonizing Methodologies: Research and Indigenous Peoples* (London: Zed Books, 1999).

in a very personal way, the differences between themselves and the people they are studying. Culture shock is quite ordinary, in fact, and often happens with tourists or travelers (as some readers may have experienced), when, for example, encountering a type of food they have never considered eating (for Powell, it was deep-fried scorpions, in China). Even though anthropologists are trained to be sensitive to other ways of life and set aside their own ethnocentrisms, they can also get caught off guard by culture shock. They may have a very uncomfortable feeling about customs and traditions that are not their own; they may feel acutely out of place; they may make mistakes in their behavior when they do not know the cultural rules; or, in the extreme, they may even experience physical ailments or illness.

Many anthropologists have written about the initial anxiety of not knowing what to do, how to act, or how to respond to cultural practices that are completely different from their own. Although anthropologists try to remain good cultural relativists (seeking to understand other cultures within their own terms and histories and not judging against one's own), anthropologists are, after all, deeply enculturated human beings who have "learned" cultural norms, in their cultures of origin. For all humans, experiencing culture shock is a natural part of encountering cultural diversity because it is derived from our own ethnocentrism, which we can never totally escape. Culture shock is important to consider because it often marks that ambiguous space between the various systems of meaning that we call "culture." Certainly, when we are passing from our own comfort zones into worlds with which we are unfamiliar, we should *expect* to experience culture shock. As anthropologists James P. Spradley and David W. McCurdy write, "Culture shock and ethnocentrism may . . . stand in the way of ethnographers. . . . Immersed alone in another society, the ethnographer understands few of the culturally defined rules for behavior and interpretation used by his or her hosts. The result is anxiety about proper action and an inability to interact appropriately in the new context."[16]

As unpleasant as it may be, culture shock can be a crucial and generative part of the fieldwork experience, if critically reflected upon as part of one's own limitations in knowledge and experience. We must ask why and how we feel this way, and not dismiss the "offensive behavior" as "gross," "weird," or "ignorant'—lest we allow the shock of difference to only entrench our ethnocentrisms. In a study that Lassiter did as an undergraduate on drug addiction and recovery, he attended Narcotics Anonymous meetings to get a sense of the recovery process. At the first meeting, he started taking notes, as any anthropologist might when doing fieldwork. Suddenly, the meeting came to an abrupt halt and all eyes turned to him; everyone wanted to know what he was doing. Because anonymity is such an important foundation of Narcotics Anonymous, the behavior of taking notes was highly inappropriate. Was he a reporter? A cop? What on earth was he writing down?

On another register, Bourgois tells a story with potentially life-threatening consequences in which he made the terrible mistake of publicly embarrassing one of his consultants—a man he calls "Ray"—by asking him to read a newspaper article in front of his friends. Unbeknownst to Bourgois, Ray could not read. Bourgois writes that "Ray's long-buried and overcompensated childhood wound of institutional failure had burst open. He looked up, regained his deadpan street scowl, threw down the paper, and screamed, 'Fuck you, Felipe! I don't care about this shit! Get out of here! All of you's!' "[17] Several days later, Ray told Bourgois, "Felipe, let me tell you something, people who get people busted—even if it's by mistake—sometimes get found in the garbage with their heart ripped out and their bodies chopped into little pieces . . . or else maybe they just get their fingers stuck in electrical sockets. You understand what I'm saying?"[18]

Though these examples may represent extremes, most forms of culture shock emerge as the more commonly felt anxiety that surfaces when you encounter cultural practices with which you are not familiar, that just make you feel uncomfortable. In the case of Melinda Wagner, being "witnessed

Philippe Bourgois in East Harlem, where he conducted his ethnographic fieldwork for In Search of Respect: Selling Crack in El Barrio. *The graffiti is a memorial to a slain youth in East Harlem. Photo by Oscar Vargas*

Surprising Forms of Culture Shock

For Karchmer, dealing with culture shock led to a critical insight that became the basis for his many years of research on traditional Chinese medicine. When Karchmer arrived in Beijing to study Chinese medicine in the mid-1990s, he was "shocked" to learn that nearly half the curriculum at the Beijing University of Chinese Medicine, as well as all other universities of Chinese medicine in China, was devoted to Western medicine, the name for modern biomedicine in China. Initially, he considered these courses a "waste of time" because they seemed like a distraction from his immediate task of learning enough Chinese medicine to do ethnographic fieldwork about this medical system. After a year of classes, he became interested in studying Chinese medicine more intensively so that he could also one day become a doctor of Chinese medicine himself, but his prejudice toward the biomedicine courses persisted. These courses had become an obstacle to him, delaying the medical training he eagerly sought. Moreover, the two medical systems seemed to be radically different. It was not clear how Western courses helped local students become doctors of Chinese medicine. If anything, it seemed like the scientific foundations of the biomedical courses often made local students less receptive to the key principles of Chinese medicine, which were rooted in the philosophy of early Chinese civilization.

Although Karchmer thought the medical school curriculum to be misguided, he never encountered a teacher or classmate that agreed with him. One day he was grumbling about this very issue to a teacher he had gotten to know quite well, when the teacher gently chided him. "Why are you so opposed to learning Western medicine? Learning both Chinese medicine and Western medicine is like learning languages. Isn't it always better to learn two languages rather than just one?" Perhaps it was the simple logic of this statement or the fact that it came from a respected teacher, but he suddenly realized his mistake. The "native's point of view" could not have been more unequivocal. Everyone agreed that a strong foundation in biomedicine was imperative to becoming a doctor of Chinese medicine. At that moment, his entire project changed. He knew it was his task to "understand" why doctors of Chinese medicine felt it was essential to learn both medical systems, not to judge this choice. An entirely new set of fascinating research questions emerged about how and why these different medical practices were being blended together, which would occupy him for years to come.

It was only after this encounter with his teacher that Karchmer realized his frustrations were actually a manifestation of culture shock. He had come to China hoping to discover the medical system of pre-modern Chinese society, not necessarily as it once existed, but as he had imagined it. Karchmer's romanticization of Chinese medicine was, in fact, based on his own dissatisfaction with biomedicine in the United States and his cultural assumptions about what an alternative medical system should look like. Although he thought he had come to China to embrace cultural difference, he found himself grappling with a reality that did not correspond to the fantasy he had constructed. His reaction was frustration and a surprising form of culture shock. Fortunately, his teacher and Malinowski's lessons led him back to a much more fruitful approach to his research.

to" by Christians was among the earliest cultural practices that made her feel uncomfortable.[19] In another ethnographic study of the occult, Wagner details how the language the participants used initially made her feel marginal and peripheral to the group. Although their language was English, their vocabulary was completely foreign to her.[20] All ethnographers have stories along these lines.

Although culture shock almost always characterizes the earliest stages of fieldwork, most anthropologists eventually learn to critically reflect upon and then overcome it. They learn the local logics for specific practices (if not exactly their "function," as Malinowski would have it) and rules for appropriate cultural behavior and get over the initial anxiety or inability to interact with others. Yet culture shock does not completely disappear; it always remains a part of the learning process of fieldwork, especially when anthropologists take time to reflect upon the *what* and the *why* of their feelings of shock, repulsion, confusion, anxiety, or estrangement.

This brings us to the next component of participation: *establishing rapport*—the development of relationships with members of a society, community, or group characterized by mutual trust. For Philippe Bourgois, pictured in the photograph above, it was difficult to convince drug dealers that he was not an undercover police officer. But Bourgois chose to live in East Harlem for five years with his family. Over time, he gained his consultants' trust and interest in what he was doing, and with their permission, began recording their conversations on tape. Not every anthropologist needs to make such an extensive commitment of time to one's fieldwork, but being present long-term in a community is certainly a key element of establishing rapport.

Having a specific skillset or knowledge related to one's research may also be important. Karchmer spent many years studying Chinese medicine in China. It was the fact that he was intensively studying Chinese medicine, understood its basic concepts and principles, and could speak the "language" of Chinese medicine that enabled him to develop rapport with the doctors he hoped to study. In this way, establishing rapport moves the ethnographer from an outsider to an insider of sorts. But there can be limits to how much of an insider one becomes—such as in Lassiter's study of Narcotics Anonymous. In this study, he was eventually incorporated into the group, invited to closed meetings that are not open to outsiders, and asked to share with the group his thoughts about drug addiction. Yet he had not experienced drug addiction and recovery personally. And from the viewpoint of his consultants, his lack of personal experience meant that there were some things about drug addiction he would never understand. Because of this lack of personal experience, he was always on the margins of the Narcotics Anonymous community which he studied.

Lassiter's experience of living and studying among members of the Kiowa Tribe—an Indigenous people originally of the Great Plains and removed to Oklahoma in 1867—was, and is, in many ways, very different from his research experience with narcotics addicts. After living and studying in the Kiowa community off and on for several years, many of his Kiowa hosts insisted that he was a community member of sorts by virtue of his long-term, meaningful participation in their community. Over many years, he developed lasting friendships with many Kiowa people, many of whom took him as a relative (i.e., as a "son," "brother," "uncle," or "nephew") and often referred to him in their language as Koy-ta-lee (which means "Kiowa boy," in the sense of being a male child who is in the process of learning Kiowa culture). Although he was not from their community, many Kiowa people often referred to their community as his home away from home. And in many ways, it certainly was; friends and relatives there have been an important part of his life, influencing not just his anthropological work but also his personal life. In fact, they have changed how he sees, interprets, and understands the world.[21] Given this, Lassiter and his Kiowa friends and consultants still recognize that he is nonetheless always marginal to their community, not being born and raised there.

We mention these personal ethnographic examples to point out that although anthropologists may live and study with a particular society, community, or group for a specified period of time (a year or more, usually), many establish rapport and relationships that last for a lifetime. And yet, these relationships—like any sustained relationships—are not uncomplicated. This is long-term commitment. Establishing rapport often turns into friendship, and friendship is characterized by ongoing intimate relationships, with all of the usual highs and lows. But in the case of relationships established during fieldwork, there are also important questions of power: Often the anthropologist is there to "write about" a community, and may arrive with resources (funding, university degrees, equipment, and flexible time and labor) that are not available to people among whom the ethnographer is living.

An important critique of anthropologists emerged in 1969 from Vine Deloria Jr., social critic, legal scholar, theologian, and member of the Standing Rock Sioux Tribe. Deloria's now-famous essay, "Anthropologists and Other Friends" (in the book *Custer Died for Your Sins*), offers a scathing caricature of anthropologists as predatory characters, doing "pure research" on Indigenous peoples, without ever doing anything relevant or locally meaningful or helpful.[22] Deloria's critique, along with the work of other postcolonial and decolonial scholars, have transformed the discipline of anthropology in important ways, the reverberations of which are still being felt today. The "reckoning" that Deloria prompted, and which has been picked up and reworked in a wide literature on decolonizing anthropology, remains an important reminder of the structural differences in power and privilege that often (but not always) exist in ethnographic encounters.[23] Friendships established in these conditions require an extra degree of self-reflection and awareness, to say the very least.

Just as culture shock and establishing rapport work in concert, so do establishing rapport and *understanding the culture*, the last of Wagner's four phases of fieldwork. But the process whereby the ethnographer moves from ethnocentrism and culture shock to an appreciation and understanding of the shared and negotiated system of meaning that, again, we call "culture" is uneven and open-ended. This happens, first and foremost, through careful documentation and reflection, which we will come to shortly, but suffice it to say now that most ethnographers assume that this "understanding" is never complete and is always tentative, ongoing, and "situated"—that is, an ethnographer's knowledge of another culture is always impacted by the ethnographer's own location, position, and lived experience. We can never presume to understand another society, community, or group in all of its complexities. Nevertheless, "understanding the culture" relies heavily on gaining entrée in the right way and then establishing rapport with consultants, who open a window into their community from the "native's point of view."

From an ethnographic point of view, "understanding the culture" does not rely on *experience* alone. As important as it is to the ethnographic method, experience is not sufficient on its own. Experience may give us an intuitive understanding of cultural practices, but, as anthropologists, we must ultimately attempt to make sense of and translate this experience into a written or visual form: a book, film, article, photo essay, or other medium. This requires close attention to a larger system of meaning that we call culture—one that frames, bridges, and articulates the experience of *others*, not just ourselves. To do this, ethnographers rely heavily on written **field notes** and **interviews** to deepen our comprehension of what we have observed, through participatory experience.

Recall that Malinowski insisted that ethnographers must document culture in order to understand it. Today, most ethnographers recognize that documentation includes observing yourself, your own biases, and how your own ethnocentrisms shape your perception and your developing understandings. It also includes documenting the public life of others, which ethnographers often do through the medium of field notes. The "typical" ethnographer is often and regularly taking notes on all that is observed and experienced. These notes are recorded in a variety of ways—in field notebooks; on laptops or smartphones; on sketchbooks; as sound files on portable audio recorders; or even on scraps of paper, if something occurs unexpectedly. However they are crafted or recorded, field notes must, as

Wagner writes, "start with what was seen, heard, tasted, smelled, and felt."[24] We emphasize the sensory as a way into description, where no detail is too small or random to be recorded.

With this in mind, some ethnographers keep a diary (for documenting self) and a separate collection of field notes (for documenting observations of cultural practices). Some keep it all in one place and later "code" their notes for descriptive, reflective, or analytical notes. Others, however, reject this arbitrary separation of "self" and "other" reflective description, recognizing that, ultimately, all documentation—because it is seen through the eyes of the observer—is subjective and situated. Nevertheless, ethnographers take notes on their observations in the same way that you might take notes during a workshop or while reading. The process is very similar. These field notes are the raw "stuff" of qualitative data and, as such, become highly valuable to the ethnographer.

Observations of self and others, however, are incomplete without ethnographic interviews. Engaging consultants in regular and ongoing conversation—either informally or formally—is the most critical component of ethnographic research.[25] It allows ethnographers, first, to check and recheck the validity of their observations, and, second, to gain a deeper understanding of cultural practices from the so-called "native point of view" as it is articulated by the members of a particular group. Ultimately, the interview is extremely important because field notes are constructed from the viewpoint of the ethnographer; they do not tell us very much about another person or group's point of view. They only point us in that direction. And the interview is not a survey with scripted questions, but more of an open-ended, lightly or semi-structured conversation around a set of themes, life stories, histories, and reflections. We might think of the interview, itself, as another mode of storytelling, this time enacted by our consultants/collaborators.

Regularly engaging consultants in conversation also allows us to confront the ethnocentrism projected by our own experience. Often, we come to believe that because we have experienced something with other people, in participant observation, our experience of that thing was the same as everyone else's. Through conversations and interviews, we may discover how our own experience is different from the experience of our consultants. Here, in the space of conversation, the ambiguity of shared experience is revealed, and differences emerge.[26] We often learn that certain assumptions we have been carrying are misguided or only part of the story.

Anthropologist Marjorie Shostak, for example, lived with and studied among the !Kung people—a group of San peoples in the Western Kalahari Desert (Namibia, Angola, Botswana)—who today, due to a range of cultural and political changes, live in settled communities in southern Africa. Her primary research interest revolved around the life of a particular !Kung woman, Nisa. In her ethnography *Nisa: The Life and Words of a !Kung Woman*, Shostak describes how her intensive conversations with Nisa helped to elaborate the point that although the two shared similarities by virtue of being women, their differences were very particular to their own societies. From sex and marriage to childbirth and family, Nisa illustrated for Shostak how being a woman in !Kung/San culture and being a White, professional woman in American culture could not at all be reduced to a common experience based entirely on a shared gender identity as "woman" (as is sometimes assumed in cross-cultural gender studies).[27]

ANTHROPOLOGY HERE AND NOW

Ethnography in Collaboration

Some of the most interesting and engaging collaborative ethnography carried out today is done by the Neighborhood Story Project in partnership with the University of New Orleans. A community-based book-writing project that utilizes collaborative ethnographic approaches, teams of community members and NSP staff work together to research and write "our stories, told by us." Take a look at their work and their many successful books and other story projects at www.neighborhoodstoryproject.org.

In addition to conducting interviews and writing field notes, contemporary ethnographers use a variety of other methods—including drawing maps, doing archival research, taking photographs, administering questionnaires, and charting kinship and other community relationships.[28] In much of our own ethnographic research, all three authors have built on the ethnographic interview and the dialogic research process it engenders, using **collaborative ethnography**, an approach that systematically engages consultants in the process of co-designing research questions and processes, thinking together during fieldwork, and in some cases, in *co-writing* (see the following section).[29] This intentionally collaborative method can deploy a variety of approaches to achieve this end—like the use of focus groups, community editorial boards, community forums and dialogues, and ethnographer/consultant teams (who go about doing ethnographic research and writing together).[30]

As anthropologist and Penobscot citizen Darren Ranco argues, collaboration is not the right arrangement in every case, and far from perfect, but given the uneven power relations that often exist between anthropologists and communities, careful and intentional collaborative methods can offer decolonial relationship-making. In his essay, "Toward a Native Anthropology," Ranco offers collaboration as one way forward for research encounters by Native and non-Native anthropologists working with Indigenous peoples, that keeps Vine Deloria's 1969 critique in mind and works against anthropology as what Ranco calls anthropology as "a hunting story."[31] In other words, collaboration can allow other kinds of stories to emerge, through the co-production of knowledge, mitigating some of the power differentials that exist. In other cases, collaboration may be impossible, as in anthropologist Laura Nader's argument that ethnographers need to "study up" and examine structural forces and institutions of dominance and power (e.g., global financial networks, big oil companies, national governments, etc.).[32] Ultimately, collaborative methods, like most ethnographic methods, point back to establishing mutual understandings on intense and ongoing conversation with our consultants, fully cognizant of the relations of power and history (noted in chapter 1) that have shaped the anthropological enterprise.

In many projects of collaborative ethnography, anthropologists and consultants work together to define research questions, outline the trajectory of a particular study, and even co-interpret and co-analyze research results as they emerge. Ethnographers have experimented with this participatory method (as it is sometimes called) for many years, but unlike other participatory approaches, collaborative ethnography also often involves consultants in the process of writing and presenting ethnography. As such, the approach mobilizes the diverse experiences, perspectives, and interests of both ethnographers and consultants to collaboratively research and write ethnography.[33]

When Lassiter was an associate professor of anthropology at Ball State University (BSU), he developed an interest in the famous "Middletown" studies of Muncie, Indiana (where BSU is located), first initiated by Robert and Helen Lynd in their 1929 book *Middletown: A Study in Modern American*

Student ethnographer Jessica Booth interviews Pastor Martel Winburn Sr. for the collaborative ethnography The Other Side of Middletown: Exploring Muncie's African American Community. *Photo by Danny Gawlowski*

Culture. His interest eventually coincided with that of local Black activist and former Indiana state legislator Hurley Goodall, who was interested in redressing the absence of the Black American experience in the original Middletown study, as well as in subsequent studies of Muncie. If Muncie somehow represented a typical American city—as some have claimed of "Middletown USA"—then why, asked Goodall, were Black Americans absent from that story?[34]

A collaborative museum exhibit, community-university theater production, and historic photograph project engendered further discussion about these issues between Goodall, Muncie community members, Lassiter, folklorist Elizabeth Campbell, and other BSU faculty and students—namely, about how a collaborative ethnographic approach might amend this problem in the Middletown literature.[35] The discussions eventually led to the collaborative ethnography *The Other Side of Middletown* (a good deal of which was written by undergraduate students in collaboration with Muncie community advisers).[36] As described in the book, faculty, students, and community members together explored the undocumented history of Muncie's Black community, the enduring legacy of race and racism in small-town America, and the many facets of contemporary Black experience in Middletown, including—as in the original 1929 study—work and home life, school-ing, leisure, and religious and community activities. Within this framework, the ethnography unfolds as a collaboratively inscribed conversation about race relations, past and present, engaged by both Black and White students, faculty, and community members—all of whom are struggling together to understand the deeper experiential complexities of race in Muncie, in par-ticular, and, more generally, in America.[37]

In sum, then, participant observation, taken broadly, allows us to under-stand the similarities and differences of culture on a very personal, intimate, embodied, and particularistic level. Ethnographic research proceeds from gaining entrée to culture shock to establishing rapport and ultimately to "understanding the culture"—with the recognition that complete "under-standing" is never fully finished. Collaboration is one manner through which "understanding" is deepened, by engaging in a co-production of knowledge, recognizing the limits of the anthropologist and the significance of consul-tants as experts in their own right.

As we conclude this section, it is important to emphasize that "understand-ing culture" is an aspiration that is never truly achieved. Rather, understand-ing culture is a dialogic and iterative process: It involves an ongoing, cyclical process of participating, observing, questioning, discussing, and reflecting, which leads to new questions and experiences for further reflection. A key stage in the immersive ethnographic experience is culture shock. It is the necessary and unavoidable distancing or displacement that the ethnographer feels, as we make the familiar strange and the strange familiar, in a cyclical process of involvement and detachment.[38] Sometimes the greatest moments of discomfort can lead to the deepest insights. Wagner's four stages of partic-ipant-observation provide a useful summary of the ethnographic process. But it is important to remember that an anthropologist might move through these stages on multiple occasions. Any of the phases might re-occur again, at any time, as the ethnographer's involvement as a participant in, and observer of, culture matures and transforms over time in relation to the changing dynam-ics of the "field site" she may be in.

ETHNOGRAPHY AS A GENRE OF LITERATURE TODAY: ON THE WRITTEN ETHNOGRAPHY

Doing ethnography through the process of fieldwork (participant observa-tion, field notes/images, and interviews) and then *writing* about culture as ethnography are two very different things. Participant observation may reveal to us an implicit understanding of culture, but translating this into text forces us to make that understanding explicit. In writing an ethnographic book or article, we are forced to ask the questions: *How do we go about describing another society, community, or group as we begin to understand it more deeply? Why even do this in the first place? How do we transform "understanding the culture"—as partial, emergent, and incomplete as it might be—into a written text (or film or video or website)? And what "work" do we hope that product might do in the world?*

As we mentioned earlier, all anthropologists write (and some make films, videos, or other media) within the bounds of a particular genre of literature. At one time, anthropologists addressed the problem of describing culture by elaborating on each of its presumed components, like Malinowski did. But most anthropologists today reject the notion that culture can be split up into clearly bounded parts; very few ethnographies are currently written this way. Nonetheless, ethnographies, like all literary genres, are still composed of chapters, paragraphs, and sentences, which are still arranged within an ethnographic tradition characterized by its own set of assumptions and goals that define the boundaries and contours of the ethnographic text and what it can do.

Although anthropologists now write ethnography with a plethora of objectives in mind, they often foreground two definitive goals of ethnography: first, to illustrate cultural diversity and the power of culture in people's lives; and, second, the imperative that ethnography teach us something about ourselves—as individuals, as groups, and as societies.[39] Both of these goals, diversity and critical reflection, remain central to ethnographic writing, even as anthropologists write to address the concerns of any number of diverse subfields of anthropology, exploring such things as political systems, infrastructures, foodways, expressive arts, cosmologies, or healing practices.

With that said, we would like to explore these points more thoroughly by returning to our story of anthropology's emergence in North America and Western Europe—first, on the call to *illustrate cultural diversity and the power of culture in people's lives.* In the decades following Malinowski's work with the Trobriand Islanders, many ethnographers (among them, Boas and his students) questioned the effectiveness of Malinowski's theoretical approach to cultural function—namely, that it was based entirely on psychological needs. Although this explanation might appear reasonable on the surface, it was very much situated with *the ethnographer's* point of view. Take Malinowski's explanation of magic, which he argued was a function of the universal psychological need to address the uncertain. This psychologically based approach really has more to tell us about ourselves and the assumptions we make about our own *disbelief in magic, captured in the very term "magic" itself,* than about the "native's point of view." Although Malinowski set forth a radical idea at the time and elaborated extensively the Trobriand point of view, in the end he had written his ethnography through a powerful ethnocentric framework: one that *presumes* that magic "can't be real" and seeks instead to explain it through rational models.[40] (We'll take up this problem again in chapter 7.)

Of course, ethnographers past and present cannot help but be ethnocentric—they are, after all, forging culture into texts that are very culturally specific to a Euro-American tradition of writing.[41] And everyone, everywhere, is ethnocentric. Even so, in their quest to be better cultural relativists, many ethnographers began to wonder how people explained their own cultural practices in *their* own minds, in *their* own terms, and how this was different from outsiders' explanations. If the goals of ethnography are to illustrate human cultural diversity, these ethnographers asked, doesn't ethnography have a role to play in elaborating on non-Western ways of explaining cultural expressions like magic or religion or economics?[42] The Trobrianders, for example, do not explain magic through Western psychology. They understand their rituals as essential for ensuring the safety and success of complex activities such as the Kula, and we should seek to understand these practices through the rationale that they provide for these activities.

By the 1950s and through to the 1970s, many ethnographers had become increasingly interested in how people articulated and shaped meaning in their own lives as actors in a cultural system. While culture shaped people's experience, conversely, how did people shape and reshape this larger system of meaning in which they lived? The central task of the ethnographer began to concern understanding how cultural practices articulated meaning to the people who engaged in them, not how they took on meaning within a psychological model (or other conceptual template) imposed by the ethnographer. One approach to this dilemma during this era (1950s–1970s) was called **symbolic anthropology**. It focused on how people actively negotiate cultural symbols—that is, cultural expressions (both verbal and nonverbal) to which people assign meaning. Instead of just focusing on experience as articulated by language, symbolic anthropologists focused on how experience was also articulated in public rituals or ceremonies (like national holidays), key symbols (like a nation's flag), or cultural metaphors (like a national pastime).[43]

The writings of British anthropologist Victor Turner and American anthropologist Clifford Geertz were particularly impactful in this regard. Their symbolic anthropology examined how people *negotiated* experience through specific symbols.[44] Turner's symbolic anthropology further examined rites-of-passage practices in which members of certain societies (he studied Ndembu peoples of Africa in former British colonies) engaged with symbols and signs in ritual processes of social transformation. Symbolic anthropologists like Turner and Geertz, as well as British anthropologist Mary Douglas, who wrote on symbols of "purity and danger," wrote their ethnographies in a way that reflected this; an entire ethnographic text might be based on a single holiday, a nation's flag, or a national pastime (or the interrelations of all three).[45] The point, however, was not to focus entirely on the symbol itself; the heart of the matter concerned how the symbol points us to deeper cultural meanings defined by and negotiated among people (in both spoken and unspoken communication).

American movies, for instance, have a lot to tell us about American culture. They have very similar story lines because they carefully (or not so carefully) play on key elements of American culture—our assumptions about romantic love, or our deep cultural attachment to the conflict between good and evil. By focusing on American movies as ethnography, we can learn a great deal about American culture—how people interpret and negotiate these cultural symbols, and how these expressions in turn affect the ways people think about and act on the meaning of their lives.[46]

By focusing on the power of symbols like this, symbolic anthropologists helped to set into motion a change in the way ethnographers would approach the writing of ethnography as primarily an interpretive endeavor, moving ethnographic writing away from its earlier attempts to be a "science of man."[47] Most notably, Clifford Geertz argued that cultural forms are symbolic systems around which people essentially build cultural stories, stories that people regularly engage to *tell themselves something about themselves.*

Given that cultural or symbolic forms are essentially culturally based stories, Geertz argued that the method of writing ethnography should proceed with this assumption in mind. Understanding culture is like reading a book, suggested Geertz in the 1970s. Both books and cultural systems are

The boat pictured above, a tatala, *is a traditional-style fishing boat of the Tao people, who live on Orchid Island (also called Lanyu), off the southeast coast of Taiwan. The livelihood of the Tao is deeply connected to fishing and seafaring. Although modern fishing boats are becoming more common on Orchid Island,* tatalas *are still being made and used according to traditional methods. The design of the boats is rich with symbolic images that represent Tao origin myths and other important aspects of sacred knowledge systems. The* tatala *has become one of the most recognizable symbols of Tao culture. Photo by Dana Powell*

composed of symbols that are *read* and *interpreted*. "The culture of a people is an ensemble of texts," wrote Geertz in 1973, "which the anthropologist strains to read over the shoulders of those to whom they properly belong."[48] Ethnographers, Geertz implied, should see themselves as interpretivists, or translators of culture.[49] And because any cultural form can have a plethora of interpretations and can be "read" from many different viewpoints, Geertz added that ethnography was better cast as a kind of "dialogue"—a metaphor for ethnography that seemed much better suited to the humanities than to the natural, physical, or lab sciences.[50]

In making this argument, Geertz cast Boas's "cultural relativity" and Malinowski's "native point of view" in a new light and thus pushed ethnography out of the stricter social sciences and into the realm of literature and the interpretive arts. Geertz opened ethnography up to a much broader range of writing methods and approaches. By the 1980s and 1990s, many ethnographers had pushed Geertz's model, called **interpretive anthropology**, even further toward literature and art. They began to experiment with new modes of ethnographic writing, experimentations that sought to more fully engage the complexities of both doing and writing ethnography, challenging the very idea of textual "representation" itself.[51]

Anthropologist and ethnographer Barbara Tedlock combined traditional ethnography with literary approaches to "the autobiography" and "the novel." In her ethnography *The Beautiful and the Dangerous: Dialogues with the Zuni Indians*, she allows the story about her friendship with her Zuni friends and consultants to frame the narrative much as would an autobiography or novel. Instead of approaching culture as a clearly bounded system, she takes us along her own process of coming to know Zuni people over several years. Tedlock leads the reader to understand that coming to know another group or community is a process, one ultimately formulated by the intimate relationships between the ethnographer and the ethnographer's hosts.[52]

This kind of experimental ethnographic writing actually had deeper antecedents in the work of one of Boas's students, Black anthropologist Zora Neale Hurston. Perhaps because of her race or her unconventional writing style, her work did not attract the attention it deserved in her day. She wrote about the US South, using local vernacular speech, blurring boundaries between fiction and nonfiction, and experimenting across numerous genres of writing. In one of her more famous novels, *Their Eyes Were Watching God*, which she wrote in 1937, we glimpse an interpretive mode of writing that is narrative- and character-driven, while also highly descriptive of "culture."[53] The interpretive turn made it possible for anthropologists to start reading her innovative work and writing style in a new light. But we need to credit Black author and critic Alice Walker for the rediscovery her work, enabling Hurston to finally achieve her place in the canons of US literature and anthropology.

Experimentation in representing culture as a meaningful, symbolic system would eventually come to dominate ethnographic writing by the end of the twentieth century. Building on and departing from Geertz, anthropologists since the 1980s have experimented with a wide variety of textual (and visual) styles and forms. **Experimental ethnography** is in many ways still vibrant and emerging, today, with anthropologists "writing culture" and writing about "cultures" as diverse as southern Appalachia, high-tech biomedicine, and mushroom harvesting.[54] Indeed, experimentation has given rise to a wide variety of forms, which are particularly well-suited for a "globalizing" world in which culture often appears fragmented, hybrid, performative, and virtual—and in many cases, politically volatile, as in the assertion of cultural-political distinctiveness by minority populations within repressive states. Experimental ethnography not only tinkers with style and form of writing but often innovates with multiple forms of media and often, multiple authors. This is a newer mode of ethnography where collaboration becomes more central to a creative process that involves text, but may also involve other media formats, such as digital interactive mapping (with ArcGIS or other platforms), video clips, still images, and web links to a wide range of other media and sources.

Apart from these experiments in digital humanistic ethnography, some anthropologists experiment with ethnographic writing in their experimental collaborations with scientists and artists who work on shared problems. For instance, in recent years as part of the American Anthropological Association's annual meetings, experimental ethnographic multimedia exhibitions are often installed in local art galleries, university halls, or even outside on the streets in mural work or performance art, widening the scope of anthropology's interpretive "field." We see this experimental inclination growing, in another example, with recent works in *multispecies ethnographies*, which aim to decenter humans and foreground the experiences of other species, and human relations with those species. This turn toward multispecies ethnography often explores other ways of knowing nature, that might decenter the (Western, Enlightenment) human being. This kind of contemporary, critical work may seem to be a far cry from Malinowski systematically documenting life among Trobriand Islanders, but they are all grounded in the field-based method of ethnography that he forged and systematized during his fieldwork.

By challenging anthropologists to view ethnography through an interpretive lens, then, experimental ethnographers remind us that whether we are the ethnographer or the reader/viewer of ethnography, we always approach the ethnography through our own experience. This is the base from which we ultimately interpret our own and others' experiences. Writing and reading ethnography allows us to broaden our interpretive lens by understanding others' points of view, but ultimately, we—the ethnographer and the reader of ethnography—are part of the process of interpretation.[55] Simply put, from doing *and* reading/viewing ethnographies, we can also gain an

Collaborative ethnography involves ethnographers and consultants in review of the developing ethnographic text. They must check for accuracy, engage in further discussion, and develop new interpretations via the process. Here, student ethnographer Michelle Anderson discusses an evolving chapter from The Other Side of Middletown *with community advisor and consultant Dolores Rhinehart. Photo by Danny Gawlowski*

understanding of ourselves—as individuals and as societies—which brings us to the second key purpose or goal of ethnography: critical self-reflection.

The second goal of ethnography, mentioned earlier, is to *teach us something about ourselves*, and this has always been implicit to the goals and purposes of ethnography. One has only to recall the implications behind Malinowski's previously cited quote: "In grasping the essential outlook of others, with reverence and real understanding . . . we cannot but help widening our own."[56] It was one of Boas's students, Margaret Mead, who made this second purpose of ethnography explicit in the writing of ethnography.[57] In 1928, Mead wrote *Coming of Age in Samoa*, an ethnography about adolescence among the Samoans in the South Pacific. She approached Samoan adolescence much as Boas approached the Inuit or Malinowski approached the Trobrianders, but, importantly, Mead added a whole section to her ethnography to suggest what understanding adolescence in Samoa should mean for Americans, and she wrote this at a time when the dominant culture of the United States had a particular anxiety over gender roles, parenting, and sexual morality.[58]

Up until Mead's study, scientists and laypeople alike generally assumed that adolescence was primarily a biological experience; thus, it followed, the experience of adolescence was the same everywhere. By this logic, every human teenager could expect to go through a turbulent period wrought by rapid changes in the body. Yet Mead found that Samoan teenagers had a very different experience with adolescence. Instead of a turbulent time characterized by dread and discomfort, Samoan adolescence was something to which both children and parents looked forward. Mead thus illustrated that adolescence was a cultural construction; although the biological changes were similar between Americans and Samoans, the adolescent experience certainly was not. Following Boas, she argued that the behavior Americans associated with adolescence was not biologically based but rather specific to American culture.

Mead directed the book at Americans, particularly educators and parents, during this period of cultural anxiety over how children developed gender identities as "women" or "men" (this was well before the wider US culture engaged in public discussions about third, or fluid, genders). She argued that because culture was learned, Americans could learn to deal with adolescence differently than they had before. If Samoan parents, girls, and boys could experience adolescence with ease, so could Americans, Mead's argument suggested. Adolescence did not have to be a turbulent, rebellious passage from childhood to adulthood, marked by distinctly gendered forms of expression. We could reshape it because it was learned and conditioned by culture.[59]

Mead's book was widely read in the United States through the 1950s and 1960s. Like other ethnographies, her work illustrated cultural diversity and the power of culture in people's lives, but, importantly, her ethnography also represented an explicit critique of American society and its gender norms. The way Mead chose to describe culture placed ethnography within a genre of literature that sought directly to challenge Americans' understandings of themselves—a technique often called **cultural critique**. It was as much about Americans as it was about Samoans.[60] Cultural critique, led by Boas and his critique of racism (see chapter 1), yet refined by his students like Mead and many others in the 1960s and 1970s, emerged as a central project for ethnography. In writing culture, anthropologists began to criticize the operations of power in relations of race, gender, class, nationality, ability, governance, and a wide range of lived experiences and institutions that could potentially be transformed by "making the familiar strange."

Mead's book was criticized for overstating the case that the adolescence experience was completely culturally determined.[61] But both her approach to writing (especially writing for a more public audience outside the discipline of anthropology) and her approach to cultural critique (especially of the ethnographer's "home" society, wherever situated) made her book a lightning rod and profoundly affected ethnographic writing. This is especially so today, as ethnographers seek ways to articulate a larger and more relevant cultural critique to a broader readership.[62] Although cultural critique is not always an explicit purpose of each ethnography, as it was in Mead's *Coming of Age in Samoa*, it remains at least implicit in the writing/filming of most ethnographic projects.

ETHNOGRAPHY'S LESSON: WHAT'S IT GOOD FOR?

In this chapter, we have discussed ethnography, or the techniques for studying and writing about culture. While we may appreciate the concept of culture itself, the study of culture is incomplete without ethnography. In that ethnography struggles to present the "native's point of view" (albeit imperfectly) from a diversity of locales, perspectives, and writing approaches, it ultimately presents us with "basic data" of how people actually share and negotiate meaning in their everyday lives. Consequently, it teaches us something about ourselves.

Ethnography's approach is distinctive: We learn about ourselves as we learn about others; conversely, we learn about others through learning about ourselves. This learning takes us into "a field site," whether down the street or around the world, where we use qualitative and empirical methods, like participant observation and semi-structured interviews, to cultivate a kind of sensibility and perspective, as scholars. Bronislaw Malinowski was one of the key figures in anthropology who helped to establish these methodological protocols. He also pioneered an early style of ethnographic writing, known as **functionalism**. Some contemporary scholars have dismissed Malinowski (and Boas, and their peers) as "handmaidens of colonialism," but we feel that their early innovations—while carried out within colonial political structures—offered a transformative critical humanism and social science, whose central method—ethnography—was a radical and vibrant leap away from earlier modes of "knowing" cultural diversity and difference.

At its best, ethnography extends to us the actual complexities of human life—our own and others'—transforming perceptions of one another (based

Cultural critique is an important part of much ethnography. In The Power of Kiowa Song, *for example, Lassiter argued that much of the imagery surrounding Indians centers on how Americans privilege what they can see—and what they expect to see—over other senses. Indeed, many Americans continue to base their knowledge of Indians on reified observations rather than on engaging the experience of Native American communities through other means. In the Kiowa community of southwestern Oklahoma, for instance, the power of what can be heard—particularly language, narrative, and song—often takes precedence over what can be seen. Individuals entrusted to disseminate this Kiowa "world of sound," like singers (shown here), can be thus enormously important to the community. Photo by Luke Eric Lassiter*

on passing intuitions and ethnocentrism) to deeper understandings of one another (based on the philosophy of knowledge that we call "culture"). Methodologically, ethnography requires that we move through at least four stages of engagement, from making entrée to culture shock to establishing rapport and, ultimately, to "understanding the culture." Anthropologists today understand these stages as iterative and ongoing. While they also seek "understanding," they are aware that such lofty finality is never fully achieved. Research is hard work and involves extensive note taking, interviewing, and collecting of relevant information. Although Malinowski's call to "grasp the native's point of view" continues to inspire anthropologists, they no longer consider the people in their research communities to be distance "natives." Rather they are friends, consultants, and, increasingly, collaborators.

As a genre of writing, ethnography helps illuminate *lifeworlds*. It can offer a glimpse—if not a perfect rendition—of ways of being and doing humanity (or, multispecies life) that create an empathetic archive of the vast diversity of experience on Earth. The subject of ethnographic writing continues to expand into ever more fascinating realms of human social experience, from economic exchanges, to institutions, medical systems, infrastructures, social movements, political parties, gangs, horticulturalists, money-lenders, snake-handlers—anything and any society where shared systems of meaning are being made, interpreted, and remade, within relations of power. With the interpretive turn of Clifford Geertz, ethnographic writing became more experimental, collaborative, and open to multimedia forms of presentation. The strong tradition of cultural critique inaugurated by Margaret Mead's work continues to flourish, keeping anthropology relevant to its popular audiences.

Finally, in addition to knowing others and their lifeworlds, knowing ourselves, critiquing power, and transforming society through action research, ethnography itself is being transformed by forces external and internal to anthropology that push for even greater reflexivity and accountability. These topics are beyond the scope of this chapter, but they remind us that ethnography operates at this crossroads, and anthropologists today are experimenting with its form, style, audience, and dissemination in a range of media and voices unimaginable to Malinowski when he transformed the field a century ago with his call to "grasp the native's point of view."

NOTES

1. Lucas Bessire, *Running Out: In Search of Water on the High Plains* (Princeton: Princeton University Press, 2021), 1–2.

2. Ibid., 2–4.

3. Carole McGranahan, *Writing Anthropology: Essays on Craft and Commitment* (Durham, NC: Duke University Press, 2020).

4. For a more sophisticated discussion of these processes, see, for example, George W. Stocking, *The Ethnographer's Magic and Other Essays in the History of Anthropology* (Madison: University of Wisconsin Press, 1992).

5. Bronislaw Malinowski, *Argonauts of the Western Pacific* (New York: Dutton, 1922), 25.

6. Ibid., 24.

7. See James L. Peacock, *The Anthropological Lens: Harsh Light, Soft Focus* (Cambridge: Cambridge University Press, 1986), 106.

8. Malinowski, *Argonauts of the Western Pacific*, 15.

9. Ibid., 515.

10. P. Kerim Friedman, "Defining Ethnographic Film," *The Routledge International Handbook of Ethnographic Film and Video* (New York: Routledge, 2020).

11. Malinowski, *Argonauts of the Western Pacific*, 518.

12. Philippe Bourgois, *In Search of Respect: Selling Crack in El Barrio* (Cambridge: Cambridge University Press, 1995), 12.

13. Melinda Bollar Wagner, *God's Schools: Choice and Compromise in American Society* (New Brunswick, NJ: Rutgers University Press, 1990), 218.

14. Ibid., 218–19.

15. American Anthropological Association, *Revised Principles of Professional Responsibility* (Washington, DC: Author, 1990).

16. James P. Spradley and David W. McCurdy, *Conformity and Conflict: Readings in Cultural Anthropology*, 8th ed. (New York: HarperCollins, 1994), 16.

17. Bourgois, *In Search of Respect*, 21.

18. Ibid., 22.

19. Wagner, *God's Schools*, 220–21.

20. Melinda Bollar Wagner, *Metaphysics in Midwestern America* (Columbus: Ohio State University Press, 1983), 191–92.

21. See Luke E. Lassiter, *The Power of Kiowa Song: A Collaborative Ethnography* (Tucson: University of Arizona Press, 1998), especially 17–65.

22. Vine Deloria Jr., *Custer Died for Your Sins* (New York: Macmillan, 1969).

23. This is a vast and growing literature. For example, see Faye Harrison, ed., *Decolonizing Anthropology: Moving Further toward an Anthropology for Liberation* (Washington, DC: American Anthropological Association, 1991); Thomas Biolsi and Larry J. Zimmerman, eds., *Indians and Anthropologists: Vine Deloria, Jr., and the Critique of Anthropology* (Tucson: University of Arizona Press, 1997); Audra Simpson, *Mohawk Interruptus: Life across the Borders of Settler States* (Durham, NC: Duke University Press, 2014); Linda Tuhiwai Smith, *Decolonizing Methodologies: Research and Indigenous Peoples* (London: Zed Books, 1999), among others.

24. Ibid.

25. See Clifford Geertz, "'From the Native's Point of View': On the Nature of Anthropological Understanding," in *Local Knowledge: Further Essays in Interpretive Anthropology* (New York: Basic Books, 1983), 55–70.

26. Cf. David Hufford, "Ambiguity and the Rhetoric of Belief," *Keystone Folklore* 21, no. 1 (1976): 11–24.

27. Marjorie Shostak, *Nisa: The Life and Words of a !Kung Woman* (New York: Vintage Books, 1981).

28. See, for example, H. Russell Bernard, *Research Methods in Anthropology: Qualitative and Quantitative Approaches*, 4th ed. (Walnut Creek, CA: AltaMira Press, 2005).

29. See, for example, Luke Eric Lassiter, *The Chicago Guide to Collaborative Ethnography* (Chicago: University of Chicago Press, 2005).

30. For a more in-depth discussion, see Luke Eric Lassiter, "Collaborative Ethnography and Public Anthropology," *Current Anthropology* 46, no. 1 (2004): 83–97.

31. Darren J. Ranco, "Toward a Native Anthropology: Hermeneutics, Hunting Stories, and Theorizing from Within," *Wicazo Sa Review* (2006).

32. Laura Nader, "Up the Anthropologist: Perspectives Gained from 'Studying Up,'" in *Reinventing Anthropology*, edited by Dell Hymes (New York: Random House, 1972), 284–311.

33. For a discussion on how collaborative ethnography fits within larger participatory approaches, see Luke Eric Lassiter, "Moving Past Public Anthropology and Doing Collaborative Research," in *Careers in Applied Anthropology: Advice from Practitioners and Academics*, ed. Carla Guerron-Montero (Washington, DC: American Anthropological Association, 2008), 70–87.

34. For a more in-depth discussion of the evolution of *The Other Side of Middletown* project, see Luke Eric Lassiter, "Introduction: The Story of a Collaborative Project," in *The Other Side of Middletown: Exploring Muncie's African American Community*, ed. Luke Eric Lassiter, Hurley Goodall, Elizabeth Campbell, and Michelle Natasya Johnson (Walnut Creek, CA: AltaMira Press, 2004), 1–24.

35. Ibid., 4–5. See also Lee Papa and Luke Eric Lassiter, "The Muncie Race Riots of 1967, Representing Community Memory through Public Performance, and Collaborative Ethnography between Faculty, Students and the Local Community," *Journal of Contemporary Ethnography* 32, no. 2 (2003): 147–66.

36. For a student retrospective of the project, see Michelle Anderson, Sarah Bricker, Eric Efaw, Michelle Johnson, Carrie Kissel, and Anne Kraemer, "Whose Book Is It Anyway? Challenges of the Other Side of Middletown Project," *Anthropology News* 45, no. 7 (2004): 18–19.

37. This brief description is excerpted, in part, from Luke Eric Lassiter, "2005 Margaret Mead Award Remarks" (paper presented at the sixty-sixth annual meeting of the Society for Applied Anthropology, Vancouver, British Columbia, March 2006). See www.sfaa.net/mead/lassiter.html.

38. On estrangement in ethnography, see Machteld de Jong et al.: https://www.inholland.nl/media/10420/artikel-jba-jongh-kamsteeg-ybema.pdf.

39. George E. Marcus and Michael M. J. Fischer, *Anthropology as Cultural Critique: An Experimental Moment in the Human Sciences* (Chicago: University of Chicago Press, 1986).

40. See chapter 7 and David Hufford, "Traditions of Disbelief," *New York Folklore Quarterly* 8 (1982): 47–55. See also the following notes on ethnoscience.

41. See Edward Said, *Orientalism* (New York: Vintage Books, 1979).

42. See, for example, Ward H. Goodenough, "Componential Analysis," *Science* 156 (1967): 1203–9.

43. See, for example, Sherry Ortner, "On Key Symbols," *American Anthropologist* 75, no. 5 (1973): 1338–46.

44. See, for example, Victor Turner, *Schism and Continuity in an African Society: A Study of Ndembu Village Life* (Manchester, UK: Manchester University Press, 1957).

45. See, for example, William Aren, "Professional Football: An American Symbol and Ritual," in *The American Dimension: Cultural Myths and Social Realities* (Sherman Oaks, CA: Alfred Publishing, 1976).

46. For fuller discussions and examples of symbolic approaches to culture, see Herbert Blumer, *Symbolic Interactionism: Perspective and Method* (Englewood Cliffs, NJ: Prentice Hall, 1969); Clifford Geertz, *The Religion of Java* (Chicago: University of Chicago Press, 1960); James L. Peacock, *Rites of Modernization: Symbolic and Social Aspects of Indonesian Proletarian Drama* (Chicago: University of Chicago Press, 1968); and Victor Turner, *Dramas, Fields, and Metaphors: Symbolic Action in Human Society* (Ithaca, NY: Cornell University Press, 1974).

47. Clifford Geertz, *The Interpretation of Cultures* (New York: Basic Books, 1973).

48. Ibid., 452.

49. Ibid., 3–30.

50. Geertz, "'From the Native's Point of View,'" 55–70.

51. See Marcus and Fischer, *Anthropology as Cultural Critique.*

52. Barbara Tedlock, *The Beautiful and Dangerous: Dialogues with the Zuni Indians* (New York: Viking, 1992). Admittedly, we are glossing over the larger critique levied against Geertz, especially his evasion of how natives of a culture actually articulated meaning to themselves. See, for example, James Clifford and George E. Marcus, eds., *Writing Culture: The Poetics and Politics of Ethnography* (Berkeley: University of California Press, 1986).

53. Zora Neale Hurston, *Their Eyes Were Watching God* (Philadelphia: J. B. Lippincott, 1937).

54. See George E. Marcus and Michael M. J. Fischer, *Anthropology as Cultural Critique: An Experimental Moment in the Human Sciences*, 2nd ed. (Chicago: University of Chicago Press, 1999). For examples of experimental ethnographies, see Annemarie Mol, *The Body Multiple: Ontology in Medical Practice* (Durham, NC:

Duke University Press, 2002); Kathleen Stewart, *A Space on the Side of the Road: Cultural Poetics in an "Other" America* (Princeton: Princeton University Press, 2017); Anna Lowenhaupt Tsing, *The Mushroom at the End of the World: On the Possibility of Life in Capitalist Ruins* (Princeton: Princeton University Press, 2017).

55. See Geertz, *The Interpretation of Cultures* and *Local Knowledge*. See also James Clifford, *The Predicament of Culture: Twentieth-Century Ethnography, Literature, and Art* (Cambridge, MA: Harvard University Press, 1988); Clifford and Marcus, *Writing Culture*; and Renato Rosaldo, *Culture and Truth: The Remaking of Social Analysis* (Boston: Beacon Press, 1993).

56. Malinowski, *Argonauts of the Western Pacific*, 518.

57. Marcus and Fischer, *Anthropology as Cultural Critique*, 1–16.

58. Margaret Mead, *Coming of Age in Samoa* (New York: Morrow, 1928).

59. Ibid.

60. Marcus and Fischer, *Anthropology as Cultural Critique*, 1–16.

61. See Derek Freeman, *Margaret Mead and Samoa: The Making and Unmaking of an Anthropological Myth* (Cambridge, MA: Harvard University Press, 1983).

62. See, for example, George E. Marcus, *Critical Anthropology Now: Unexpected Contexts, Shifting Constituencies, Changing Agendas* (Santa Fe, NM: School of American Research Press, 1999).

KEY THEMES
IN CULTURAL
ANTHROPOLOGY

Cultural Adaptation and Globalization

The Roots of Our World System

Recall that in chapter 2, we suggested that while anthropologists may study an individual society, community, or group—like families in Japan or Protestant churches in the southern United States—their ultimate purpose is to advance a deeper understanding of larger cultural issues, issues like race and ethnicity; or religion; or politics and economics; or kinship, marriage, and family; or ecology; or gender; or the nature of violence, conflict, and peace. When it comes to the study of culture, these are the larger and highly complex human issues in which anthropologists are ultimately interested. This is because the similarities of culture that bridge the human experience are best understood through comparative approaches, which highlight larger human patterns and relationships.

In the second half of this book, we turn to a discussion about the larger realm of human cultural issues. We can compare these issues cross-culturally—an approach, you'll remember, that is built on ethnographic methods. We plan to introduce a few of the vast number of human cultural issues that anthropologists explore, such as gender and power; family and kinship; and knowledge and belief. But first we need to clarify the larger context within which all human issues operate: a broad and dynamic **world system**.

We all know that our world is becoming smaller every day due to information, media, and transportation technologies and that we live in an incredibly complex and multifaceted world. For twenty-first-century life, **globalization** is now a well-established fact. But we would like to tell the story from an anthropological point of view, one that takes into account the deep historical trajectory of globalization—which is not so new after all—and the world system that supports it. This is a story that includes a consideration of all the world's societies as they have come to participate in this system, albeit in uneven ways.

Many anthropologists have argued that the world system, as we know it today, is not a creation of the technological achievements of the last century, nor even a product of European imperialism of the last five centuries. Rather, anthropologists trace the emergence of the world system to the invention of agriculture ten thousand years ago! They emphasize that the human exploitation of nature (its land and resources) over time generated human societies that became ever more interconnected and reliant on each other, culminating in today's system of nation-states.

The invention of agriculture was one of the most transformative events in the history of human beings. It enabled the great achievements of many societies, but it also led to the unequal distribution of resources, benefiting certain groups and societies far more than others. Our anthropological story of how this world system emerged will help us better grasp how scholars understand the inequalities and uneven development that exists in the contemporary world system.[1] At the end of this chapter, we will consider briefly the problems of the so-called **Anthropocene**, a term that has become popular to describe the man-made crises afflicting the planet, such as climate change, mass extinction, and emergent pandemics (like COVID-19). So from the invention of agriculture, to the emergence of the world system, to the crisis of the Anthropocene, we explore how human cultural adaptations produced the globalized world we know today—for better or for worse.

IN THE BEGINNING: ADAPTATION, CULTURE, AND HUMAN SUBSISTENCE

The world system in which we live today springs from events that were set into motion ten thousand to twelve thousand years ago with the development of **agriculture**. Our modern world is often thought to be the product of the relatively recent historical events of **industrialization** and **capitalism**. Depending on one's perspective, the modern world may represent the crowning achievement of human civilization or the origins of multiple crises confronting societies around the world, including climate change, biodiversity loss, overpopulation, poverty, hunger, lack of health-care access, terrorism, and intensified ethnic conflicts.[2]

On May 21, 2022, K-pop superstars BTS joined the White House press briefing to speak out against anti-Asian hate crimes and promote cross-cultural understanding. For a long time, it was assumed that globalization meant the spread of Western products and values to the rest of the world. In recent decades, the direction of that flow has become more multiple and complex. Even in the realm of entertainment, performers, such as the Korean pop stars of BTS, now have an enthusiastic following in the United States. MediaPunch Inc. / Alamy Stock Photo

Before we get too immersed in a debate about modernization, we want to reframe this and other related discussions through the lens of anthropology. In particular, we will explore human adaptations before and after agriculture, the ramifications of a settled life (particularly the interdependence created by economic trade as a result), the constant rise and fall of complex civilizations, the problem of growing populations, and how the rise of our current world system can be understood within this cultural framework, *a framework that continues to evolve*, as the crisis of COVID-19 has reminded us. Our intention is to offer you the larger cultural context in which all the world's people now live. We must understand and appreciate this larger cultural context and its historical precedents before we start on our more intensive and particularistic discussions of gender and power, marriage and kinship, and knowledge and belief in the chapters that follow.

Like all anthropological stories, the story about the world system is a story of constant fluctuation and change; it's a story about biological and cultural adaptation, selection, and reproduction. Like all other living organisms, human beings have continuously evolved physical and behavioral characteristics that allow us to survive and reproduce. And, like all other living organisms, our past and present relationship with the physical environment is mediated by the complex evolutionary workings of natural selection, variation, and other biological processes (see chapter 1). But unlike most other living organisms, the relationship between human beings and our changing environments is also mediated by another process: culture.

Recall for a moment the definition of culture offered in chapter 2: Culture, in an anthropological sense, is a shared and negotiated system of meaning informed by knowledge that people learn and put into practice by interpreting experience and generating behavior. Although we have used, and will again use, this definition of culture broadly in the upcoming chapters, we focus on one aspect of this definition in this chapter—specifically, the manner in which the acquisition of knowledge has helped human societies to adapt to their physical environment and pass this knowledge through social means to succeeding generations. Indeed, as human beings, we are absolutely dependent on this aspect of culture. Infants are not born with the knowledge of how to hunt or how to build a fire or how to cook; they are not born with the knowledge of how to converse, read, or use a computer; they are not born with the knowledge of how to treat illness and heal disease. No, the human *collective* (in a general sense) generates and transmits this knowledge for survival. Without it, we would perish.

To survive, we reproduce, change, and add to this knowledge, passing it from generation to generation. Technically, this process is called **cultural reproduction** (as compared to biological reproduction), and it appears to have emerged as an adaptation in human evolution around two million years ago among early ancestors of modern *Homo sapiens* (that's another story, however).[3] Since then, the phenomenon of culture has been that which, like natural selection, mediates our relationship with our surrounding environments—no matter who we are. It is the intermediary or the liaison between our species and the diverse environments in which we find ourselves.

Of course, culture is not always adaptive. Even as we recognize the capacity for culture as an aspect of human biological evolution, we also acknowledge that culture often produces and reproduces **maladaptive practices**, practices that threaten the very survival of our species (and others) rather than enhance it. Generally, however, we use culture to adapt to environmental conditions,

Culture is not just adaptive to human survival; it also generates maladaptive practices. For example, mountaintop removal (shown here)—literally, the removal of mountaintops to access coal—has brought about devastating and irreversible damage to both the environment and the local communities surrounding mountaintop removal sites. Orjan Ellingvag / Alamy Stock Photo

to reproduce, and to survive in a way different from any other living creature. With culture, we have enormous flexibility (over the long haul) to adapt, reproduce, and change. *Homo sapiens* have learned to adapt to nearly every possible climate; we now live and reproduce in almost every part of the globe.

GATHERING, HUNTING, AND MOVING: ON FORAGING

The earliest known cultural adaptation began with what anthropologists call **foraging**, which may have begun as long ago as 1.5 million years—well before the emergence of *Homo sapiens*.[4] In cooperating groups, people gathered undomesticated plants and hunted wild animals (including those that swim and fly). They lived in small, non-settled groups (usually composed of a few dozen or less), moving from place to place. Men were usually but not exclusively the hunters (hunting both small and large game), and women were usually but not exclusively the gatherers (collecting wild plant food such as nuts, berries, or insects). The foraging diet consisted primarily of gathered foods; meat only supplemented this diet. This is why some anthropologists prefer to call this strategy "gathering and hunting" instead of the more popular nomenclature "hunting and gathering."[5]

It might sound like a bleak existence, but what anthropologists know about foraging may surprise you. Foraging is the most stable form of adaptation ever practiced by human beings. In fact, up until ten thousand to twelve thousand years ago, the entire world's population consisted of gatherers and hunters. Today, very few modern foragers remain, often because of forced settlement and land dispossession by modern **nation-states**.[6] Though wild, foraged foods do remain highly significant for cultural heritage and dietary needs in a wide range of Indigenous populations around the world. For example, in Guangfu Township, on the highly developed island of Taiwan, the "wild edibles" open market, run and sourced by Amis foragers, offers culinary delights from mushrooms to tubers, and from scores of wild greens and herbs, none of which can be found in commercial supermarkets.

Much of what we know about foraging comes from intensive ethnographic study over the past several decades with these modern foragers. One foraging group whom anthropologists have studied intensively since the 1950s are the !Kung or Ju/'hoansi (which means "real people") of southern Africa. The !Kung are part of a much larger population called the San, who today number well over ninety thousand, and although nearly all !Kung San were foragers in the 1950s, few hunt and gather full-time today, due to transformations in the local and wider economy, access to land, and other forms of social and political pressure.[7] Nevertheless, one of the first things that shocked the world about the !Kung's foraging way of life was how healthy it was. Most scholars and laypeople alike had imagined gathering and hunting to be a nasty, brutish, day-to-day struggle for the most basic sustenance. But, as it turns out, people like the !Kung had equally as nourishing or even far better diets than most modern Americans. Consider the following.

Richard Lee, an ethnographer who closely followed and measured the !Kung diet in the 1960s, concluded that "meat and mongongo nuts comprised the major part of the diet, contributing 31 and 28 percent of the weight respectively. About 20 species of roots, melons, gums, bulbs, and dried fruits . . . made up the remaining 41 percent of the diet. In all, the work of the Ju/'hoansi made available a daily ration of 2,355 calories of food energy and 96.3 grams of protein to each person. . . . The caloric levels were more than adequate to support the Dobe population and to allow the people to live vigorous, active lives without losing weight."[8]

ANTHROPOLOGY HERE AND NOW

San People Today: From Foraging to Settled Communities

The lives of San peoples—today living in countries in southern Africa such as Namibia and Botswana—have changed dramatically since the times when they were extensively studied as foragers in the mid-twentieth century. Many anthropologists who studied and worked directly with the San have also worked as advocates during these transition times, helping to develop projects that directly benefit the San and other Indigenous peoples of the region. One such organization is the Kalahari Peoples Fund, which has launched a variety of projects, ranging from water and land development to linking San people with computers and the Internet. You can learn more about the organization and their various projects at www.kalaharipeoples.org.

Another thing that shocked many people about the !Kung and other foragers was the relatively small amount of work they put into getting what they needed to survive comfortably. This was another thing that Lee studied closely. On average, all the work that men did in a week—including hunting, making tools, and "housework" (i.e., as Lee writes, "food preparation, butchery, drawing water and gathering firewood, washing utensils, and cleaning the living space")—averaged to 44.5 hours; all the work that women did—including gathering, making tools, and "housework"—averaged to 40.1 hours. The combined average for both men and women was 42.3 hours.[9] When you compare this to our own work lives, in which we now work forty to sixty hours per week (if not more) just at our workplace, not including housework (like cutting the grass or cleaning the bathroom or repairing things), the foraging lifestyle of the !Kung begins to look rather undemanding, doesn't it? In fact, it is (or was). Lee reported that the vast majority of the !Kung's time was spent in leisure: eating, resting, playing with the kids, and visiting. "In summary," wrote Lee, "we have learned from the study of Ju/'hoan subsistence that despite the popular stereotype [of foragers], the Ju do not have to work very hard to make a living. In assuming that their life must be a constant struggle for existence, we succumb to the ethnocentric notions that place our own

Western adaptation at the pinnacle of success and make all others second or third best. Judged by these standards, the Ju are bound to fail. But judged on their own terms, they do pretty well for themselves."[10]

When compared with dozens of other studies on foragers, it seems that what Lee learned about the !Kung was also true for other foragers.[11] We now know that, in general, people today (both as individuals and as societies) work far more than we ever have. This was true fifty years ago; it also seemed to be true hundreds of years ago, and even thousands of years ago. With the emergence of agriculture, people started laboring more and more to get what they needed to survive, and the trend hasn't stopped.

But we're getting ahead of ourselves. Back to foraging.

It may surprise us that the !Kung and other foragers did not work as much as we might think to get what they needed to survive comfortably, and, in addition, they were amazingly healthy. It may surprise us even more that they did not suffer disease on the same levels as did people in the Middle Ages or during the industrial revolution or even in today's world. Their secret was mobility. Although there were perhaps thousands of San people, for instance, they never lived in one spot as a single population (until very recently). Recall that one of the characteristics of a foraging way of life is that people live in small, non-settled, mobile groups, moving from place to place. This was the case for the !Kung San: They lived as small, mobile groups gathering and hunting and did not move about as one giant mass. So because the !Kung—like most foragers—never gathered as a population in one locale for any extended period of time, any one disease could not easily flourish and spread. Although a communicable disease could affect one or more of these small, mobile groups, wiping out a few dozen people, the disease could not spread to the population as a whole because of the demographic and geographic distance between the smaller, mobile populations.[12] Anthropologists have a name for this type of organization—that is, for foragers who live in small, non-settled, mobile groups: a **band**.

While the band is often associated with small, mobile, foraging groups, the band also describes a particular social, political, and economic organization. When people are organized in this way—moving about in small, mobile groups, like the !Kung once did—certain social, political, and economic patterns manifest repeatedly. Interestingly, in almost every foraging society known to anthropologists, social, political, and economic relations have very similar characteristics.[13] Consider the following three patterns.

First, in a social sense, these bands are not haphazard collections of a few dozen people; they are almost always organized around **kinship**. That is, everyone in a particular band is related to almost everyone else either through birth or marriage. Social ties *between* bands, however, are also based on kinship. Men and women can marry outside their own band, for example, because they may be too closely related to those in their own band. This cements the ties between bands, each of which is connected to other bands through kinship ties.[14]

Second, politically speaking, leadership in bands is very loosely defined. Leadership decisions are most often made by elder members of the band (usually men). Beyond gender, the leadership role is determined by age, individual skill, and accumulated respect; it is not predetermined (e.g., through birth or royalty), as it can be in other societies. Because the band is relatively egalitarian, any elder can be a leader. (There are exceptions to this rule, but rarely do we find, for instance, the passing of a leadership role from father to son, as we find in agricultural societies.) While a band leader may make decisions about where to camp or when to hunt, these same leaders have no *real* power; they cannot make others follow orders against their will. In case of conflict, any person can leave one band and join any other band, feeling right at home with close or distant relatives. Among most foraging bands like the !Kung, the social and political makeup of any one band is constantly changing because of this fluidity of people.[15]

Third, and finally, the overall health and survival of a band heavily depends on a particular kind of economic exchange. What we mean by *economic* here is that which concerns how resources are *obtained* and *distributed* between and among people. Within the band, all resources that become available to any one individual (hunted meat, gathered fruits) pass through a system called **reciprocity**, the exchange of goods and services between two or more people without the use of money. Reciprocity implies that there is a social obligation to return or reciprocate exchange and giving as part of a larger social commitment.[16] Such "sharing economies" have been the subject of a number of anthropological studies, for many reasons, including the way that they offer alternatives to our ingrained but very modern assumptions about the nature of economic exchange as supposedly driven by profit alone.[17]

Let us explain exactly what we mean by this. Among foragers like the !Kung, when all the men in a particular band go hunting, everyone understands that not everyone will bring back a kill. Whoever does bring back a kill must share it with the entire group. To put it personally, if I don't bring back a kill this time, my brother may, and my family and I will get some of it; when I bring back a kill, I also share it with everyone. Hunting is "for" the collective rather than "for" the individual hunter.

We could say that the property of any one person belongs to the whole band. But this reciprocity is not some cool "commune thing." It's a little more complicated than that. In some foraging groups, for example, sharing is moderated by closeness to certain relatives—that is, the more closely related you are to me, the better selection of meat you might get from my kill. But, as in so many other things, what goes around comes around, and the sharing tends to even out over the long haul in most foraging societies. Thus, reciprocity is a system of exchange that lies at the very heart of the way a foraging band survives. Without this exchange of goods and services (and the constant expectation of reciprocation), the social and political system of the band breaks down, along with everything else—including well-balanced diets and short workweeks. We need to point out that reciprocity works in a variety of ways and that foragers can also engage in other forms of reciprocal exchange, like trade. Of course, all humans—including us, the authors—engage in reciprocity all the time (as when we invite someone over for dinner and then they invite us back), but, importantly, foragers depend on reciprocity for their very survival.[18]

THE DOMESTICATION OF PLANTS AND ANIMALS

About ten thousand to twelve thousand years ago, a few human groups began to abandon the exclusive use of foraging and to take up the practice of domesticating plants and animals for food. We write *the practice of domesticating* because everything we know about foragers points to the probability that humans most likely knew about **domestication** long before but chose not to practice it. Foragers like the !Kung have apparently known about farming for hundreds, if not thousands, of years from their contacts with settled peoples. But they never took it up. After all, why should they take the time to grow food when they could just gather it? As we will see, it takes more effort to grow your own food than to gather and hunt for it.[19]

Why *did* foragers start domesticating plants and animals for food? A good many anthropologists believe that it was not until humans were forced to start settling—forced by the need of more food to feed growing populations. Remember that humans have always been, in almost all cases, in contact with other humans; we know of no group that has been isolated from any other group long enough to be considered a completely isolated population. As foraging bands grew larger and larger, they needed more and more land on which to hunt and gather. But these lands were also being used by other foragers. As foragers moved from camp to camp, hunting and gathering on vast expanses of land, competition for land and resources increased, and people started settling down to raise their own food. Although it took more work, the returns were high. A population growing crops, say, could feed more people on less total land than that needed by foragers. More food for more people, however, did not necessarily mean better-quality food for higher numbers of people. There was, in the end, a price to be paid for this higher production.[20] But more on that later.

The domestication of plants and animals probably first emerged as a way to subsidize foraging. Anthropologists identify two different but closely related adaptive strategies that did just this: **horticulture** (or *swidden agriculture*) and **pastoralism** (or *herding*). The former involves the small-scale, nonindustrial cultivation of plants (often with crop rotation); the latter involves the domestication, control, and breeding of a specific herd of animals. *Horticulturalists* (people who practice horticulture) and *pastoralists* (people who practice pastoralism) are still found throughout our world, and anthropologists have studied them extensively, but their numbers, like foragers, continue to dwindle as nation-states seek to integrate horticulturalists and pastoralists (often forcibly) into a larger **political economy**.[21]

Horticulture and pastoralism produced larger populations than did foraging, and some of these populations were settled in one spot for long periods of time. But this did not mean that mobility and migration was suddenly halted. Many pastoralists have remained nomadic until the present. Economically, horticulturalists and pastoralists depended heavily on reciprocity, just like foraging bands of hunters and gatherers. Politically, kinship still played an important organizational role among both horticulturalists and pastoralists. But beyond these similarities, there were important differences.[22]

Unlike foragers, large families in time and space—called **descent groups** or **lineages**—could (and today, in many societies, still do) have power above and beyond any one individual. While individual leaders had not previously had much power, the descent groups to which they belonged often did. That is, the descent groups extended beyond the boundaries of any one settled village of horticulturalists or any one nomadic pastoralist band. (More on descent

A woman and her twin daughters aerate a manure pile in preparation for spring plant-ing in the mountain village of Walabi in Yunnan Province, China. Photo by Danny Gawlowski

groups in chapter 6.) And they could use their dominance to control re-sources, especially land and natural resources, influence decisions, or resolve conflict in ways that a band leader working alone could not.[23]

Aside from descent groups, horticulturalists and pastoralists also orga-nized themselves through other political means that transcended individual communities, political organizations that might have little to do with kin-ship. Religious societies and warrior organizations found among many historical Native American societies are examples: Although people might be related in a particular warrior or religious organization, membership was determined by virtue of being a warrior or a particular kind of religious practitioner, not necessarily by being related.[24] Anthropologists call this kind of integration—in which different settled or nomadic communities are united through descent groups or common organizations (like warrior or religious societies)—a **tribe**. We could certainly say that the foraging bands like the !Kung are unified by connections among relatives, but among so-called tribes, the integration of communities can be much more formal than that found in most bands.[25]

Band, tribe, hunter-gatherer, horticulturalist, pastoralist, and so on—these terms are part of the lexicon of anthropology and, like all professional terminology, established to enable the sense-making of the analyst (the anthropologist) rather than for the societies or individuals being studied or written about. For this reason, some of these terms have fallen out of favor today or seem "outdated" when used in contemporary, critically inflected anthropology. They are, however, instructive for appreciating how culture came to be understood as adaptive and how certain forms of political organization (e.g., band or tribe) corresponded across very different locations and populations, with similar kinds of subsistence practices (horticulture, agriculture, foraging). It is important to bear in mind our discussion from chapter 1, and remember that these forms of human organization do not represent developmental "stages" on some kind of unilinear pathway toward "progress" or "civilization" or "the state," but are, instead, descriptors of social formations expressed in diverse ways the world over, both in the past and present.

AGRICULTURE AND THE EMERGENCE OF THE STATE

Horticulture and pastoralism set the stage for the large-scale domestication and cultivation of crops, an agricultural practice that emerged all over the world: in the Middle East, Eurasia, and Africa between seven and a half thousand and twelve thousand years ago, and in North, Central, and South America well over six and a half thousand years ago.[26] With this emergence would eventually come the most complex forms of political and economic organizations: **states**.

These states did not just appear out of thin air, however. **Prestates**—which anthropologists often call *chiefdoms* or *kingdoms*—first developed by integrating horticulturalists, pastoralists, or other food producers (such as "intensive fishermen") into a hierarchical political and economic structure, with a "chief," "lord," or "king" who occupied the highest position. People were ranked under this centralized leader, who could have considerable power and influence, much more than band or tribal leaders.[27]

An interesting example in the archaeological record is Cahokia, a city of mounds that existed where East St. Louis is located today.[28] Emerging around AD 1050, Cahokia consisted of thousands of people. It had collapsed by 1500, but at its peak, around 1150, more people lived at Cahokia (about twenty thousand people) than in London at that time.[29] Like other chiefdoms,

Cahokia was characterized by hierarchy: Below the chief, an elite class of sub-chiefs (who were most likely related to the chief) ruled the leaders of family clans, who, in turn, ruled the commoners.[30] Not only was this ranking nominal, but it was also inscribed into the landscape: Atop the largest mound—which, at about one hundred feet tall, rose above everything and everyone else in the city—the chief administered Cahokia.[31]

ANTHROPOLOGY HERE AND NOW

The Mounds at Cahokia

You can learn more about the fascinating mounds at Cahokia—their history, as well as continuing archaeological research at the site—at www.cahokiamounds.org.

Economically, the people who lived in prestates like Cahokia practiced reciprocity. But unlike foraging bands or tribal pastoralists or horticulturalists, some people had access to power, prestige, and even resources (such as food) that others did not, primarily because of their rank in the social order. This is where an economic system called **redistribution** comes into play. In this type of economic exchange, resources (e.g., crops at Cahokia) flowed into one central locale (e.g., the chief at Cahokia), and then they were redistributed again to support, for example, full-time warriors or religious specialists. (In some ways, the process works like taxes do today, although this modern practice is much more depersonalized.) Importantly, while resources flowed back out to the masses from the chief (though certainly not in the same form), the act of redistribution often increased the wealth, power, and prestige of the chief and his subordinates. Consequently, chiefs, lords, or kings often had the power to control land and resources in ways that tribal or band leaders did not.[32]

Chiefs, lords, and kings often maintained their political and economic domination through coercion and warfare.[33] In this regard, some so-called chiefdoms or kingdoms were very much like **ancient states**, which expanded through large-scale conquest. But, in contrast to chiefdoms or kingdoms, these ancient states consisted of much larger populations.[34]

Cahokia Mounds, ca. AD 1150. Courtesy Cahokia Mounds State Historic Site / Painting by William R. Iseminger

Ancient states—hierarchical political systems characterized by centralized governments—arose primarily around large-scale agriculture and first emerged about five to six thousand years ago. Many of these developed independently of one another in places all over the world: Mesoamerica (Central America), South America, Africa, Mesopotamia, and Southeast Asia. These states had centralized power—that is, a consolidated authority was organized around a ruling bureaucracy rather than just one chief, king, or lord. For comparison, while Cahokia had a centralized authority—a chief—the Mayan civilization of Central America (which collapsed around AD 900) had a ruling body of individuals that was spread throughout the state.[35] Like ancient Rome (also an ancient state), the Mayans had bureaucrats who governed outlying towns and cities in what is present-day Guatemala, Mexico, Honduras, Belize, and northern El Salvador.

Political centralization was only the beginning, however. Integrating people within a centralized, ruling bureaucracy often included state-sponsored religion (the separation of church and state is a very recent phenomenon), the presence of a highly organized military (for both expansion and defense), reciprocity (as in bands and tribes), redistribution (as in chiefdoms or kingdoms), and **market exchange**—that is, the exchange of goods and services through the use of money. In times past, "money" included items such as shells, beads, animal skins, precious metals, and rice.[36]

The development of markets was especially important to the development of states. Indeed, the state depended (and today still depends) on market exchange (or in today's terms, import and export trade) to survive. As people settled, their diets were increasingly limited to a few crops. They were able to produce more food for more people, but their diet had to be subsidized through trade. In addition, unlike foragers, who could just move to another locale when their food became scarce, agriculturalists were often stuck in one spot. When crops failed, food shortages ensued, making trade all the more significant.[37]

The market, then, was (and still is) an incredibly important factor in maintaining the state's political system. Ever since the first agricultural states emerged, they have depended on trade—internal or external—for their survival and maintenance. Human cultural adaptation, politics, and economics, then, are intimately linked.[38] While there can be self-sufficient foragers, *there have never been any completely self-sufficient agricultural states.*[39]

AGRICULTURAL TRENDS AND THE EMERGENCE OF SOCIAL CLASS

As people shifted from foraging to domestication (horticulture, pastoralism, and large-scale agriculture), political systems (e.g., leadership), economic systems (e.g., dependence on trade), and social systems (e.g., community size) got more complex. *Complex* here does not mean more developed but simply a much wider array of culturally governed relationships between and among people. For instance, tribal political organization is more complex than band political organization because there are more political institutions (descent groups, warrior societies) through which people must navigate their lives. The state is much more complex than the band, primarily because the political economy that maintains a state—whether it be ancient or modern—is responsible for the survival of geometrically larger populations.

Some anthropologists have used the term **cultural evolution** to describe the transition from foraging to domestication of plants and animals.[40] For contemporary anthropologists, evolution means only *change*—hence, cultural evolution means cultural change. To imply that evolution means "progress" would misrepresent the facts. As humans adopted domestication, political and economic trends accompanied this change in adaptation. Among these were the growth of permanent settlements, an increase in population density, chronic food shortages (which were relatively low among foragers like the !Kung), a higher dependence on trade, full-time specialization (such as political leadership), and inequities in wealth. Such changes, of course, were ultimately brought on by a technology—agriculture—that involved harnessing food resources to support larger and larger populations.[41]

Heavy prices were paid for the adoption of agriculture, however—among them, worsened health, disease, and social inequality.[42] As people focused on fewer types of crops, overall nutrition decreased. In addition, because people were living in close proximity, poor sanitation and its concomitant health threats became problems. The practice of trade helped spread disease across great distances, which could often have devastating effects within an agriculture state. In terms of social inequality, stored food helped to create, for the first time in human history, substantial economic divisions between groups of people. Some people had greater access than others to the dietary reserve, which could increase their and their families' health, well-being, *and* social status. To be sure, the emergence of **class**—that is, the division of people into groups with differing access to resources—accompanied large-scale agriculture where, generally, no such grouping had existed among foragers.[43]

Of the many important consequences of the agricultural revolution, we want to give some additional attention to the phenomenon of class. Scholars of all stripes, including anthropologists, are deeply interested in the role of

The scale, complexity, and effects of agriculture only continue to grow. Photo by Danny Gawlowski

class in social and cultural activities. Class differences within a society are an important reminder of the inherent multiplicity of culture that we discussed in chapter 2. The lifestyles, values, and interests of different classes within a society may be so different that the two groups believe they have little in common with each other. Perhaps the individual most responsible for bringing attention to the phenomena of class is Karl Marx, the well-known nineteenth-century economist whose critique of capitalism inspired communist revolutions around the globe in the twentieth century. In 1848, Marx and his collaborator Friedrich Engels wrote in *The Communist Manifesto*, "The history of all hitherto existing human society is the history of class struggles."[44] Regardless of what one may think about Marx's larger project to bring about communist revolution, his attention to class as a driving social force in modern societies has been extremely influential.

We also do not have to subscribe to Marx's revolutionary agenda to recognize the powerful role of class in our social existence. We are all acutely aware of the social hierarchies that pervade one's society, even if we are not accustomed to describing them in terms of class. Rich, poor, or middle-class; executive, worker, or professional; urban, rural, or suburban—we not only know well the strata of society from which we hail but can quickly recognize this background in others. The mannerisms, the way of speaking, the style of dress, the place of residence and work, just to name a few traits, can quickly inform us about the class background of someone we have just met.

In our folk notions of social class, however, we often think social rank is determined by individual wealth. But this one marker of class cannot begin to explain how class shapes lived experience and individual behavior. In recent years, anthropology has contributed significantly to the study of class, particularly through the work of Pierre Bourdieu, a French anthropologist who began his career studying the Kabyle, a Berber ethnic group in northern Algeria. Bourdieu was particularly interested in how the everyday practices of the Kabyle tended to reproduce predictable patterns of behavior (i.e., culture) through what he termed "durable dispositions."[45] When he turned his intellectual interests toward the study of French society, he applied this same notion of "durable dispositions" (for which he coined the term "habitus") to the analysis of the production and reproduction of French class hierarchies.

Bourdieu's unique approach to the study of class helped scholars to see the processual, ongoing nature of class distinctions within a society. He showed how class divides were continually being produced and reproduced through questions of "taste" in music, art, fashion, decor, food, and so on. Bourdieu expanded significantly on Marx's treatment of class. According to Marx, capitalist economies were creating two great opposing classes: the bourgeoisie, who owned the means of production, and the proletariats (or workers), who owned nothing but their own labor. In contrast, Bourdieu argued that class was not just shaped by the nature of one's work but also created through consumption. One's education, upbringing, place of residence, and various lifestyle choices, Bourdieu argued, produced the "durable dispositions" of one's class status.

Perhaps most importantly, class hierarchies in a society are intimately related to questions of power. The higher one's rank in a society, the greater access one has to important resources. On this issue, Bourdieu also contributed many unique insights. He argued that individuals mobilize various forms of "capital" as they struggle and compete within various social arenas. Like Marx or other traditional theorists of class, Bourdieu recognized the importance of wealth or what he called "economic capital." But he also understood that other forms of capital could be just as powerful. For example, he argued that one's "cultural capital" would be determined to a large extent by one's education. A college degree can be leveraged for important work opportunities and strongly shapes one's lifestyle preferences, choice of spouse, and how one raises one's children. Other forms of capital include "social capital," derived from one's network of acquaintances, and "symbolic capital," based on how one deploys certain symbols of status. The ability, or lack thereof, to mobilize these various forms of capital is closely related to one's class disposition (or "habitus") and can either enable or constrain one's access to important resources in society.[46]

AGRICULTURE AND WORLD SYSTEM THEORY

To return to our story about the various implications of the agricultural revolution, one of its most dangerous consequences has been population growth—agriculture's "catch-22." As population increases, the need for high agricultural yields increase; as yields increase, populations increase, which brings about a need for even higher agricultural yields. Consequently, since the time when agriculture emerged, the world's population has steadily grown. As anthropologist John H. Bodley points out,

The relatively rapid growth in population that accompanied and perhaps contributed to the adoption of farming is one of the most significant demographic events in human history. It marked the end of the long period of relative population equilibrium that foraging peoples established and initiated a period of almost continuous population growth and a rapid series of interrelated changes that led successfully to politicization, the emergence of large-scale urban culture, and finally, the rise of industrial global cultures.[47]

About five hundred years ago, the Age of Exploration among European seafaring nations forged the links between the Old and New Worlds. With the rise of industrialization by the eighteenth and nineteenth centuries, the world slowly but surely became fused into one international, global market economy. Global trade began with ethnobotanical resources (spices, tea, camphor, quinine, etc.) and shifted toward guns, enslaved humans, and even ice (for instance, from the Arctic to Hawaii), but moved steadily toward the exchange in energy resources and other industrial materials. With the increased mechanization of agriculture, the growth of manufacturing, the development of complex factory systems, and the expansion of urban centers, the world population grew exponentially. Since the end of World War II (1945), the rate of trade and consumption has increased as never before—and population has risen similarly. From 1950 to 2000, the world's population doubled nearly two and a half times, from 2.5 billion to well over 6 billion people.[48] Today it has surpassed 8 billion.

The differences between ancient states and contemporary nation-states are significant, of course. Today, we live as residents of nation-states that occupy every part of the globe, incorporate millions of people into multifaceted political systems, and in many ways resemble one another (e.g., McDonald's in Beijing is not so different from McDonald's in Mexico City). This integration has led scholars to theorize the political and economic relationships of nation-states to each other through what is known as "world systems theory." According to these theorists, the various national economies play different and uneven roles in the world system that can be classified into three basic types—core, semi-periphery, and periphery. The world's wealthiest and most powerful nation-states make up the **core** and tend to engage in high-skill, capital-intensive production. The world's poorest nation-states constitute the **periphery** and provide raw materials and low-skill production. Other nation-states that mediate the flow of economic resources between the core and the periphery are considered the **semi-periphery**.

World systems theorists, like Andre Gunder Frank and Immanuel Wallerstein, have helped us visualize how uneven flows connect the different regions of the world. While raw materials tend to flow *out of* the periphery countries and *into* the core countries, the economic benefits tend to accrue to core countries (also known as the First World, or Global North) rather than the periphery (also known at the Third World, or Global South). At the same time, the ecological costs of globalization tend to be "outsourced" to the periphery nations (or periphery locations within the core nations), leaving the poorest nations and peoples to suffer with the consequences of deforestation, habitat destruction, and toxic waste disposal.

The flows of the world system also include human beings themselves. People are moving from the periphery and semi-periphery to the core and from rural areas to city centers as never before; the planet is seeing a surge in urbanization. Modern nation-states are facing unprecedented rates of immigration (people coming in) and emigration (people going out). Ethnic, linguistic, and religious groups are in contact as never before, and, as referenced in chapter 2, the context of our world system is now forcing people with radically different cultural values, attitudes, and practices to negotiate their values, attitudes, and practices on an international scale—again, as never before. Most recently, the COVID-19 pandemic has reminded us that microorganisms and their associated diseases are also part of our global flows. To be sure, we can no longer understand the complexities of people and the dynamics of culture outside of this ever-emergent system.[49]

LESSONS FOR THE ANTHROPOCENE

Modern nation-states and ancient states do share some characteristics. Although trade and the exchange of goods and services exist on a much broader and more complex level, and although international trade is for the most part framed by a capitalist world economy (with its own unique history), one characteristic persists: fragility. Exhaustion of resources, famine, social unrest, institutionalized inequality, food shortages, conquest, mass genocide—these are cultural artifacts that have led to the demise of states. When we examine the evidence, we see that throughout the past five or six thousand years, states have consistently risen and fallen because of political and economic pressures.

The prestate Cahokia, for example, most likely collapsed because of the exhaustion of its surrounding resources, food shortages, and/or class conflict.[50] When states fall, survivors have presumably taken up less complex ways of organizing themselves—as foragers, pastoralists, or horticulturalists.

Today, however, the situation we face is very different from that of ancient states. In a relatively short amount of time, nation-states (and the international trade that supports them) have produced and reproduced larger and larger populations that can never go back in large measure to foraging, pastoralism, or horticulture. Because all the world's people are today integrated into a transnational political economy, we face some difficult questions in the twenty-first century, questions that humans have never had to face before, although the questions were generated long ago. Science writer Jared Diamond, who is most famous for articulating this point of view, puts it this way:

> Archaeologists studying the rise of farming have reconstructed a crucial stage at which we made the worst mistake in human history. Forced to choose between limiting population or trying to increase food production, we chose the latter and ended up with starvation, warfare, and tyranny. Hunter-gatherers practiced the most successful and longest-lasting lifestyle in human history. In contrast, we're still struggling with the mess into which agriculture has tumbled us, and it's unclear whether we can solve it. Suppose that an archaeologist who had visited us from outer space were trying to explain human history to his fellow spacelings. He might illustrate the results of his digs by a 24-hour clock on which one hour represents 100,000 years of real past time. If the history of the human race began at midnight, then we would now be almost at the end of our first day. We lived as hunter-gatherers for nearly the whole of that day, from midnight through dawn, noon, and sunset. Finally, at 11:54 p.m., we adopted agriculture. As our second midnight approaches, will the plight of famine-stricken peasants gradually engulf us all? Or will we somehow achieve those seductive blessings that we imagine behind agriculture's facade, and that have so far eluded us?[51]

We must recognize that living in modern nation-states (wherever they may be, however small or large) means that we are necessarily dependent on political and economic "others" (both individual people and individual societies) for our continued survival. The *real* threats to the survival of eight billion people have much more to do with politics and economics than with things like "moral decay," "lack of sufficient resources," or other misguided popular assumptions.

Core nations produce enough food to feed the entire world, but people are starving because of the political and economic inequities in distributing resources, not because there are too few resources to feed them. And within these cores, extreme poverty and dispossession of land and resources persist for many, while in some periphery nations, there exists a concentrated minority of staggering wealth. So these inequalities exist not only *between* nations but *within* nations. This is one reason why, when the social movement to "Occupy Wall Street" erupted in 2011 in New York City (with anthropologists like David Graeber and Michael Taussig participating), the criticism was not only of the wealthiest 1 percent of the USA but the wealthiest 1 percent of a global elite, who are connected—and often protected—across the globe by financial and political networks. Indeed, if this story about the evolution of the state has anything to teach us, it is this: Self-dependence, self-sufficiency, and isolation are illusions. Nation-states simply cannot go it alone.[52]

Thus, the culture that mediates our relationship with our environments, writ on an international scale, is today powerfully shaped by historical and contemporary political (state), economic (market), and ecological (natural) systems. What at first glance might appear to be very "localized" aspects of culture in reality have extensive political, economic, and ecological influences. Anthropologists today remain cognizant of these wider relations of power, history, and influence even as they study topics that may seem to be far removed from those wider forces. As it turns out, the political-economic-ecological forces shaping nation-states have direct impacts on the everyday sociocultural lives of people in even the most seemingly "out of the way" places.

Our relationships and survival with the environment cannot be considered outside this construct. Climate change has made this abundantly clear in recent years. For example, increased sand dunes and sandstorms in the Colorado Plateau region of the US Southwest (northern Arizona and New Mexico) may appear to be isolated ecological oddities, affecting a few rural Diné (Navajo) families whose roads or homes become blocked or buried in the moving sands. Yet as a team of geologists and hydrologists has shown, these are not isolated or random events but are part of a wider regional drought and ecological mutation, leading to widespread desertification and water shortages.[53] Moreover, as ethnographers have shown, increasing water shortages have turned courtroom "water rights" settlements between the Navajo Nation, other Colorado River nations, and the state of Arizona into a legal and economic battlefield.[54] This has further exposed the impacts of water contamination across the reservation, left behind from uranium mining and milling on the Colorado Plateau, during the US–USSR Cold War (1945–1991).[55] Thus, what appear to be "local" problems turn out to be regional and often planetary in scope.

It's no wonder, then, that many anthropologists take very seriously the study of this larger cultural framework. They seek to understand how human groups—small or large—respond to and shape the processes of economic, political, and ecological globalization on a daily basis. Biological and archaeological anthropologists are increasingly calling on all of us to recognize how the evolving physical, sociopolitical, and economic environment presents us with among the most important challenges of our time.[56] Linguistic anthropologists are increasingly calling on all of us to recognize the cultural complexities of integrating diverse peoples with diverse languages and backgrounds within common political and economic systems.[57] Sociocultural anthropologists are increasingly calling on all of us to recognize the ways in which people can (and do) both mediate and resist the larger structural powers that dominate them and their lives.[58] Ultimately, what this means for the study of cultural issues like gender and power, marriage and family, and knowledge and belief is that our interconnections with others exist not only in our common biology or our common encounters with universal human problems (like the food quest), but also in a shared political, economic, and ecological world culture.

So where do we go from here? In recent years, the human impact on the world's environment has become an inescapable fact. The outbreak of the COVID-19 pandemic in 2020, the rise in temperatures, intensifying typhoons, droughts, and other climatic events remind us how deeply entangled all societies are with the globalization processes we have discussed here. Geologists have termed our era the **Anthropocene**, an epoch in which the activity of humans has radically transformed the planet's ecosystems, potentially altering the well-being of the planet and all its life forms. The "Anthro" in the term, of course, denotes the human. Anthropologists debate the usefulness of this term but recognize its power in affirming the human-centered and human-driven responsibilities for this unprecedented degree of planetary change. And while environments have always changed, and humans along with them, the loss of species and dramatic seasonal shifts mean that cultures, too, are

ANTHROPOLOGY HERE AND NOW

Climate Change and Indigenous Peoples

One of the many problems of globalization and climate change that anthropologists address today concerns how Indigenous peoples organize to defend their lands and customary ways of life, in the face of (a) intensifying pressures to assimilate and/ or relinquish traditional homelands; and (b) rising sea levels or droughts that threaten their ability to maintain healthy traditional territories. Anthropologists who are also ethnographic film-makers have responded to this double challenge, highlighting how communities assess and adapt to these conditions. Brian McDermott's film *We Are All Related Here* shows this struggle among Yup'ik peoples in Newtok, Alaska, as permafrost melt has necessitated relocation. Charles Menzies (also known as hagwil hayetsk) works on issues of Indigenous traditional territories, political economy, and natural resource management. He directs the Ethnographic Film Unit at the University of British Columbia, which uses "the language of documentary video to explore issues of environmentally and socially responsible resource use that prioritizes collaborative community-based projects." You can learn more about the film unit and its various film projects at anthfilm.anth.ubc.ca.

changing, in response. In her essay, "Gone the Bull of Winter," Susan Crate carefully details how her Viliui Sakha research partners in northern Siberia fear that warming temperatures and loss of snowfall will impact one of their most important cultural stories: The "bull" who personifies the winter season may now be lost, given the dramatic seasonal changes transforming their cultural relationship with their environment. Crate diagnoses the urgency for anthropology in these times as nothing less than "a state of emergency," as we witness and experience the harsh impacts of global processes on peoples' lives. She continues: "We ask what our proper responses and responsibilities to our research partners are in these revelations. How do we translate, advocate, educate and mediate between our research communities and the larger global community?"[59]

This is a question not only for warming Siberian temperatures but for the role of anthropology in the Anthropocene as new forms of social and environmental harm affect global relations. In our efforts toward understanding cultures, we increasingly see how cultures are at risk, both from long-standing threats of war, genocide, contamination, assimilation, and dispossession, and from newly emerging threats that follow from a consumer-driven, energy-hungry global culture, which has resulted in grave environmental and social dangers. What are anthropologists to do, given these conditions? We witness how local actions are increasingly global actions, and vice versa—so much so that a declaration like "Think globally, act locally" might better be posed as "Think globally, *act* globally." At the same time, acting globally is no longer simple (if it ever was). Declining empires and shifting international relations, recent wars and invasions, the disintegration of the global finance and trade system, renewed movements for re-localization (cooperatives, local foods movements), and the surge of new working and social habits following COVID-19, suggest that we may be entering what some call an age of "de-globalization."

CONCLUSION

In this chapter, we have covered an enormous timeline, from the foraging strategies of early *Homo sapiens* to the dangers of climate change. But we have argued that the globalizing processes that we can see in operation all around us have their origin in a unique moment in the history of human beings: the invention of agriculture. This cultural adaptive strategy has enabled an unprecedented expansion in human population and led to the development of complex societies and economically interdependent nation-states. Anthropologists are still exploring the consequences of these developments—from the emergence of class hierarchies, to the uneven flows of the world system, to the devastating ecological impacts of globalization. Whatever the future of the globalizing processes that we have described in this chapter, we believe that anthropology can play a meaningful role in finding ways to understand and manage the coming challenges. We hope that you will carry a heightened awareness about the urgency, ethics, and global relevance of anthropological theory and ethnography with you, as we turn to specific topics of research and action, in the final few chapters.

NOTES

1. A profusion of literature takes up the history of the modern world system from a number of disciplinary perspectives. For a more thorough discussion of world-system theory, see, for example, Giovanni Arrighi, *The Long Twentieth Century* (London: Verso, 1994); Christopher Chase-Dunn and Thomas Hall, *Rise and Demise: Comparing World-Systems* (Boulder, CO: Westview Press, 1997); and Immanuel Wallerstein, *The Modern World System: Capitalist Agriculture and the Origins of European World-Economy in the Sixteenth Century* (New York: Academic Press, 1974) and *Geopolitics and Geoculture: Essays on the Changing World-System* (Cambridge: Cambridge University Press, 1991).

2. The darker perspectives on the negative influences of the invention of agriculture have been most popularly articulated by Jared Diamond—see, for example, *The Third Chimpanzee: The Evolution and Future of the Human Animal* (New York: HarperCollins, 1992), 180–91, and especially *Guns, Germs, and Steel: The Fates of Human Societies* (New York: Norton, 1997). But archaeologists and other anthropologists have long argued that agriculture initiated a human way of life that continues to have a multiplicity of consequences today. Admittedly, we present a simplified introduction of this important topic. For more nuanced discussions of the complexities of agriculture and its consequences (as well as the diverse anthropological arguments surrounding its development), see Mark Nathan Cohen, *Health and the Rise of Civilization* (New Haven, CT: Yale University Press, 1989); Mark Nathan Cohen and George J. Armelagos, eds., *Paleopathology at the Origins of Agriculture* (Orlando, FL: Academic Press, 1984); Brian Fagan, *Floods, Famines and Emperors: El Niño and the Fate of Civilizations* (New York: Basic Books, 1999); Elman Service, *Origins of the State and Civilization: The Process of Cultural Evolution* (New York: Norton, 1975); Julian Steward, *Theory of Culture Change: The Methodology of Multilinear Evolution* (Urbana: University of Illinois Press, 1955); Joseph A. Tainter, *The Collapse of Complex Societies* (New York: Cambridge University Press, 1990); Leslie White, *The Evolution of Culture: The Development of Civilization to the Fall of Rome* (New York: McGraw-Hill, 1959); and Eric Wolf, *Peasants* (Englewood Cliffs, NJ: Prentice Hall, 1966).

3. For easily read introductions to the evolution of *Homo sapiens*, see Donald Johanson and Maitland Edey, *Lucy: The Beginnings of Humankind* (New York: Simon & Schuster, 1981), and Donald Johanson and James Shreeve, *Lucy's Child: The Discovery of a Human Ancestor* (New York: Avon, 1989).

4. Cf. Richard Lee and Irven DeVore, eds., *Man the Hunter* (Chicago: Aldine, 1968); G. Philip Rightmire, *The Evolution of* Homo erectus: *Comparative Anatomical Studies of an Extinct Human Species* (Cambridge: Cambridge

University Press, 1990); and Robert J. Wenke and Deborah I. Olszewski, *Patterns in Prehistory: Mankind's First Three Million Years*, 5th ed. (Oxford: Oxford University Press, 2006).

5. See Frances Dahlberg, ed., *Woman the Gatherer* (New Haven, CT: Yale University Press, 1981).

6. For a fuller discussion, see Peter P. Schweitzer, Megan Biesele, and Robert K. Hitchcock, eds., *Hunters and Gatherers in the Modern World: Conflict, Resistance, and Self-Determination* (New York: Berghahn Books, 2000).

7. Richard Lee, *The Dobe Ju/'hoansi*, 2nd ed. (Fort Worth, TX: Harcourt Brace, 1993), 9–22.

8. Ibid., 59–60.

9. Ibid., 58.

10. Ibid., 60.

11. See, for example, Lee and DeVore, *Man the Hunter*.

12. Cf. George Armelagos and J. R. Dewey, "Evolutionary Response to Human Infectious Diseases," *Bioscience* 157 (1970): 638–44.

13. Steward, *Theory of Culture Change*.

14. Ibid.

15. Lee, *The Dobe Ju/'hoansi*, 61ff. Cf. Marjorie Shostak, *Nisa: The Life and Words of a !Kung Woman* (New York: Vintage Books, 1981).

16. Marcel Mauss, *The Gift: The Form and Reason for Exchange in Archaic Societies* (New York: W. W. Norton & Company, 1990).

17. See Marcela Vasquez-Leon, Brian J. Burke, and Timothy Finan, eds., *Cooperatives, Grassroots Development, and Social Change* (Tucson: University of Arizona Press, 2017).

18. For a fuller discussion, see Marshall Sahlins, *Stone Age Economics* (Chicago: Aldine-Atherton, 1972).

19. Much of the following discussion is based on Mark N. Cohen's *The Food Crisis in Prehistory: Overpopulation and the Origins of Agriculture* (New Haven, CT: Yale University Press, 1977).

20. Ibid.

21. See, for example, the recent works about the Nuer, pastoralists of eastern Africa. Among these are Jon D. Holtzman, *Nuer Journeys, Nuer Lives: Sudanese Refugees in*

Minnesota (Boston: Allyn & Bacon, 2000), and Sharon Hutchinson, *Nuer Dilemmas: Coping with War, Money and the State* (Berkeley: University of California Press, 1996).

22. Steward, *Theory of Culture Change.*

23. See, for example, the literature on segmentary lineage systems, most notably E. E. Evans-Pritchard, *The Nuer: A Description of the Modes of Livelihood and Political Institutions of a Nilotic People* (New York: Oxford University Press, 1940), and Marshall Sahlins, "The Segmentary Lineage: An Organization of Predatory Expansion," *American Anthropologist* 63 (1961): 322–45. But see also Adam Kuper, "Lineage Theory: A Critical Retrospective," *Annual Review of Anthropology* 11 (1982): 71–95, and Henry Munson, "On the Irrelevance of the Segmentary Lineage Model in the Moroccan Rif," *American Anthropologist* 91 (1989): 386–400.

24. See, for example, Robert H. Lowie, *Indians of the Plains* (Washington, DC: American Museum of Natural History, 1954).

25. See Marshall Sahlins, *Tribesmen* (Englewood Cliffs, NJ: Prentice Hall, 1968); Service, *Origins of the State*; and Steward, *Theory of Culture Change.* But see also Morton Fried, *The Notion of Tribe* (Menlo Park, CA: Cummings, 1975).

26. For a discussion on the complications attendant on dating the emergence of agriculture—among other debates—see Bruce D. Smith, *The Emergence of Agriculture* (New York: W. H. Freeman, 1995). See also T. Douglas Price and Anne Birgitte Gebauer, *Last Hunters, First Farmers: New Perspectives on the Prehistoric Transition to Agriculture* (Santa Fe, NM: School of American Research Press, 1995).

27. For a more thorough discussion of prestates and their deeper complexities, see, for example, Timothy Earl, ed., *Chiefdoms: Power, Economy, and Ideology* (Cambridge: Cambridge University Press, 1991).

28. For a fuller discussion of Cahokia, see Timothy R. Pauketat, *The Ascent of Chiefs: Cahokia and Mississippian Politics in Native North America* (Tuscaloosa: University of Alabama Press, 1994), and Timothy R. Pauketat and Thomas E. Emerson, eds., *Cahokia: Domination and Ideology in the Mississippian World* (Lincoln: University of Nebraska Press, 1997).

29. Claudia Gellman Mink, *Cahokia: City of the Sun* (Collinsville, IL: Cahokia Mounds Museum Society, 1999), 24.

30. Mink, *Cahokia*, 20; see also Pauketat and Emerson, *Cahokia*, 3–5.

31. Mink, *Cahokia*, 24–25.

32. Elman Service, *Primitive Social Organization: An Evolutionary Perspective* (New York: Random House, 1962); see also Timothy Earl and J. Erickson, eds., *Exchange Systems in Prehistory* (New York: Academic Press, 1977).

33. See Robert Carneiro, "The Chiefdom as Precursor of the State," in *The Transformation to Statehood in the New World*, ed. Grant Jones and Robert Kautz (Cambridge: Cambridge University Press, 1981), 37–97, and Jonathan Haas, *The Evolution of the Prehistoric State* (New York: Columbia University Press, 1982).

34. For a full discussion of states, their emergence, and the consequences of their political economies, see Morton Fried, *The Evolution of Political Society: An Essay in Political Anthropology* (New York: Random House, 1967); Allen Johnson and Timothy Earle, *The Evolution of Human Societies: From Foraging Group to Agrarian State* (Stanford, CA: Stanford University Press, 1987); and Service, *Primitive Social Organization*.

35. See John S. Henderson, *The World of the Ancient Maya*, 2nd ed. (Ithaca, NY: Cornell University Press, 1997).

36. Sahlins, *Stone Age Economics*.

37. Cf. Mark Cohen, *The Food Crisis in Prehistory Overpopulation and the Origins of Agriculture* (New Haven, CT: Yale University Press, 1977) and *Health and the Rise of Civilization* (New Haven, CT: Yale University Press, 1989).

38. For a more nuanced discussion of the market and its relationship to political economy, see, for example, Terence D'Altroy and Timothy Earle, "Staple Finance, Wealth Finance, and Storage in the Inka Political Economy," *Current Anthropology* 26 (1985): 187–206.

39. Cf. Johnson and Earle, *The Evolution of Human Societies*.

40. See, for example, ibid.

41. See White, *The Evolution of Culture*.

42. See, for example, Diamond, *The Third Chimpanzee*, 180–91.

43. Diamond, *The Third Chimpanzee*; see also Diamond, *Guns, Germs, and Steel*. Cf. Cohen, *The Food Crisis in Prehistory* and *Health and the Rise of Civilization*.

44. Karl Marx and Friedrich Engels, *The Communist Manifesto* (New York: International Publishers, 1979 (1948), 9.

45. Pierre Bourdieu, *Outline of a Theory of Practice* (Cambridge, UK: Cambridge University Press, 1977).

46. Pierre Bourdieu, *Distinction: A Social Critique of the Judgement of Taste* (Cambridge, MA: Harvard University Press, 1984).

47. John H. Bodley, *Anthropology and Contemporary Human Problems*, 3rd ed. (Mountain View, CA: Mayfield Publishing, 1996), 151–52.

48. For a more detailed discussion of problems surrounding population growth, see Bodley, *Anthropology and Contemporary Human Problems* (especially chapter 6).

49. See Arrighi, *The Long Twentieth Century*; Chase-Dunn and Hall, *Rise and Demise*; and Wallerstein, *The Modern World System*.

50. Cf. Pauketat, *The Ascent of Chiefs*, and Pauketat and Emerson, *Cahokia*.

51. Jared Diamond, "The Worst Mistake in the History of the Human Race," *Discover* 8 (1987): 66.

52. Cf. Diamond, *Guns, Germs, and Steel*.

53. See, for example, Margaret Hiza Redsteer, Rian C. Bogle, and John M. Vogel, "Monitoring and Analysis of Sand Dune Movement and Growth on the Navajo Nation, Southwestern United States: US Geological Survey Fact Sheet 2011–3085," 2011; and Margaret Hiza Redsteer, Kirk Bemis, Karletta Chief, Mahesh Gautam, Beth Rose Middleton, and Rebecca Tsosie, "Unique Challenges Facing Southwestern Tribes," in *Assessment of Climate Change in the Southwest United States: A Report Prepared for the National Climate Assessment*, ed. G. Garfin, A. Jardine, R. Meredith, M. Black, and S. LeRoy (Washington, DC: Island Press, 2013).

54. Andrew Curley, "Unsettling Indian Water Settlements: The Little Colorado River, the San Juan River, and Colonial Enclosures," *Antipode* 53 (4) (2019).

55. Dana E. Powell, *Landscapes of Power: Politics of Energy in the Navajo Nation* (Durham: Duke University Press, 2018); and Teresa Montoya, "Yellow Water: Rupture and Return One Year after the Gold King Mine Spill," *Anthropology Now* 9 (2017): 91–115.

56. See, for example, Carole Crumley, ed., *New Directions in Anthropology and Environment: Intersections* (Walnut Creek, CA: AltaMira Press, 2001).

57. See, for example, Walt Wolfram, *American English: Dialects and Variation* (Malden, MA: Blackwell, 1998).

58. See, for example, Jennie M. Smith, *When the Hands Are Many: Community Organization and Social Change in Rural Haiti* (Ithaca, NY: Cornell University Press, 2001).

59. Susan A. Crate, "Gone the Bull of Winter?: Grappling with the Cultural Implications of and Anthropology's Role(s) in Global Climate Change," *Current Anthropology* 49 (4) (2008): 569–95.

5

Sex, Gender, and Inequality
Cross-Cultural Perspectives

As human beings, we take a lot for granted. While we may appreciate that culture creates a world of meaning and difference around us, we often still assume that our actions, behaviors, and thoughts are natural or right. We should appreciate that this, too, is a part of our ethnocentrism, an idea we explored in chapter 2. Even with this understanding of the range of expressive possibilities in being human, it can be difficult to break free from the deeply held assumptions we hold about the world and ourselves.

One of the more powerful among such assumptions is that of **gender**. Human beings almost everywhere tend to think the differences between humans we classify as "women" and those we classify as "men" are differences that are natural, inherent, and inborn; moreover, many human societies take the categories of "woman" and "man" as unquestionable facts of "nature." Even if we appreciate that culture establishes the contours through which we live and express our lives, people have tended to be less willing to extend such understandings to something as basic and, presumably, as biological as gender. Yet when anthropologists have sought to understand societies around the world, the vast differences we see among human expressions of gender conclusively illustrate that these taken-for-granted differences are more cultural than they are biological.

From anthropology, we can begin with a classic example presented by Franz Boas's student Margaret Mead in her 1935 book, *Sex and Temperament in Three Primitive Societies.* Mead undertook this ethnographic study in the 1930s, an era when Western gender norms were particularly rigid and the roles of women and men strictly defined. In this way, Mead's project was in response to what she saw as the cultural conservativism of US society. As a young female scholar in the intensely male-dominated academy, she was no doubt already inclined to question the strictly gendered habits of her own profession.

In this well-known study, Mead sought to understand diverse (and non-Western) expressions of gender identities and sexual behavior by comparing three peoples of New Guinea: the Arapesh, the Mundugumor, and the Tchambuli. In each of these groups, men and women exhibited personality traits that were very different from what Americans might expect. For instance, Arapesh women and men behaved in ways that Mead's readers may have expected American women to act: both genders displayed "a personality that . . . we would call maternal in its parental aspects, and feminine in its sexual aspects."[1] Mundugumor men and women, however, behaved in ways that many of Mead's US-based readers might have expected only men to act—in the extreme: "Both men and women developed as ruthless, aggressive, positively sexed individuals, with the maternal cherishing aspects of personality at a minimum. Both men and women approximated to a personality type that we in our culture would find only in an undisciplined and very violent male."[2]

In marked contrast to the Arapesh and the Mundugumor (both of whom downplayed the contrast between men and women), Mead found that the Tchambuli drew clear lines between the two genders. But unlike Americans, Tchambuli harbored stereotypical attitudes that were the exact *opposite* of 1930s American gender stereotypes: There was "a genuine reversal of the sex-attitudes of our own culture, with the woman the dominant, impersonal, managing partner, the man the less responsible and the emotionally dependent person," Mead found.[3] In the end, Mead's study illustrated that culture (rather than biological sex alone) had an enormous role in shaping the contours of how women and men were assigned particular roles. Mead wrote:

> These three situations suggest, then, a very definite conclusion. If those temperamental attitudes which we have traditionally regarded as feminine—such as passivity, responsiveness, and a willingness to cherish children—can so easily be set up as the masculine pattern in one tribe, and in another be outlawed for the majority of the women as well as for the majority of men, we no longer have any basis for regarding such aspects of behavior as sex-linked.[4]

For Mead, linking the behavior of women and men (expressions of gender identities) entirely to biology—that is, seeing them as "sex-linked"—missed how culture powerfully shapes the behavioral profiles of what societies take to be a "man" and a "woman." Moreover, Mead's findings of gender diversity cast a mirror back on US society itself, exposing the deeply rigid construction of a strict **binary gender system** in America, and the associated cultural norms that she—and many others of the time—found highly troubling. In long-standing traditions in Western thought, binaries are usually also perceived not only as two distinct categories but as *oppositional* as well (in this case, women as fully distinct from and therefore the "opposite of" men). Dualistic binaries have been foundational in Euro-American philosophy since René Descartes penned his famous phrase, *Cogito ergo sum* ("I think, therefore I am"), confirming the dualism of the mind and the body.

In the gender binary society of Mead's time, for instance, men of a certain social class were seen as "natural" wage earners, working in the "public" sphere (masculine, outward-facing, amplified, social, and visible), and women were seen as "natural" homemakers, whose work remained largely hidden in the "private" sphere (feminine, domestic, out of sight, protected, and familial). Yet as Mead and other ethnographers showed, these seemingly "natural" roles and dualist binary positions become overturned by empirical evidence from other places and peoples. Mead's work helped to expose the rigidly structured binary gender system of US society and the many oppressions being enacted in the name of "appropriate" or socially acceptable expressions of gender.

Although Mead's original studies have been criticized for overstating the case, countless other anthropologists since Mead have illustrated that culture operates to construct gender and sexuality. Importantly, this legacy includes other women anthropologists who studied with Boas and examined cross-cultural gender roles, like Zora Neale Hurston, working in the Black South, and Ella Cara Deloria (also known as Aŋpétu Wašté Wiŋ), working in her own Yankton Sioux Nation in South Dakota.

Take, for example, religious practice. In many societies around the world, men and women may have separate access to the gods, take on separate religious functions, maintain different kinds of sacred knowledge, and even have separate expectations placed on their spiritual development. In all the major religions of the contemporary world, priesthood roles have traditionally been the prerogative of men. That is no surprise to those of us brought up in Judeo-Christian, Western, or other **patriarchal traditions** in which men are the primary holders of social power. What may surprise you, depending on your own background, is how often religion corresponds with gender—and in a number of different and interesting ways.

In some Native American traditions, certain religious practices are the sole activity of men, who, as representatives of large families, are charged to pray for their entire nation (both women and men)—an activity not engaged in by the women. Among many Pueblo peoples of the southwestern United States, men attend the most sacred rituals held in the kiva—a room (usually underground) where ceremonies take place.[5] Compare this with Christian worship in mainstream America, where women constitute the majority of church membership, though men still hold the vast majority of positions as ministers or pastors. National opinion polls in the United States suggest that men as a whole are less devoted to their churches than women. Indeed, religion would, on the surface, appear to be more important to women than men. According to these studies, women apparently pray more, and women more often and more deeply examine their faith, spiritual growth, and relationship to God. Although men overwhelmingly hold priesthood and pastor roles, it turns out (in this logic) that women are the more "spiritual" gender in American churches.[6]

In another example of cultural associations between gender and spirituality, people of the Ryūkyū Islands just south of mainland Japan would agree that females are more inclined toward spiritual matters than males. Ryūkyūan, the islanders' Indigenous religion, accords women a special ability to communicate with the supernatural. Women thus dominate religious rituals and even represent their families in prayer at the household hearth.[7] This attitude linking gender (in this case, women) with spirituality is also similar to some Hindu beliefs. Among the *hijras* of India, men who want to take up worship of the mother goddess Bahuchara Mata must renounce their "maleness" by undergoing a castration ceremony before they can be considered a true *hijra*, transitioning to a **nonbinary** or **third gender**—"neither man nor woman," as anthropologist Serena Nanda describes.[8] After becoming a *hijra*, worshippers take female names and adopt female dress and behavior, becoming what anthropologists term a "third gender" that is, in this case, associated with the sacred.

These examples suggest that religion can sometimes be as much about the ideas surrounding diverse expressions of gender as about the search for

Among the hijras *of India, men who want to take up worship of the mother goddess Bahuchara Mata renounce their "maleness," take female names, and adopt female dress and behavior. Rohit Bhakar / iStock*

spiritual meaning. Remember, we are not born with these ideas or identities; rather, we learn them, often slowly and over time, through processes of shared meaning-making and enculturation, as we discussed in chapter 2. Cross-culturally, then, the linking of human sexuality and gender identity with institutions like religion, politics, or economics is not really that surprising. But interestingly, these examples also illustrate that people conduct their lives at the most basic and complex levels in reference to their ideas about the relationship between gender, sex, and sexuality. Almost everywhere, with few exceptions (the Arapesh and the Mundugumor apparently being some of the few), women and men (and in some societies, third genders) can have wholly different expectations placed on them by society, wholly different functions and roles, and often, as a result, may experience wholly different lives. These gendered experiences are powerful and often enduring, but they are not fixed and may change over time. They may also vary considerably within a society, depending on many factors, such as intersections with an individual's race, class, nationality, ethnicity, or ability.

Let's look at another example—one that may seem extreme by US standards. Among several Indigenous peoples of the South American Amazon and the New Guinea highlands, men and women live in separate houses. Women and their children live in their own houses separate from men, who live in "men's houses." Women and men interact in everyday life, of course, but their relations are often socially suspect. In some groups, men and women are said to thoroughly distrust one another; their sexual relations, for instance, are very infrequent. By contrast, in American society, the typical nuclear family household is often established on a male–female (binary gender–based) marriage (though this heterosexual marriage norm has been challenged legally and socially in recent years). The household in many societies in the Amazon and New Guinea highlands, however, is founded on a *commonality* rather than difference, with people of the same gender. This cultural practice is also strictly structured by age: The exception to this gender exclusivity in household dwelling is for persons under a certain age, as is the case with boys who live in their mothers' houses but have not moved or been initiated into the men's houses.[9]

In another example, Diné (Navajo) creation stories state that in a previous world the "separation of the sexes" on opposite riverbanks followed a spell of intensive quarreling, constituting one of the most formative moments for understanding the significance of the eventual reunification of the two genders (and the other nonbinary genders that are also part of the story) and the ability of humans to take their place, ultimately, in the contemporary world.[10] This includes, as Diné anthropologist Harry Walters explains, a thoughtful understanding of the *five* genders constituting Diné society and their ongoing relevance despite efforts by colonial authorities to reduce this multiplicity into a male/female binary.[11] Diné historian Jennifer Denetdale extends this critical perspective on colonialism's disruptions of Indigenous systems of gender, showing how contemporary interpretations of Navajo "traditional

Men building a women's house in highland Papua, New Guinea. From left to right, the house consists of a hearth room, pig stalls, and a bedroom for women and children. Photo by Ruth C. Wohlt

culture" are often manipulated in a manner to favor a patriarchal status quo.[12] In sum, despite the supposedly "natural" basis of gender, sociocultural constructions of gender are not fixed but are ongoing negotiations of culture, power, and identity.

While many of us may be unfamiliar with these kinds of gender arrangements, they are not at all that surprising when we begin to compare societies around the world. In actuality, humans have regularly created sex- and gender-based groups. For example, ethnographers and videographers Susannah M. Hoffman, Richard Cowan, and Paul Aratow report that in 1970s Kypseli (a small traditional Greek village), women and men clearly constituted separate groups in day-to-day life. During the day, men hunted, tended their fields (which they alone owned), and visited and transacted business in the village square (where women rarely, if ever, congregated). While the men were away from home, women's activities dominated the smaller village courtyards, where they gathered to visit and work. When the day came to a close, however, women lost control of the courtyards as the men returned and began visiting with each other. While the home was primarily the prerogative of women—that is, homes were given female names, owned by women, and were passed from mother to daughter—inside the home, men and women also had their own male and female sections. The inner parlor was the province primarily of men, and the kitchen was strictly a women's space. Religion, too, paralleled these divided worlds. In the village churches, men and women gathered as separate groups: Men almost always sat closer to the church's altar, and women sat or stood in the back of the church.[13]

Contrast Kypseli with the village of Nazaré in Portugal, where a working-class group of fishermen live in ways very different from that found in Kypseli.[14] Instead of men dominating public space, women do. But in addition, women dominate private, domestic space as well. Ethnographer Jan Brøgger reports that men—who are the fishermen in this small Portuguese village—fish for their families. But their wives are responsible primarily for selling the fish in the public marketplace. In the home, there is no men's assigned space, as in Kypseli. Men are expected to wake in the morning, have a quick breakfast, and exit the home as soon as possible. At home they are considered "in the way"; in many respects they are marginal members of the home.

The working-class Nazaré are primarily **matrilocal**: After marriage, the newly married couple moves to live within the wife's family's household (we will discuss this and other kinds of residence patterns further in the next chapter). Many a married man, then, enters a household entirely controlled by women who are related to one another: his wife, his wife's mother, his wife's married or unmarried sisters, and their children. Both he and his wife's father are considered "strangers" in the household: They are from altogether different families; in a sense, they are unrelated. And *their* families have no property rights in a home owned primarily by the women of the house. In other words, the entire space of the home is the prerogative of women. Coupled with women's dominance in the marketplace, Brøgger concluded that the working-class community of Nazaré (in contrast to the bourgeoisie of the village, who mirror the rest of Europe) represents a case in which,

> unlike the situation that traditionally prevails in both the United States and Europe, the women are also in charge of the economy outside the household. Many women among the stratum of fishermen are business-people in the true sense of the word. This unconventional division of roles between men and women makes the situation in Nazaré particularly interesting. . . . [T]he dominant position of women has important consequences for the conjugal [i.e., married] relationship and the family structure.[15]

Enough of the Nazaré and Kypseli, men's houses, sex-based religion, and Margaret Mead. We mention all of these examples because of the questions they raise. Are women's and men's worlds always divided? What of the worlds that involve "neither male nor female" (as in the *hijras* of India, or Navajo five genders, discussed above)? Are gendered worlds always characterized by power relations? Are men or women more often the dominators, and in what cases is this relationship undermined, reversed, or more egalitarian? These are questions we will take up shortly.

SEX AND GENDER: BEYOND THE BINARY

As we hope you have gathered from these diverse examples, the human experience of sex, gender, and sexuality—just like everything else—is shaped by culture. Before we dive deeper into this central aspect of the human experience, it is important to clarify our terms. Although we will mention "sexuality"—the quality of being physically attracted to other people—in this chapter, our main emphasis will be on the two fundamental terms of "sex" and "gender." In casual conversation, these two terms are sometimes used interchangeably, but we will stick to the more technical definitions—with some caveats. Most scholars use "sex" as a reference to the biological basis of human reproduction and "gender" as a term for the culturally mediated expression of sex. In short, sex is based in nature; gender reflects cultural influences. We will follow this usage, but we also want to caution readers against an overly rigid understanding of these two terms. As we will see, it will be important to also embrace some ambiguity when it comes to discussions of sex and gender.

Our main caution with regard to the above definitions of sex and gender is that it can be hard to disentangle them from their specific history in Western societies, which has emphasized a strict male/female binary. It has long been assumed in Western thought that sex (secondary sexual characteristics, reproductive organs, chromosomes) is purely biological and includes only two sexes: male and female. Because gender roles were assumed to be derived from their biological origins, they were also rigidly dualistic. Anthropologists, along with many other scholars, reject this line of reasoning as a form of fallacious thinking called **essentialism**. An "essentialist" argument claims that certain human behaviors, such as gender roles, are determined by "natural" processes. Essentialism has a long history in Western thought. The rigid dualisms of "male" and "female" gender roles are just one example. As we have seen above, anthropologists, in their observations of the diverse ways of being human in the world, have challenged the dualism of gender roles as "natural" or as having any essential connection to biological sex. Gender theorist Judith Butler has famously argued that gender could be best understood as a "performance" rather than an "essence." Like Butler, anthropologists have tracked gender's "performance" in diverse settings, across space and time.

The idea of gender as performance may be surprising to some readers, especially when each of us might individually feel that one's gender identity is so deep-seated. But consider your own social world. How is gender socially reinforced, affiliated with power? When you tinker or innovate with your clothing, hairstyle, way of walking or sitting or speaking, have you received (perhaps unwanted) feedback from parents, peers, or educators that would discipline you back into behaviors that they expect from you, into an "appropriate" expression of your gender? "Don't throw like a girl," "Sit like a lady," or "Speak like a man" are all-too-familiar admonitions, sanctions for deviating from cultural norms. They serve as warnings that someone perceives you (or another) to be gender-nonconforming. Such admonitions vary across cultures, but all societies exert some forms of social conformity to regulate gender expression and, in some cases, punish those who fall "out of line." While this has changed radically in recent years in Western societies and many urban areas around the world, with androgynous superstars having transformed global popular culture (consider the gender aesthetics of the K-pop "boy band" BTS), gender nonconformity is still highly risky for many individuals in many societies.

If gender roles are not absolutely fixed, how and why does culture assign diverse behaviors, roles, and values to biological sex in the first place? The answer resides partly in how culture works, which, you'll remember from chapter 2, is inextricably bound to social interaction and power. We must associate with other people to reproduce ourselves, our societies, and our cultures from generation to generation. Because of this, we are always passing through life *in relation* to other people. From the time we are born, we are someone's child or grandchild, brother or sister, nephew or niece, friend or foe, student or teacher, mate, father or mother, uncle or aunt, or grandfather or grandmother. As human beings, we cannot escape this—whether we assign these categories to ourselves or whether others assign them to us.

Being a member of certain groups and being expected to act in certain ways is fundamentally human. Because gender so pervades our lives, it weaves in and out of our social interactions; each and every person must negotiate

Anthropologists have argued that gender roles are not biologically determined but are learned, negotiated, and shaped by various sociocultural forces and power relations. Photo by Danny Gawlowski

a "gendered" position in society, no matter how or where they live. Indeed, people *negotiate* many culturally defined positions, including gender. In some societies, gender is considered immutable; in others, it is quite flexible. But whether immutable or flexible, our ideas about gender are always shaped by the groups of which we are a part. They always vary, if only by degrees, from people to people and from place to place.

To better understand this process of negotiation, let's briefly examine what anthropologists have often termed **third genders**, or, more recently, **nonbinary genders**. These genders don't fit within the male/female binary that has dominated Western societies in the modern era. Above, we have already mentioned the *hijras* of India, a third or alternative gender in which emasculated men and intersexed individuals become accepted members of a sacred group of worshippers. We also discussed the existence of *five* genders in Navajo (Diné) society. Another case in point are so-called "Two Spirit" persons (formerly known by the pejorative French term, *berdache*) of many other North American Indigenous peoples, who reject or transcend exclusively male or female gender roles. In the past, colonizing forces and Christian missionaries often targeted Two Spirit persons in an effort to eradicate these genders. But ethnographers have recorded historical and contemporary cases of a broad range of **alternate genders** in over 150 different North American Indian societies.[16] In many of these nations, individuals occupied a separate, often named category, apart from that of "man" or "woman." The majority of recorded cases document biologically sexed males who assumed female dress, occupations, and/or behaviors, specific to their societies. But these persons did not have the same status as women; they inhabited an intermediate status, one often imbued with supernatural powers and/or responsibilities.[17] For example, among the Hidatsa—a northern Plains people—the "man-woman," or *miati*, dressed and worked like Hidatsa women but also took on special religious and ceremonial roles. "Their roles in ceremonies were many and exceeded those of the most distinguished tribal ceremonial leaders," wrote ethnographer Alfred Bowers. "There was an atmosphere of mystery about them. Not being bound as firmly by traditional teachings coming down from the older generations through the ceremonies, but more as a result of their individual and unique experiences with the supernatural, their conduct was less traditional than that of the other ceremonial leaders."[18]

The *miati* assumed their separate status, unconventional ceremonial roles, and special associations with the supernatural through repeated dreams and visions that preceded and necessitated their gender transformations.[19] Such vision experiences encouraging or obliging gender transformations were common in many other Native North American groups as well, such as the Arapaho, Miami, and Ute.[20] Other documented cases of gender transformations also cite childhood interests in the activities of the other genders, which could develop over time.[21] Among the Mohave of the Greater Southwest, women who were pregnant might dream that their children might become *alyha* or *hwame*, the gender variants for males and females, respectively. But it wasn't until those children began to express interests in the dress, activities, and behaviors of the other gender as they grew up that the alternate, third-gender status became socially recognized and affirmed.[22]

Like the Mohave, some groups, like the Cheyenne and Diné, had variant gender categories for both males and females (having, in effect, four or more genders).[23] But even in societies with only one alternate gender (which in most cases was assumed by males) or no gender variants at all, some individuals (often female) could adopt the dress, occupations, and/or behaviors of the other without making a full transition into a separate, alternate, or third-gender category. This kind of fluidity unsettled colonial administrators tasked with taking census data following a European binary gender system and controlling Indigenous populations as part of the project of settlement. In several Plains nations, for instance, women would at times assume masculine activities and/or behaviors without shifting their status as "women" within their societies. These "manly" or "manly hearted" women eschewed conventional female roles and extended their influence into male-dominated arenas of property ownership, ceremonial leadership, and even warfare.[24]

When considered alongside the third-gender variants available for males in many Plains groups, these alternatives "offered men and women opportunities," as Standing Rock Lakota anthropologist Beatrice Medicine once noted, "for displaying cross-sex talents in socially approved ways, and in doing so, they were probably essential to the psychological well-being of peoples who lived in societies with highly dichotomized gender expectations."[25] Medicine, like Mead before her, understood that anthropology not only offered a lens into "the unfamiliar" but also offered a mirror back onto dominant societies in a mode of reflection that would, one day, be known as cultural critique. Studies such as Mead's and Medicine's suggested other ways to live, to organize human life, and to thrive. The same could be said today for the many North American Native peoples who must negotiate social roles as nonbinary, third genders, or Two Spirits within a larger settler society that, in most quarters (including in many contemporary Native communities), makes little room for alternatives when it comes to gender.[26]

ANTHROPOLOGY HERE AND NOW

Two Spirits, the Documentary

Two Spirit persons continue to carve out space for themselves in society. Even in contemporary Native communities, where their roles were traditionally more understood and celebrated, they can be the victims of horrific violence. *Two Spirits* is a documentary of a young Diné teen, Fred Martinez, who was murdered because of his third-gender identity. The film explores the multiple gender roles found in traditional Diné society and the movement for awareness against hate crimes that Martinez's death inspired. You can learn more about Martinez, the film, and alternate genders the world over at www.pbs.org/independentlens/two-spirits.

"Woman Jim" (also known as "Squaw Jim" and "Finds Them and Kills Them") was a well-known bote (a third-gender role among the Crow of the northern Plains), famous for accomplishments as a warrior, artist, and religious and spiritual leader. Photo 1928, courtesy of the National Anthropological Archives, Smithsonian Institution (INV 00476400)

The existence of nonbinary genders remains present cross-culturally. Other instances include the *xanith* of Oman, who are said to exhibit both masculine and feminine characteristics; the *mahu* of Tahiti, men who, like the *hijras*, take on women's behavior and activities (but without emasculation surgery); and the "Sworn Virgins" of the Balkans, women who abstain from sexual relations and refuse marriage and motherhood to assume the dress and activities of men.[27]

These broad-ranging examples illustrate a central conclusion of the anthropology of gender: The experience and expression of gender can be highly variable, with only a tentative correspondence with biological sex. Culturally constructed categories for gender identification might be better understood as falling along a continuum, with "male" and "female" at the two poles, among a range of possibilities that include alternate genders as points in between. In 2014, global social media giant Facebook decided to move past the male or female binary to offer fifty-eight different possible gender identifications, ranging from agender to trans person to two-spirit. Facebook's proliferation of gender identity options made international news, affirming the demand among users worldwide for more suitable gender terms. Facebook's decision certainly reflects the greater tolerance toward nonbinary genders and alternative sexual orientations in the West, but it may take some time until we understand its true significance. In the meantime, gender roles continue to be influenced by social forces; we don't become who we are in a vacuum, but rather in relation. And they continue to be subject to questions of power, as we will discuss in greater detail in the next section.

We have discussed at length the malleability of gender thus far, without saying much about sex. We so often imagine biology to be beyond the reach of culture, but as it turns out, sex is far more complex than we have assumed. **Biological sex** usually refers to the physical differences associated with reproduction, such as chromosomes, hormones, genitalia, secondary sex characteristics (body and facial hair, pelvic build, muscle mass, etc.), and so on. But biology must always be interpreted by physicians, parents, and others, and therefore it cannot escape the realm of culture. A full discussion of human biology is beyond our scope, but suffice it to say that there exists a wide range of differences in genetic expression and sex development across bodies that seem to exceed the classic male/female binary. For example, there is growing recognition of the phenomenon of "intersex," individuals born with biological attributes that would traditionally be ascribed to both male and female. Reflecting on the intersex experience, gender and sexuality scholar Anne Fausto-Sterling has provocatively argued that a five-sex system would be a better reflection of human biological sexual diversity.[28] As Fausto-Sterling has pointed out, the ambiguities of biological sex have already become a contentious issue for major international events, such as the Olympics, which are structured around a binary model of sex.[29] The activism of South African Olympic runner and gold medalist, Caster Semenya (see the box insert), have exposed the limitations and challenges confronting such international events. While sex and gender remain key terms for thinking about one of the most important aspects of the human experience, they are also imperfect terms. We must learn to use them, while also recognizing their limitations.

GENDER, INEQUALITY, AND POWER

In the context of everyday interaction, the culturally defined positions that we hold in relation to other people cannot be separated from the process of **power**. In fact, these relations are often *defined* by power, at the level of states (as legislation, policy, education) and at the level of everyday social life (work, family, religion, and other relationships). Whether we are talking about a mother or a daughter, a member of one ethnic group or another, or someone young or old, one culturally defined position is impacted by its association with other culturally defined positions, and often mediated by institutions

ANTHROPOLOGY HERE AND NOW

Is Sex Itself a Problematic Category?

International sports-governing bodies have strangely found themselves at the center of a growing debate about the biological definitions of male and female. Should the sex of athletes be determined by physical appearance, genitalia, DNA, hormones, or some other biological marker? Should every competitor be required to "prove" their biological sex or just those competitors whose sex might be considered "ambiguous?" Consider the case of two-time Olympic gold medalist, South African runner Caster Semenya, who was not allowed to compete in the 2020 Tokyo Games—as a "woman." She burst onto the international track-and-field scene in 2009 at age eighteen, winning the gold medal at the World Championships in the women's 800 meters. Her sudden rise in the sport and remarkable performance improvements over a short period of time led to suspicions of drug use. Semenya was required to submit to drug tests and a sex verification test, which she "passed." She went on to win gold medals in the 2012 and 2016 Olympics in the 800 meters, but the controversy around her achievements has never ceased.

Semenya was raised female, identifies as female, and is legally female in South Africa. But as an athlete, her sex remains in question. In 2018, the International Association of Athletics Federations (IAAF), now known as World Athletics, determined that women with "differences of sexual development," as athletes like Semenya are now being called, and who have elevated levels of testosterone, must now take medication to lower those levels in order to compete in the track races from 400 meters to 1 mile. Semenya has previously been required to take this medication in 2011 and described the experience as excruciating. "It made me sick, gain weight, [have] panic attacks. . . . It was like stabbing yourself with a knife every day."[1] She challenged the 2018 IAAF ruling in the Federal Supreme Court of Switzerland and the European Court of Human Rights, but to no avail. Many have pointed out that the leading women athletes affected by the IAAF policy are all from the Global South, raising suspicions that covert racism may be behind these new rules.

Runner Caster Semenya competing for South Africa at an international track-and-field competition. "Womens 800m—ISTAF 2011" by André Zehetbauer from Schwerin, Deutschland, licensed under CC BY-SA 2.0

So who gets to decide what determines one's sex and gender? Physicians? International athletic organizations? Semenya has become increasingly vocal about the issues at stake in her case. She credits her track-and-field success to her intense training regimen, not her testosterone levels. In her twitter account @ caster800m, she wrote on February 21, 2021: "This fight is not just about me; it's about taking a stand and fighting for dignity, equality and the human rights of women in sport. All we ask is to be able to run free as the strong and fearless women we are!! Thank you to all of those who have stood behind me."

Note

1. "Caster Semenya Offered to Show Officials Her Vagina to Prove She Is Female," *The Guardian*, May 24, 2022.

ANTHROPOLOGY HERE AND NOW

The #MeToo Movement and Sexual Assault

Questions of gender and power were brought into the public spotlight, particularly in relation to the problem of sexual violence, in just the past few years with the rise of the #MeToo movement on social media. This movement was kindled by allegations of sexual assault against the famous film producer Harvey Weinstein in October 2017. American actress Alyssa Milano posted on Twitter in response to these public allegations, asking followers to respond "Me too" if they had been sexually harassed or assaulted, leading to the emergence of the new hashtag #MeToo. The phrase "Me Too" was first coined by sexual assault survivor and activist Tarana Burke in 2006, as a way to bring awareness and elicit empathy for a serious social problem that has long been hidden due to the shame of the victims and the all-too-frequent impunity of its perpetrators.

The courage of celebrity women bringing attention to the problem of sexual assault ignited a cultural wildfire that went global. The #MeToo movement led to a surge of legal actions against perpetrators and brought a heightened level of collective awareness to the insidious and frequently hidden nature of gender-based sexual violence. This was, of course, not a "new" problem. Scholars and feminist activists had diagnosed this violence long before, and struggled for policy changes. The United States government took important action against gender-based violence with the 1994 USA Violence Against Women Act, which has been reauthorized in 2000, 2005, 2013, and 2022 to expand its legal protections. Nonetheless, the #MeToo movement has shown that much more work remains to be done to protect women and other nonbinary genders against assault.

(schools, churches, courts, prisons, etc.). All of these positions are shaped by history and at the same time being challenged, reformed, and remade in present conditions.

When we think of power, we often tend to think of domination or subjugation. Within the world of gender, this kind of inequality may result in sometimes horrific physical violence, as the #MeToo movement has reminded us. But it is important to recognize that anthropologists understand the concept of power in a broader context, as effects that are visible in the most mundane aspects of everyday life. Anthropologists have known for many years that in any given society, because men, women, and, in many cases, nonbinary genders are assigned certain tasks and roles, these activities take on particular values that people use to rank the status of certain activities over other activities. Anthropologists call this phenomenon the **sexual division of labor** and find such divisions to be a primary organizer of cultural life in all societies—though the precise arrangements vary considerably across societies. In itself, there is nothing "wrong" about the sexual or gendered division of labor; the issue of power emerges when some activities are highly valued while others are devalued.

Although notable exceptions have surfaced in ethnographic literature (e.g., the case in Nazaré), in most societies, the tasks and roles associated with the sexual division of labor generally place men's activities above the activities of women. Even among relatively egalitarian societies like the !Kung (the foragers of southern Africa discussed in the previous chapter), men's activities have been valued above women's. Although !Kung women did the majority of work collecting food, the meat hunted by men was often more highly valued within !Kung society.[30] In our own so-called "progressive" times, within democratic societies, things are not so different. Throughout our world, most women's labor is largely undervalued—whether the woman is a corporate executive, stay-at-home parent, teacher, factory worker, computer engineer, or nurse, her labor is socially constructed as less valuable than men's at the same tasks. In the workforce, men consistently get paid more than women for the same job performed across most sectors of employment. And women, regardless of whether they are employed in the external workforce, still do most of the world's domestic labor and housework—including care of children, a task that is devalued and generally unpaid no matter what country she lives in.[31]

Even in the most presumably "modern" and purportedly egalitarian societies, women—no matter what other jobs they might have—still for the most part maintain primary responsibility for housework and child care. Photo by Danny Gawlowski

The global diaspora of migrant workers from the so-called Global South to the United States and Europe has made this sexual division of labor visible at a larger scale. Women's work in this often black-market economy has become the subject of several important anthropological studies.[32] In addition to the sexual division of labor that occurs within all societies, a global division of labor occurs among different ethnic groups and social classes of workers. Many migrant men may be subject to grueling work in construction and agriculture in this low-wage global economy. Migrant women may find difficult work situations in other industries, such as housekeeping, textile production, packaging, and child care. Gender, from this view, is much more than personal identity; it is deeply intertwined with societal and transnational issues of power and other forms of social inequality.[33]

So why do so many societies the world over consistently devalue women's tasks and activities? Is it "natural"? Does it have to be this way? To address these questions, we need to fast-forward from anthropological elders like Boas, Malinowski, and Mead to the early 1970s and the height of the feminist movement. Several women anthropologists took inspiration from Mead (and other scholars who had written about gender) and began to address questions like these, not only in societies where they were doing fieldwork but also in their own professional lives in a male-dominated discipline.[34] These researchers questioned how anthropological knowledge could be applied to problems faced by women in the United States. They knew that their own lives were characterized by professional inequality and wondered if women's lives everywhere were characterized by this kind of inequality. Though sometimes blind to their own privilege (many were highly educated, White women), several scholars took up these questions and forged a new path that became known as **feminist anthropology.**

Several anthropological books and essays appeared on the scene. Among the most prominent was a work titled *Women, Culture, and Society*, edited by Michelle Rosaldo and Louise Lamphere.[35] This cross-cultural comparison was significant because it brought together solid ethnographic examples, key questions about gender-based inequality, and suggestions for thinking about and acting on the current civil and human rights struggles of women in the United States. As anthropologists, the authors of *Women, Culture, and Society* argued based on the vast amount of ethnographic information collected about the world's people that the sexual division of labor was universal: Some division occurs in all societies. In the mid-1970s, gender-based inequality also appeared to be universal, with women's work generally devalued in societies around the world. The authors thus began with a key assumption that although there were a few notable exceptions, male domination and female subordination were generally universal. Several of the authors sought to address *why* male dominance seemed to be so widespread and persistent. The ethnographic evidence could not support an entirely biological explanation for the origin of **gender-based inequality**—that is, women were not "essentially" or "naturally" inferior to men. Indeed, biological differences between men and women are minuscule compared to the culturally based differences. Although factors like relative strength (due to secondary sex traits like muscle mass) may play a role in some sexual divisions of labor, culture and not biology creates the *learned differences* among the genders and, in turn, the *social values* that people place on gendered roles and activities.

Instead of relative strength, several of the authors (most notably, Michelle Rosaldo and Sherry Ortner) argued that other biological trends—chief among them, childbirth—are the broad base on which culture *builds* and *maintains* a division of labor and, thus, gender-based inequality. While childbirth is biological, the culturally defined positions relative to men—the meanings and the roles built around the act of reproduction—are not. The authors argued that, by virtue of childbirth, women are associated with children, the home, and the "hearth," over and over again, from foraging bands to agriculture states; in a word, they are seen as *domestic*. Men, by virtue of not bearing children, are usually free from the responsibilities of child care (in many societies, they have absolutely nothing to do with it beyond conception). Because they are "child free," men are more mobile, free to roam away from the home. Men are rarely associated with the domestic. Instead, they are associated with that which is *public*, like religion. Out of this biological base, then, culture not only constructs gender but also constructs learned, gender-based inequalities and values. Men do not get the idea that their work may be more important than women's work from their biology; rather, they learn it through enculturation as they grow up. Women, similarly, are enculturated to learn that their labor is less important and less valuable—and this is constantly reinforced in systems that support and celebrate men's knowledge and achievements while diminishing those of women.

Having established that women's social subordination seemed to be universal, and that culture, not biology, was most responsible for gender-based inequality, feminist anthropologists engaged in cultural critique of their own (European/North American) society. Taking inspiration from Margaret Mead (who, as you'll remember, argued in *Coming of Age in Samoa* that ethnography provides alternatives to our own cultural assumptions and convictions about gender), these scholars suggested that this knowledge (women's subordination, its cultural construction, and its potential for cultural critique) could work to *change* women's subordination in our own society—that is, *if gender-based inequality is learned, it can be changed.*

Coming at the height of the women's movement in the United States, this contention was an important component of *Women, Culture, and Society*. For example, one of the authors, Michelle Rosaldo, argued that nearly everywhere, both men and women consistently valued that which was public, and thus, that which was the domain of men. In the United States, this meant the workplace. Rosaldo argued that Americans value it more highly than the domestic, notably child care. (Consider the importance of money in our society, and how one's salary is a measure of "success," and then compare the income of business executives [still mostly men] to the income of homemakers [still mostly women].) During the women's movement of the 1970s, many feminists sought to carve out an equal place for women in the workplace—an equal place that has yet to be fully achieved. While Rosaldo argued that this was indeed important to women's rights, she focused on the way our society consistently devalued the domestic (especially child care) and valued work outside the home:

> American society is in fact organized in a way that creates and exploits a radical distance between private and public, domestic and social, female and male. It speaks, on one level, of the conjugal family, while on another it defines women as domestic (an invisible army of unemployed) and sends its men into the public, working world. This conflict between ideal and reality creates illusions and disappointments for both men and women. . . . This conflict is at the core of the contemporary rethinking of sex roles: we are told that men and women should be equals and even companions, but we are also told to value men for their work. So far, women concerned to realize their equality have concentrated on the second half of this paradox, and have sought grounds for female solidarity and opportunities for women in the men's working world. . . . Yet as long as the domestic sphere remains female, women's societies, however powerful, will never be the political equivalents of men's; and, as in the past, sovereignty can be a metaphor for only a female elite. If the public world is to open its door to more than the elite among women, the nature of work itself will have to be altered, and the asymmetry between work and the home reduced. . . . [M]en who have in the past committed their lives to public achievement will recognize women as true equals only when men themselves help to raise new generations by taking on the responsibilities of the home.[36]

Cross-cultural, comparative studies like *Women, Culture, and Society* were important and groundbreaking because of the questions they raised and the discussions they helped to initiate among anthropologists about gender, power, and inequality.

INTERSECTIONALITY

Over time, anthropologists began to question the assumptions underlying early feminist anthropology research, challenging the very idea of male dominance and female subordination. By the late 1970s and early 1980s, anthropologists were arguing that this assumption was based on a narrow either/or proposition. It ignored the diversity and complexity of **gender roles** within societies around the world. For instance, among the Onondaga and other Iroquois nations, men serve as public political leaders; yet they were (and still

Anthropologists have called attention to how all gender roles are learned. Questions of power inequality are inevitably tied to these gender roles, but they also intersect with other factors, such as race, class, sexual orientation, language, nationality, ability, and so on. Photos by Danny Gawlowski

are) elected by clan mothers—women who head large extended families or clans. From the outside, it *appears* that men have more power to make binding decisions for the tribal government and, thus, for the nation as a whole, but their power is mediated by clan mothers who elect them and have the right to remove them if they wish.[37] This new research showed that gender relations were, and are, much more complex than identifying one society or another as straightforwardly "male-dominated." Clearly, women have little power relative to men in some societies; yet in many others, men may dominate some activities while women dominate others.

Other scholars also pointed out that the assumption of universal male dominance and female subordination lacked a critical historical perspective. Peggy Reeves Sanday demonstrated that certain patterns of female power and male dominance were not solely built on biological differences (such as childbirth) but emerged most powerfully through historical processes. Sanday argued that many tribal societies change their "sex-role plan"—the template for defining gender, power, and its relationships—as they encounter political or economic stress such as migration, food shortages, or colonialism. Many tribal societies were transformed from relatively egalitarian societies to hierarchical ones through the processes and structures of colonization. Male dominance, then, was not necessarily universal but had a historical relationship with the violence of colonization. Gender-based inequality was least pronounced among foragers and small "shifting cultivation economies." Sanday argued that it increased markedly as societies became "associated with increasing technological complexity, an animal economy, sexual segregation in work, a symbolic orientation to the male creative principle, and stress."[38]

As we suggested earlier in our discussion of the colonial suppression of third genders, many dimensions of gender inequality appear to have been produced and intensified by colonialism. As a total disruption of social, ecological, and political relations, colonialism "remade gender" in the image of Eurocentric patriarchal and heterosexual norms and employed (as is still often the case in conditions of war) overt sexual violence as a tool to dominate aboriginal populations.[39] Indigenous feminist scholars like Joanne Barker, Mishuana Goeman, and Jennifer Nez Denetdale, among others, have taken up this analysis and offer critical examinations of contemporary gender oppressions and gender-based violence against Native women, as a function of colonial histories.[40]

Early feminist anthropologists tended to be narrowly focused on the question of gender, and perhaps because they were predominantly White and upper-middle-class, they glossed the complex lives of women of color. These anthropologists were part of what is now called "second-wave feminism," the movement in the 1960s and 1970s to struggle for greater women's equality. ("First-wave feminism" refers to the nineteenth- and early-twentieth-century efforts to secure the legal right to vote for women.) More contemporary feminist scholars, partly from postcolonial, Indigenous, or racial minorities, have been critical of second-wave feminists for failing to account for the privileges of their racial and socioeconomic status. These new scholars argued that most women across the globe confront complex "intersections" of lived inequalities, related to their race, ethnicity, class status, and so on. They rejected the assumption that all women are virtually the same and thus suffer and enjoy the same experiences because of their common biological sex. Black feminists, in particular, argued that an assumption of "sameness" undermined the larger liberatory project to uncover the workings of gender and, in turn, to address inequality broadly. "The way the gender of the black woman is constructed," wrote Hazel Carby, "differs from constructions of white femininity because it is also subject to racism."[41] The study of gender, Carby and other Black feminists argued, could not be separated from history, race, and class. Indeed, the category of "woman" was just as problematic and ethnocentric as the categories of "male dominance" or "women's subordination."[42]

In this vein, Kimberlé Crenshaw, a professor of law, is credited with coining the term **intersectionality** in 1989 as a new concept for understanding oppression, a way of analyzing intersecting and interlocking social inequalities that include gender and sexuality but also extend to consider race, class, and other forms of inequality. The critical debate that emerged around the concept of intersectionality has deeply impacted anthropology. Around the same time, anthropology as a discipline was also facing widespread challenges to its colonial underpinnings (see Talal Asad, *Anthropology & the Colonial Encounter*) and forms of representational practice (see James Clifford and George Marcus, *Writing Culture*).[43] The confluence of these debates has been pushing the discipline forward in complex ways since that are beyond the scope of this book. But most broadly we can say that the impact of intersectionality theory, together with the emergence of post- and decolonial critiques, has pushed feminist anthropologists to reposition analyses of gender and power within wider fields of entangled forms of historical violence.

ANTHROPOLOGY HERE AND NOW

What Is Postcolonial Feminist Anthropology?

If you are interested in understanding more about how feminist anthropology and postcolonial critique are pushing the discipline of anthropology, we recommend that you check out *Cultural Anthropology*'s podcast, "AnthroBites," featuring Christa Craven and Siobhan McGuirk, who provide a succinct, fifteen-minute discussion on the state of postcolonial feminist anthropology.[1]

Note

1. Siobhan McGuirk, "AnthroBites: Feminist Anthropology," AnthroPod, *Fieldsights*, March 15, 2018, https://culanth.org/fieldsights/anthrobites-feminist-anthropology.

For anthropologists, this heated discussion—at once related to academics, social movements, literature, and policymaking—began to define a new era for understanding gender more fully within its cultural and political contexts, within which genders were neither biologically determined nor diametrically opposed but were always in the process of being negotiated in tandem with other forms of human experience and relationships of power. A renewed emphasis on ethnography ensued so that anthropologists might more fully elaborate the negotiation of gender in local contexts, with attention to the granular particularities of specific social formations.[44] Anthropological theories and methods, it turned out, had a lot to offer wider societal debates about gender equity. For example, Carla Freeman's ethnography, *High Tech and High Heels in the Global Economy: Women, Work, and Pink-Collar Identities in the Caribbean*, showed how globalizing economic processes had particular consequences for the labor of women and female embodiment in the Global South.[45]

The anthropology of gender has come a long way from Mead's early-twentieth-century studies. It has opened a new window into the utilization of ethnographic methods and anthropological knowledge for understanding gender-based inequality, in particular, and larger systems of inequality in general.[46] Importantly, this discussion has shifted firmly away from the study of "women," as rooted in an assumption about common biology or shared experience, and forcefully toward "gender," as grounded in a more broadly based knowledge, one that accounted for the diverse cross-cultural, historical experiences found in a continuum from "male" to "female." As anthropologist Henrietta Moore notes,

> Feminist anthropology is more than the study of women. It is the study of gender, of the interrelations between women and men, and the role of gender in structuring human societies, their histories, ideologies, economic systems and political structures. Gender can no more be marginalized in the study of human societies than can the concept of "human action," or the concept of "society." It would not be possible to pursue any sort of social science without a concept of gender.[47]

Today, anthropology is just one discipline of many that explores issues related to gender. Out of the second-wave feminism of the 1960s and 1970s, a new field of women's studies emerged. These academic programs have gradually expanded to study a wide range of issues related to gender and sexuality, far beyond the traditional notion of "woman." Likewise, the field of gender studies has become incorporated into most humanities and social science disciplines. Anthropologists continue to bring their uniquely, ethnographically grounded methodologies to the exploration of these issues. At the same time, the insights from the study of gender continue to influence and shape aspects of anthropology that might have once been assumed to have little relation to the issues of women.

LESSONS FROM THE ANTHROPOLOGY OF GENDER

What can we learn from the deeper and more nuanced intricacies of gender, power, and inequality? We would like to conclude with four key lessons.

First, being aware of the cultural processes of gender gives us unique insight into one of the most basic human phenomena. While not all people everywhere and in all times (past and present) share the experience of socioeconomic class (see chapter 4) or race (see chapter 1), all people in all places and at all times have shared the experience of being part of a society or culture in which sex and gender must be negotiated. Indeed, gender is one of the cornerstones of all societies, from marriage to family to kinship, which are the subjects of the next chapter.

ANTHROPOLOGY HERE AND NOW

More Resources on Feminist Anthropology

You can learn more about the field of feminist anthropology, including publications, current research activities, and other topics, at the website of the Association for Feminist Anthropology, posted at www.aaanet.org/sections/afa (see especially "Links and Resources").

Second, feminist anthropology offers both a perspective for understanding gender-based inequality more deeply and a call to action.[48] Anthropologists studying gender and power have not been content with *just* understanding or conducting research on the relationships between gender, power, and other forms of inequality. They have been involved in social movements, policy change, and wider cultural critique to change the conditions of gender inequality and oppression. This complex and hotly debated knowledge has necessitated a more complex redress of women's and gender issues on local and international stages alike. Although a lot has changed since the efforts of the second-wave feminists of the 1960s and 1970s, much work remains to be done. The #MeToo movement is a poignant reminder of how problems like sexual violence persist despite years of advocacy. The Pulse nightclub in 2016 in Orlando, Florida, and Club Q in 2022 in Colorado Springs, Colorado, were both sites of horrific mass shootings directed at homosexual people and persons with nonbinary genders. Beyond these high-profile events, it is important to remember that microaggressions of gender inequality occur every day, often "below the radar," which can make school, work, or home unsafe environments. The stark reality of violence against women and people with different sexual orientations is that it is far from a "purely academic" issue.

Third, this call to action is not limited to the study of gender. Through the concept of intersectionality, feminist scholarship has opened new ways to understand and act on the deeper complexities of all types of human difference and human inequalities in our world—a project to which anthropology has been deeply committed since its inception. Rather than seeing gender as an entity to be studied in isolation, scholars now understand that gender is experienced in diverse and often contradictory ways, and always within the contexts of race, class, language, ability, sexuality, ethnicity, and nationality. In a sense, anthropologists now take "intersectionality" as a given—as a starting point for an inquiry rather than a significant "finding" in itself. This holistic approach, in which gender is just one of several important social categories of analysis, has become central to the study of any form of social inequality. It has widened our ability to understand how various social forces shape both individual and collective actions.

Lastly, the fourth key lesson: The anthropology of gender and intersectionality can help deepen our understanding of the concept of culture and lead us to sometimes surprising, insightful analysis. In her famous essay, *Do Muslim Women Really Need Saving?*, written in the aftermath of the 9/11 tragedy and the subsequent US military operations in Afghanistan, Lila Abu-Lughod demonstrates precisely this point. Abu-Lughod criticized the US government for justifying its war on the grounds of "liberating" Afghan women, which she argued echoed colonial discourses of "saving" people of color from their supposed backwardness. The argument that Afghan women were being oppressed, made by both President Bush and First Lady Laura Bush, turned on the Muslim practice of female veiling and the reputation of the Taliban government of Afghanistan for requiring all women to wear a *burqa*, a near-total form of veiling. To the average US citizen who knew little about Islam, the *burqa* seemed to symbolize the extremes of Taliban oppression, the absolute repression of women's rights.

Abu-Lughod brought her deep ethnographic experience studying Islamic veiling and a keen awareness of intersectional analysis to her essay on the Afghanistan War. In her earlier research in a Bedouin community in the Western Desert of Egypt, she had lived with a large family, experiencing the strict sexual division of labor and participating in veiling and other female activities of her host family. She came to understand the subtleties of veiling, when and where it was done, the agency of women in modulating the practice, and its deep connections to the values of family honor and female modesty.[49] In her essay, she correctly predicted that Afghan women would have little interest in abandoning these values—and therefore veiling—regardless of their political leanings for or against the Taliban. She also explained that styles of Islamic veiling have close connections with ethnicity and socioeconomic status. *Burqas* are a form of veiling that happens to be popular among the Pashtun ethnicity of southern Afghanistan and northern Pakistan, the region where the Taliban first emerged as a political movement. But even among the Pashtun, the *burqa* was considered the preferred veiling style of reputable, well-to-do families and not unsuitable for women of lower-class status.[50]

Although the Taliban sought to require all women to wear *burqas*, it was hardly the symbol of repression that Americans imagined it to be. The tragedy of 9/11 is of course complex, and the response of the US government should not be reduced to an incorrect understanding of Islamic veiling. But the point here is that complex questions of gender often require the grounding of an ethnographic perspective. US politicians were quick to blame "Islamic/Afghan culture" and take up the mantle of "women's liberation" in mobilizing popular sentiment for war. Abu-Lughod's article reminds us that reductionist descriptions of any culture always slip into stereotype or worse. Likewise, questions of gender and power can lead to empty slogans—and in this case, misguided policies—unless they are understood within the wider social, historic, and political terrains in which they are situated.

NOTES

1. Margaret Mead, *Sex and Temperament in Three Primitive Societies* (New York: Morrow, 1935), 279.

2. Ibid.

3. Ibid.

4. Ibid., 279–80.

5. Elsie Clews Parsons, *Pueblo Indian Religion* (Chicago: University of Chicago Press, 1939), 9ff.

6. See George Gallup Jr. and D. Michael Lindsay, *Surveying the Religious Landscape: Trends in U.S. Beliefs* (Harrisburg, PA: Morehouse Publishing, 1999).

7. Susan Starr Sered, *Priestess, Mother, Sacred Sister: Religions Dominated by Women* (Oxford: Oxford University Press, 1994), 13–14.

8. Serena Nanda, *Neither Man nor Woman: The Hijras of India*, 2nd ed. (Belmont, CA: Wadsworth, 1999), especially 24–37.

9. Cf., for example, Raymond C. Kelly, "Witchcraft and Sexual Relations: An Exploration in the Social and Semantic Implications of the Structure of Belief," in *Man and Woman in the New Guinea Highlands*, ed. Paula Brown, Georgeda Buchbinder, and David Maybury-Lewis (Washington, DC: American

Anthropological Association, 1976), 36–53; and Robert F. Murphy, "Social Structure and Sex Antagonism," in *Peoples and Cultures of Native South America*, ed. Daniel R. Gross (Garden City, NY: Doubleday, 1973), 213–24.

10. Paul Zolbrod, *The Diné Bahane* (Albuquerque: University of New Mexico Press, 1987).

11. Wesley Thomas, "Navajo Cultural Constructions of Gender and Sexuality," in *Two Spirit People: Native American Gender Identity, Spirituality, and Sexuality*, ed. Sue-Ellen Jacobs, Wesley Thomas, and Sabine Lang (Urbana: University of Illinois Press, 1997).

12. Jennifer Denetdale, "Chairmen, Presidents, and Princesses: The Navajo Nation, Gender, and the Politics of Tradition," *Wicazo Sa Review* 21 (1) (2006): 9–28.

13. Susannah M. Hoffman, Richard Cowan, and Paul Aratow, *Kypseli Women and Men Apart: A Divided Reality* (Berkeley: University of California Extension Media Center, 1973).

14. Jan Brøgger, *Nazaré: Women and Men in a Prebureaucratic Portuguese Fishing Village* (Forth Worth, TX: Harcourt Brace Jovanovich, 1992).

15. Ibid., 16.

16. Will Roscoe, *Changing Ones: Third and Fourth Genders in Native North America* (New York: St. Martin's Press, 1998), 7, 223–47.

17. See Charles Callender and Lee M. Kochems, "The North American Berdache," *Current Anthropology* 24, no. 4 (1983): 443–70.

18. Alfred W. Bowers, *Hidatsa Social and Ceremonial Organization* (Washington, DC: Bureau of American Ethnology, 1965), 167.

19. Ibid., 166–67; Callender and Kochems, "The North American Berdache," 451.

20. See Callender and Kochems, "The North American Berdache," 451–53.

21. Ibid.

22. George Devereux, "Institutionalized Homosexuality of the Mohave Indians," *Human Biology* 9: 498–527. For a concise description, see also Serena Nanda, *Gender Diversity: Crosscultural Variations* (Prospect Heights, IL: Waveland Press, 2000), 21–23. The placement of the Mohave in the Greater Southwest follows Alice B. Kehoe, *North American Indians: A Comprehensive Account*, 2nd ed. (Englewood Cliffs, NJ: Prentice Hall, 1992), 103–59.

23. In addition to Devereux, "Institutionalized Homosexuality of the Mohave Indians," see George Bird Grinnell, *The Cheyenne Indians: Their History and Ways of Life*, 2 vols. (New Haven, CT: Yale University Press, 1923), 39–47; and Wesley Thomas, "Navajo Cultural Constructions of Gender and Sexuality," in *Two-Spirit People: Native American Gender Identity, Sexuality, and Spirituality*, ed. Sue-Ellen Jacobs, Wesley Thomas, and Sabine Lang (Urbana: University of Illinois Press, 1997), 156–73. Cf. Roscoe, *Changing Ones*, 213–47.

24. See Beatrice Medicine, "'Warrior Women': Sex Role Alternatives for Plains Indian Women," in *The Hidden Half: Studies of Plains Indian Women* (Lanham, MD: University Press of America, 1983), 267–80.

25. Ibid., 276.

26. See, for example, Brian Joseph Gilley, *Becoming Two-Spirit: Gay Identity and Social Acceptance in Indian Country* (Lincoln: University of Nebraska Press, 2006).

27. Nanda, *Neither Man nor Woman*, 130–37. See also Unni Wikan, "Man Becomes Woman: Transsexualism in Oman as a Key to Gender Roles," *Man* 12 (1977): 304–19; Niko Besnier, "Polynesian Gender Liminality through Time and Space," in *Third Sex, Third Gender: Beyond Sexual Dimorphism in Culture and History*, ed. Gilbert Herdt (New York: Zone, 1996), 285–328; and Antonia Young, *Women Who Become Men: Albanian Sworn Virgins* (Oxford: Berg, 2000).

28. Anne Fausto-Sterling, "The Five Sexes," *The Sciences* (March/April 1993): 20–25.

29. Anne Fausto-Sterling, *Sexing the Body: Gender Politics and the Construction of Sexuality* (New York: Basic Books, 2000).

30. See Marjorie Shostak, *Nisa: The Life and Words of a !Kung Woman* (New York: Vintage Books, 1981), 243.

31. See Martha Ward, *A World Full of Women* (Boston: Allyn & Bacon, 1996), 218–22.

32. Linda J. Seligmann, *Peruvian Street Lives: Culture, Power, and Economy among Market Women of Cuzco* (Chicago: University of Illinois Press, 2004).

33. See United Nations Population Fund, *The State of World Population 2000* (New York: United Nations Population Fund, 2000), especially chapter 3, "Violence against Women and Girls: A Human Rights and Health Priority."

34. In addition to Mead's *Sex and Temperament*, see also Simone de Beauvoir, *The Second Sex*, trans. H. M. Pashley (New York: Knopf, 1953), and Margaret Mead, *Male and Female* (New York: Morrow, 1949).

35. Michelle Zimbalist Rosaldo and Louise Lamphere, eds., *Women, Culture, and Society* (Stanford, CA: Stanford University Press, 1974). Other important books included Ernestine Freidl, *Women and Men: An Anthropologist's View* (New York: Holt, Rinehart and Winston, 1975), and Rayna Reiter, *Toward an Anthropology of Women* (New York: Monthly Review Press, 1975). The following discussion is drawn from several sources, including Micaela Di Leonardo, *Gender at the Crossroads of Knowledge: Feminist Anthropology in the Postmodern Era* (Berkeley: University of California Press, 1991); Louise Lamphere, "Feminism and Anthropology: The Struggle to Reshape Our Thinking about Gender," in *The Impact of Feminist Research in the Academy*, ed. Christie Farnham (Bloomington: University of Indiana Press, 1987), 11–33; Henrietta Moore, *Feminism and Anthropology* (Minneapolis: University of Minnesota Press, 1988); Sandra Morgen, "Gender and Anthropology: Introductory Essay," in *Gender and Anthropology: Critical Reviews for Research and Teaching*, ed. Sandra Morgen (Washington, DC: American Anthropological Association, 1989), 1–20; and Michelle Rosaldo, "The Use and Abuse of Anthropology: Reflections on Feminism and Cross-Cultural Understanding," *Signs* 5, no. 3 (1980): 389–417.

36. Rosaldo and Lamphere, "Women, Culture, and Society: A Theoretical Overview," in *Women, Culture, and Society*, 42.

37. Cara E. Richards, personal communication. See also Peggy Reeves Sanday, *Female Power and Male Dominance: On the Origins of Sexual Inequality* (Cambridge: Cambridge University Press, 1981), 24–28.

38. Sanday, *Female Power and Male Dominance*, 171.

39. Andrea Smith, *Conquest: Sexual Violence and American Indian Genocide* (Durham, NC: Duke University Press, 2005).

40. Denetdale, "Chairmen, Presidents, and Princesses," 9–28; Mishuana Goeman, *Mark My Words: Native Women Mapping Our Nations* (Minneapolis: University of Minnesota Press, 2013); Joanne Barker, ed., *Critically Sovereign: Indigenous Gender, Sexuality, and Feminist Studies* (Durham, NC: Duke University Press, 2017).

41. Hazel Carby, "White Women Listen! Black Feminism and the Boundaries of Sisterhood," in *The Empire Strikes Back: Race and Racism in '70s Britain*, ed. Birmingham University Centre for Contemporary Cultural Studies (London: Hutchinson, 1982), 214.

42. In addition to Carby, see, for example, Patricia Hill Collins, *Black Feminist Thought: Knowledge, Consciousness, and the Politics of Empowerment*, 2nd ed. (New York: Routledge, 2000); Gloria Hull, Patricia Bell Scott, and Barbara Smith, eds., *All the Women Are White, All the Blacks Are Men, But Some of Us Are Brave* (Old

Westbury, NY: Feminist Press, 1982); and bell hooks, *Yearning: Race, Gender, and Cultural Politics* (Boston: South End Press, 1990). Also important to this critique—and not discussed here—was the issue of feminist anthropologists choosing to speak for other women through ethnography and other modes of representation. Ethnographers, in particular, began to grapple with the very real differences in agendas between themselves and the women they studied. For a particularly intriguing discussion of this ethnographic problem, see Elaine Lawless, "'I Was Afraid Someone Like You . . . an Outsider . . . Would Misunderstand': Negotiating Interpretive Differences between Ethnographers and Subjects," *Journal of American Folklore* 105 (1992): 301–14. Cf. Elaine Lawless, *Holy Women, Wholly Women: Sharing Ministries through Life Stories and Reciprocal Ethnography* (Philadelphia: University of Pennsylvania Press, 1993), especially 1–7.

43. Talal Asad, ed., *Anthropology & the Colonial Encounter* (New York: Humanities Press, 1995); James Clifford and George E. Marcus, eds., *Writing Culture: The Poetics and Politics of Ethnography, 25th Anniversary Edition* (Berkeley: University of California Press, 2010).

44. See, for example, Joan Newlon Radner, ed., *Feminist Messages: Coding in Women's Folk Culture* (Urbana: University of Illinois Press, 1993).

45. Carla Freeman, *High Tech and High Heels in the Global Economy: Women, Work, and Pink-Collar Identities in the Caribbean* (Durham, NC: Duke University Press, 2000).

46. See UN Population Fund, *The State of World Population 2000,* especially "Violence against Women and Girls."

47. Henrietta Moore, *Feminism and Anthropology* (Minneapolis: University of Minnesota Press, 1988), 6. For a host of other developments both in feminist anthropology and in the anthropological study of gender not discussed here, see Lila Abu-Lughod, *Writing Women's Worlds* (Berkeley: University of California Press, 1993); Sherry Ortner, *Making Gender: The Politics and Erotics of Culture* (Boston: Beacon Press, 1996); and Peggy Reeves Sanday and Ruth Gallagher Goodenough, eds., *Beyond the Second Sex: New Directions in the Anthropology of Gender* (Philadelphia: University of Pennsylvania Press, 1990).

48. See, for example, Moore, *Feminism and Anthropology.*

49. Lila Abu-Lughod, *Veiled Sentiments: Honor and Poetry in a Bedouin Society* (Berkeley: University of California Press, 1988).

50. Lila Abu-Lughod, "Do Muslim Women Really Need Saving? Anthropological Reflections on Cultural Relativism and Its Others," *American Anthropologist* 104 (3) (2001): 783–90.

6

Work, Success, and Kids
On Marriage, Family, and Kinship

So many of us in today's world find our lives revolving around the same problem: We need money in order to survive, and we must have a job in order to make money. This imperative is reflected in the way we think about ourselves and others; increasingly, we define ourselves by the jobs we do. In the United States, one of our first questions on meeting another is "What do you do?" which, of course, means "What's your job?" This conversational move is fast spreading through our contemporary world.

We follow jobs from city to city, or country to country, bringing our families along—our small, *portable* families. Two parents may work full-time to rear one, two, or more children, or, often, a single parent (almost always the mother) works one, two, or more jobs and is responsible at home for rearing the children. For most of human history, this was very unusual—that is, one or two people, off by themselves, rearing children alone—but, increasingly, it is now par for the course.

At first glance, our small, portable families may seem similar to small foraging bands that also followed "the job" of gathering and hunting. But in function, purpose, and consequences, our families—as arranged around the search for work within an international capitalist economy—are relatively new in the human scheme of things. Indeed, when we compare people from around the world, past and present, this kind of family is extremely unusual. Today, mainstream America's family ideal hinges on the union or marriage of two people who establish their household separate from other family households and who rear children within this separate space. These children are expected to grow up, leave their parents' home, and establish independent households, where they will repeat the process.

For mobile Americans, then, the abandonment of the extended family is the norm. We view those who remain ensconced within their families as aberrations, deviates, or losers. It is within this base of experience that we view talk shows regularly featuring sensationalist topics like "Grown Men and Women Who Haven't Left Home." A forty-year-old man who still lives with his mother. Positively shocking. "My God, get out of the house, man!" an audience member yells when she finally gets the microphone. "You can't depend on your mom forever. You should be ashamed of yourself!"

If the rest of the world were watching (and many of them are), they would (and sometimes do) view such displays with bewilderment. Why would anyone want to leave their family to establish their own household and remake a brand-new family? What was wrong with the old family? Why would Americans condone such wholesale abandonment of their families? And this is a place that claims to have "family values"? What is wrong with these people?

Lassiter remembers addressing these questions with one of his Kiowa consultants, Billy Evans Horse. They were talking about the meaning of success in America. For Lassiter, success meant the well-known American equation of "Get a job + make money + get out of the house + start your own family = success," but Billy Evans Horse defined success as raising his children so that they would stay in the house, take care of their parents, and raise the next generation of Horses in that *same* house, where three-plus generations had raised their families in the Horse household. For traditional Kiowa people like Billy Evans Horse, choosing to live with your family—instead of leaving home to establish your own—constituted true family values. How could most Americans claim to have family values, he asked, when they consistently choose jobs and money and independence (and getting out of the house) over their families?[1]

When we do cross-cultural comparisons of both past and present human concepts of family, we find that most of the world would agree with Billy Evans Horse. He is expressing value not just for a Kiowa tradition but also for a human tradition in which family is the primary social commitment and the basis of personal identity. The desire to leave your old family behind and make a new one is relatively novel in the human scheme of things.

Billy Evans Horse. Photo by Luke Eric Lassiter

INTRODUCING FAMILY: ON KINSHIP

For most of human history (and presently for many of the world's people), "family" has conventionally consisted of large networks of relatives, or kin—networks that anthropologists call **kinship**. Cross-culturally, kinship is based on the relationships created by marriage (or **affinity**) and birth (or **consanguinity**). Both of these human phenomena, we will find, are—like everything else human—constructed by culture. While we may find many societies that assign relatedness of children to both parents and their families equally, we find others that assign relatedness of children more to the mother and her family than to the father and his family, and vice versa. Humans build on marriage and birth to construct "family" in amazingly diverse ways.[2]

Take an example close at hand: the Kiowa. Like most Americans, Kiowa people reckon kinship through each side of the family, assigning relatedness more or less equally through both males and females (any given individual is more or less equally related to both mother's and father's brothers and sisters). Unlike most Americans, though, many Kiowa people put into practice a way of reckoning family that is more specific to their own Kiowa tradition.[3] For instance, many of those whom most Americans would call "cousins" are often called (in English) "brothers" and "sisters" in the Kiowa community. Many of the relatives whom most Americans would call "uncles" and "aunts," Kiowas would also call, in English, their "fathers" and "mothers." Your mother's sisters are called "mother," and your father's brothers are called "father." And *their* spouses also can be, and sometimes are, called "mother" or "father."[4] (There are separate Kiowa-specific terms for mother's brothers and father's sisters in the Kiowa language, but today these individuals are often called, in English, "aunts" and "uncles." Bernadine Herwona Toyebo Rhoades puts the contemporary practice succinctly: "Your mother's sisters are called 'mother' and her brothers are your uncles. Your father's brothers are addressed as 'father' and his sisters are your aunts."[5])

ANTHROPOLOGY HERE AND NOW

Information on the Kiowa Tribe

You can learn more about the Kiowa Tribe of Oklahoma—including various cultural organizations (many of which are descent organizations)—on their official tribal office website at www.kiowatribe.org.

Kiowa people today may embrace several different variations on this theme—especially because the Kiowa way of reckoning kin, particularly in its older form, can be incredibly involved and complex, with numerous specific terms for different relatives. Kiowa people currently build on this older system and often combine it to varying degrees with the way of reckoning kin in mainstream American families (e.g., using English terms like "aunt," "uncle," "sister," "brother," "mother," and "father").[6] The point here is that, even today, any individual in the Kiowa community can conceivably have several dozen brothers, sisters, mothers, and fathers (and aunts and uncles).

The Kiowa kinship system gets more interesting when we add more "vertical" relatives. Among the Kiowa, you don't have just two sets of grandparents: your grandparents' brothers and sisters can also be your grandparents. Of course, it works the other way, too. Just as an elder can conceivably have dozens of grandchildren, grandchildren can have as many grandparents.

We'll get to what this means shortly. But let's add another generation. (This is where it gets really interesting.) Your great-grandparents may be addressed in the same way as your siblings, as "brothers" and "sisters." In fact, you may call your great-grandmother "big sister," and she may call you "little brother" or "little sister," depending on your gender.

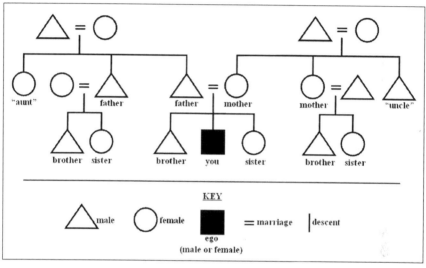

Relatives most Americans would call "cousins" are often called (in English) "brothers" and "sisters" in the Kiowa community. Many of the relatives whom most Americans would call "uncles" and "aunts" Kiowas would also call, in English, their "fathers" and "mothers." Your mother's sisters are called "mother," and your father's brothers are called "father."

Taking all of this into account, imagine having dozens of brothers and sisters, fathers and mothers, grandparents, and "big brothers" and "big sisters." It works in the other direction, too. Even if you are not married, you can conceivably have a good many sons and daughters (who are your brothers' or sisters' children), grandchildren, and even perhaps "little brothers" and "little sisters." Can you even imagine keeping up with a system like this from day to day? Well, many Kiowas do, even today. "That Kiowas put a lot of stock in how they are related to other Kiowas is pretty well known in southwestern Oklahoma," writes Kiowa and anthropologist Gus Palmer Jr. "As it turns out,

Kiowas are actually one big family in ways that puzzle most non-Indians. They can't believe you have so many grandpas and uncles and brothers."[7]

Significantly, the terms that Kiowa relatives call one another are not merely labels. They also imply certain kinds of relationships with and responsibilities to others. As an individual in the Kiowa world, your many parents may have responsibilities for you just like your biological parents; they may discipline you, they may take care of you if your parents die or divorce, and they may help out, if they are able, with your education, just like your biological parents. The relationship between grandparents and grandchildren is a bit different: You are meant to spoil one another. In the same way that grandparents spoil their grandchildren, grandchildren, as they grow up, may reciprocate by indulging their grandparents; grandchildren take their grandparents to pow-wows, take them to the movies, and may even care for them if they become ill.

Your relationships with your dozens of brothers and sisters can be the most significant in your life; historically, the Kiowa brother–sister bond was the most important of all, often more important than your relationship to your fathers or mothers, or even to your spouse. "A woman can always get another husband," it was said, "but she cannot get another brother."[8] Even today, a sister may ask anything of her brother, and he will respond, and vice versa. And your relationship with your "big sister" or "big brother" can be much like your relationship with your brothers and sisters: You take care of one another, whatever the cost. In the Kiowa world, no one is left unrelated; hence, no one is left uncared for. "Almost every Kiowa is related to another Kiowa in one way or another," writes Palmer.[9]

This particular way of reckoning kinship is also found in other parts of the world—other Indigenous groups have similar ways of reckoning kin—but even within this system there can be an amazing amount of diversity. Anthropologists make a number of distinctions concerning how kin are labeled from society to society. In general, anthropologists refer to kin systems that reckon each side of the family as being similarly related through both male and female links (like the usual American family—"cousins" are "cousins" on each side) as **bilateral kinship**. While both mainstream Americans and Kiowa Americans may have very different ways of labeling and referring to their kin, they do generally share a system of bilateral kinship with many other groups around the world.

Even still, anthropologists have identified a great variety of kinship systems along these lines, many of which are also based on **descent**—that is, the assignment of relatedness traced through common ancestry. Some bilateral groups may reckon descent more or less informally through both male and female links—what anthropologists often call **cognatic descent**. (For example, the Kiowa community has several family descendant organizations whose members trace their relatedness to each other back to prominent Kiowa leaders.[10]) Other groups, however, may trace descent much more formally through either male or female links exclusively, a way of reckoning kinship relations that can be very different from that found among bilateral groups—a kind of kinship that anthropologists often call **unilineal descent**. These two ways of reckoning descent, through either the father's or the mother's family, are referred to as **patrilineal descent** and **matrilineal descent**, respectively.

Let's consider matrilineal descent. In societies that practice matrilineal descent, all people—male and female—trace their kinship relations through their mother's side of the family. As a member of a matrilineal society, regardless of your gender, you are (of course) related to your mother and your father. Although you may recognize your father and his kin as related through marriage, by birth you are considered more directly related to (and are a member of) your mother's family. This means that your relatedness to the unilineal kin on your father's side stops, in a way, with your father. Although, again, you may (depending on what society you reside in) recognize his kin as distant relatives through marriage, you are not directly related to his parents, his brothers and sisters, or their children. Simply put, they are outside the membership of your mother's kin, which consists of your mother's relatives.

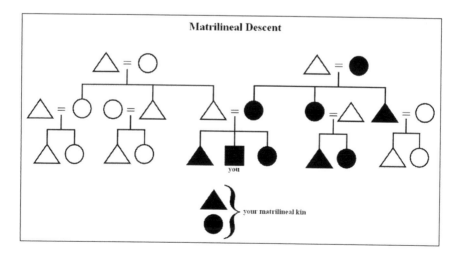

Matrilineal Descent

In this system, then, you are closely related to your mother, her parents, her brothers and sisters, and the children of your mother's *female* relatives. Because in the matrilineal system descent does not pass through male relatives, you are not closely related to any children (cousins) of your mother's *male* relatives.

Patrilineal descent is the exact opposite of matrilineal descent: All people, both male and female, reckon their unilineal kin through their father's side of the family. Kinship is not traced through female relatives—which means, of course, that you are *not* closely related to any children (cousins) of your father's *female* relatives. Of the two unilineal descent systems, matrilineal descent is rarer, but ethnographers have described both in various forms all over the world—from Africa to Europe, Asia, the South Pacific, and North and South America.

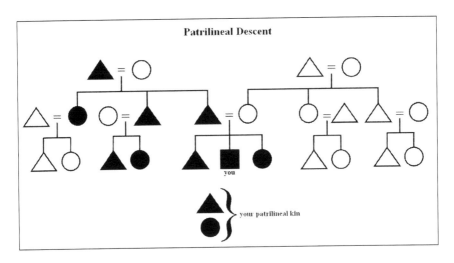

Unilineal descent can get very complicated. In the bilateral system—the one most Americans, including the Kiowas, follow—the boundaries of families (where they begin and leave off) can be ambiguous. Yet in many unilineal societies (patrilineal or matrilineal), families in space (who is alive and a member of the family right now) and time (who was a member of the family in the past, or who will be a member of the family in the future) are often much more formally organized as **lineages**—larger descent groups made of several patrilineal or matrilineal families who often have power above and beyond any particular family within the lineage. This larger family lineage, then, can extend back in time and will continue into the future—that is, everyone will be born into a lineage, not just a family. The lineage can be important for organizing several villages within a tribal political structure, for instance, or the lineage can be important for passing property or land from fathers to sons or from mothers to daughters.

Lineages can be organized (and often are) into much larger collective units, called **clans**, which are composed of several lineages. When we start talking about clans, we're no longer talking about hundreds of people; we're talking about thousands of people. Indeed, among those people who practice clan descent rules, the clan may stretch back to the beginning of time and may continue, presumably, well into the future.

In the clan system, people remember and keep up with what clan you are from and to which clan you belong from the time you are born. In these societies, it is among the first things you learn. In many unilineal Native American groups, among the first things that people ask one another is to which clan they belong. Such questions are significant for a number of reasons, among the most important being to determine whom you can and cannot marry.

THE INCEST TABOO, EXOGAMY, AND ENDOGAMY

Generally, all people past and present have made a distinction between whom they may and may not marry. While people define and practice **marriage** in a diversity of ways (which we'll address in the next section), prohibitions are universally based on three things: the **incest taboo** (which regulates sex and/or marriage between people considered kin), **exogamy** (marriage outside a certain group), and **endogamy** (marriage within a certain group).[11]

The incest taboo is perhaps the most important of these. Like everything else cultural, the incest taboo is constructed differently from society to society, from culture to culture. In America today, incest is commonly defined as having sexual relations with someone closely related, such as a sibling, parent, grandparent, aunt, uncle, or cousin. As bilateral people, we tend to see everyone as generally equally related to everyone else on both our mother's and our father's side of the family. In this context, it makes sense that we would not want to have sexual relations with them.

Among many other people of the world, the incest taboo isn't this simple. In many unilineal descent systems, the incest taboo can be defined quite differently from the way it is defined among those who practice bilateral kinship. In these systems of descent, certain so-called cousins (from our bilateral point of view) are outside the incest taboo: They are not directly related to you because descent cannot be passed through males (in matrilineal descent systems) or females (in patrilineal descent systems). Thus, in matrilineal societies, the incest taboo does not apply to cousins on your father's side of the family or cousins who are your mother's brother's children. They are considered *exogamous* (outside your own lineage). In some matrilineal societies, these cousins can be considered ideal marriage partners (a marriage practice that anthropologists call **cross-cousin marriage**)—ideal because such an arrangement helps to continue already-established relationships between and among families.

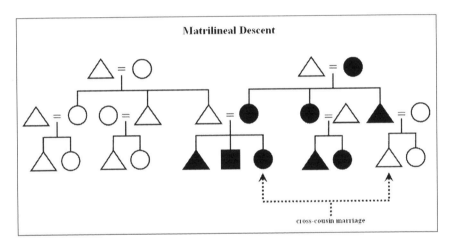

The same pattern of cross-cousin marriage can occur in patrilineal societies. Here, cousins on the mother's side of the family and the father's sister's children are not directly related; thus, they are outside the incest taboo. But in a few patrilineal societies (e.g., among some Arab groups), there is a rare exception to the rule. In these societies, because property is passed through the male line, a marriage to the father's brother's children is ideal because it maintains and strengthens the passage of property within the lineage (anthropologists call this marriage practice **parallel-cousin marriage**). Although parallel cousins are endogamous (inside the lineage), they are still considered marriageable partners. Marrying "within" family happens elsewhere as well. Extreme cases include brother–sister marriage, such as that among royalty in ancient states (remember Cleopatra?). Nevertheless, when we examine the practices of marriage around the world, cousin marriage is not as unusual as it sounds to us.

But this brings us back to an important point: The incest taboo, and thus exogamy and endogamy, are incredibly variable when viewed through a comparative lens; what seems strange to us is so because we view the world through a bilateral system. But even among those of us who share a bilateral system, considerations of "family" and "marriage" can be highly variable, as the Kiowa example illustrates. How much more important it is, then, that we recognize that those who live within a patrilineal or a matrilineal system view the world through their kinship systems as strongly as we do.

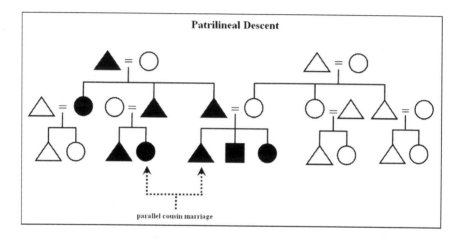

DEFINING MARRIAGE CROSS-CULTURALLY

Obviously, part of the purpose of the incest taboo, exogamy, endogamy—and, ultimately, marriage—is to regulate sex and to produce offspring, but cross-culturally, past and present, marriage has a range of purposes that far exceed the regulation of sex or the production of offspring. Marriage is critical to kinship for a number of reasons; perhaps most important, it is through marriage that kin groups build and maintain family through time. Anthropologists have long struggled to define marriage because its practice is so diverse, it takes on so many different forms, and it serves so many purposes.[12]

Many modern Americans tend to think about marriage as the union of a man and woman who may or may not produce offspring. Simple enough. But in addition to being ethnocentric, this idea of marriage does not easily account for all the forms of marriage that we find in the ethnographic record, past and present. Take, for example, the widespread occurrence of "female husbands" or **woman marriage** in many African societies.[13] Among the Nuer, patrilineal pastoralists of Sudan, a woman unable to have children may take a "wife" who enters into sexual relations with a man to bear children. The children, in turn, refer to the first woman (the one who has taken a wife) as "father" and inherit property (e.g., cattle) through her father's patrilineal lineage (because children cannot inherit property through women). Among the Nandi, patrilineal pastoralists of Kenya, a woman who does not bear sons for her husband—which is critical for passing property from father to son—may enter into a nonsexual marriage with another woman, who, as in the Nuer case, enters into sexual relations with a man to bear children. Again, as in the Nuer case, the children can now inherit property through their female "father." In parts of West Africa, a wealthy married woman who works outside the home may marry another woman who will take care of the home and children. Among some Bantu peoples of southern Africa, "woman marriage" takes several different forms: Among the Zulu, when a father dies and has no male heirs, his eldest daughter may take his place and marry another woman who will bear male heirs on his behalf.[14]

This certainly does not match the definition of marriage we have in mind when we think about marriage in the United States, does it? While the "female husband" or "woman marriage" may seem bizarre to most Americans, this kind of flexibility shows up rather often in the ethnographic record, past and present. (So, too, does inflexibility; for instance, in some patrilineal societies, a woman could face death for not producing male heirs.) With these kinds of examples in mind, we might think about marriage cross-culturally as a union between a *socially acknowledged* (if not biological) "male" and "female." But the human practice of marriage is much more diverse than what this might imply. Many modern nation-states recognize same-sex unions, which do not always involve the social or legal acknowledgment of one person as "husband" and the other as "wife." Or consider the much more common practice of **polygamy**, which is marriage of one person to two or more spouses.

Polygamy has been described all over the world. Generally, it takes on two forms: **polygyny** (one man married to more than one woman) and **polyandry** (one woman married to more than one man). Polyandry is the rarer of the two, and anthropologists have described it in cultures primarily in south Asia. In the Himalayas, for instance, several brothers may marry one wife to keep from splitting up their property (especially land, which can be limited) among their children. Additionally, the wife always has a husband at home if the brothers must travel for long periods of time.[15]

ANTHROPOLOGY HERE AND NOW

Traditional Same-Sex Marriage in Kenya

BBC recently ran a story about the traditional practice of same-sex marriages between women in Kenya, and how the passing of property via these traditional marriage arrangements has been recently bolstered by a high-court ruling. The story, "Kenya's Legal Same-Sex Marriages," can be accessed at www.bbc.co.uk/news/world-africa-16871435.

The more common form of polygamy is polygyny. Unlike polyandry, it has surfaced all over the world, from Asia to Africa to the Americas. Consider the Rashaayda Bedouin, Arab pastoralists of eastern Sudan. Here, a man may enter into a marriage with several co-wives, each of whom may have her own household where she and her children live. Tensions do arise between co-wives, but the husband is bound by tradition to provide for each wife equally. Ethnographer William C. Young reports that "if a polygynously married woman finds any sign of unequal treatment, she will complain to her brothers, who will also resent the slight of their family and will, consequently, back her in a quarrel with her husband and support her if she leaves him and asks for a divorce."[16]

When we consider that the husband must treat each wife equally—which includes providing for each of them and their children—you might reason that all Bedouin men would neither want nor be able to enter into a polygynous marriage. Well, you would be reasoning correctly. While polygyny may be the Bedouin ideal, in actuality very few men and their families can afford it. This raises an important point about polygyny in general: Among the world's people for whom polygyny is the ideal, few men and their families actually enter into the practice because they do not have the resources to do so.[17] As Americans, we tend to view such polygamous unions (both polyandrous and polygynous ones) through our own concepts of marriage, which found the institution on the sexual relations between two people. But polygamy is about much more than different sexual partners. Among some Plains Indian tribes, men often took the unmarried sisters of a first wife as co-wives. These sisters might otherwise have been left uncared for in a warrior-based society in

Many Americans think that same-sex unions, like the public ceremony pictured here, are a modern phenomenon. But in some parts of the world, same-sex marriages—such as the widespread occurrence of "female husbands" or "woman marriage"—actually represent a very old practice. Photo by Danny Gawlowski

which shortages of men were common.[18] And among the Rashaayda Bedouin, men often engage in polygyny to enlarge the size of their families, which can further their political careers.[19]

Like everything else cultural, people all over the world today debate and negotiate these marriage customs. An international debate rages about the purposes and meanings of polygamy, especially concerning polygyny and its relationship to women's subordination.[20] While this might seem to be a "no-brainer," it is actually a complex issue. Consider what US journalist, attorney, and polygynist Elizabeth Joseph says about what she calls her "ultimate feminist lifestyle":

> I've often said that if polygamy didn't exist, the modern American career woman would have invented it. Because, despite its reputation, polygamy is the one lifestyle that offers an independent woman a real chance to "have it all." . . . As a journalist, I work many unpredictable hours in a fast-paced environment. The news determines my schedule. But am I calling home, asking my husband to please pick up the kids and pop something in the microwave and get them to bed on time just in case I'm really late? Because of my plural marriage arrange-

ment, I don't have to worry. I know that when I have to work late my daughter will be at home surrounded by loving adults with whom she is comfortable and who know her schedule without my telling them. My eight-year-old has never seen the inside of a day-care center, and my husband has never eaten a TV dinner. And I know that when I get home from work, if I'm dog-tired and stressed-out, I can be alone and guilt-free. It's a rare day when all eight of my husband's wives are tired and stressed at the same time. . . . Polygamy is an empowering lifestyle for women.[21]

Regardless of where you stand on this issue, marriage seems a little more complex when we attempt to put aside our own ethnocentrisms and seek to understand (not necessarily agree with) "the native point of view."

This brings us back to a point about the purposes of ethnography (from chapter 3): While a study of culture allows us to appreciate others' way of life, it also should teach us something about ourselves. When we work to comprehend the cross-cultural role of marriage in a larger world context, we begin to understand that marriage can be much more than two people "bound in a sacred union" who produce *their* children, who, in turn, are *their parents'* sole responsibility. When we consider the complexity of the ethnographic record, marriage has been most often conceived among most humans within much larger networks of kin. Simply put, in the larger human scheme of things, marriage is not about sex or love in the way that most Americans think about it; *cross-culturally, marriage is about creating and maintaining social rather than sexual relations.* It is more often social (i.e., again, conceived within much larger networks of kin) because it involves more than the husband-wife-children triad through which many Americans judge our own and others' experiences with marriage and family.

WHAT MARRIAGE CREATES AND MAINTAINS: MORE ON MARRIAGE AS A SOCIAL UNION

Just as family can be extremely important in defining social commitment and personal identity, the people with whom a family enters into marriage can also be significant. In actuality, they do not exist entirely outside of family ("not related to us") just because they are not marriageable. Chief among the things to consider about marriage are its consequences and ramifications, especially the responsibilities to other families that these unions engender.

Take, for example, the !Kung San—who, you'll remember, live in southern Africa and who, up until relatively recently, were hunter-gatherers. After a

!Kung marriage, a new couple may, ideally, live with or near the bride's family for a time (in general terms, anthropologists call this **matrilocal** or **uxorilocal residence**). In the meantime, a !Kung man must hunt for his wife's family, a service that anthropologists call **bride service**. As you might imagine, it is in the family's best interest to have daughters marry because their husbands will help to provide for the larger family. The wife's family reciprocates by providing the couple with a place to live and raise children in the first years of the marriage. Through this system, all married people are essentially tied to a large network of people to whom they are immediately responsible.[22]

The practice of bride service is not found only among the !Kung; in fact, it's widespread. Compare the !Kung case with the Kiowa, who practiced a kind of bride service in certain cases. Recall that the brother–sister relationship was key to Kiowa kinship. Marriage was sometimes constructed around this most important relationship. Elite and high-status warriors could beseech their sisters to marry in order to oblige their sisters' new husbands to aid them in battle. Simply put, an elite warrior could put less prestigious warriors in his service through marriage; essentially, he could put the new brothers-in-law to work for him and his family. In a raid for horses, the less prestigious warrior was bound to give a good number of his captured horses to his wife's brother. For less prestigious warriors trying to increase their status, it was in their best interest to be associated with a wife's brother who was a prestigious warrior.[23]

Bride service is widespread, but it is not the only kind of marriage/family responsibility. Many unilineal societies (and some bilateral folks, too) practice what anthropologists often call **bridewealth**, a practice in which the husband's kin gives gifts to the wife's kin at marriage. For many societies, the importance of bridewealth is that it sets up a reciprocal relationship that can last for the lifetime of the marriage. In some matrilineal societies, the wife's matrilineage is obligated to reciprocate the original bridewealth by helping out the husband's matrilineage when there is a death or birth in the family. The husband's matrilineage is also obligated to help the wife's matrilineage in times of need. This back-and-forth reciprocation continues throughout the life of the marriage; each family has a responsibility to help the other in child care, to help pay for family ceremonies, or anything else that the matrilineage may face or enter into.

Imagine living in a society in which you have responsibilities both to your own family and to the families with whom you are connected through marriage. In many societies past and present, this responsibility is inescapable.

You live your entire life through a network of kin relations, a network composed of relatives in your immediate family and relatives through marriage. Everyone lives and dies within the collective charter of multiple responsibilities and commitments generated and maintained by marriage.

This pattern is also pervasive in patrilineal societies. In many traditional European and Asian societies, the wife's family is expected to give the woman's inheritance to the husband's family, a practice that anthropologists often call **dowry**. You might imagine that it would be in the best interest of the husband's family to marry. But it is also in the best interest of the husband's family to *maintain* the marriage, because the wife's family can ask for the dowry back if there is a divorce. These families—especially the men, who often run the show—have a great deal invested in this marriage.

Take another example from traditional China, in which marriage and the production of sons is seen as absolutely crucial to the longevity of the patrilineage. After a marriage, the wife resides with the husband's family (in general terms, **virilocal** or **patrilocal residence**), and her primary role is to produce children (especially males) to continue the patrilineage. Here, unlike the ideal brother–sister relationship among the Kiowa, the key relationship is between a father and son. Daughters will presumably leave the home to produce children for another patrilineage.[24]

The practice of producing children for the patrilineage is widespread among patrilineal societies, but it takes on a number of forms. The African "female husband" practice is one example; although, as you'll remember, the insistence that property or children pass through males is not as strict as it is (or was) in traditional China. Today, of course, these practices are increasingly being negotiated on an international scale. Within the past several decades, Chinese legislators have passed laws to deemphasize the role of the male in the traditional patrilineal system, and the dowry has been outlawed in some nation-states.[25] Changing something as basic as the ways people structure family does not come easily. Imagine if the US Congress passed a law decreeing that we would reckon kinship matrilineally from here forward. We'd go crazy. "What, men taking the surnames of their wives?" There would be rioting in the streets.

Nevertheless, regardless of how we view these practices, these examples illustrate, once again, that marriage cross-culturally is not as much about the sexual union of two people as it is about generating and maintaining larger social networks. The larger social exchanges that pass through marriage can-

Marriage doesn't just unify individuals; it can also strengthen relationships between and among groups. Building on traditions both old and new, a bride and groom exchange rings during a Coast Salish wedding at Lummi Nation in Washington State (top). Members of the bride's family prepare a canoe, filled with groceries and other gifts, to give to the groom's family (bottom). Photos by Josie Liming

not be underestimated, especially when the exchanges are being negotiated between large and powerful families.

With this in mind, it is easy to understand why many of these larger family groups have an interest in maintaining marriage; it is because maintaining marriage means maintaining larger social networks. In some societies, when the wife dies, the widower may marry a sister or another woman from his wife's family (a widespread practice that anthropologists call **sororate**), in this way maintaining his relationship with the family. For instance, among the Kiowa, if a wife died, it was not unheard of for an unmarried sister to take over where her sister had left off. After all, the children were as much hers as her sister's. (Remember, because she was the deceased woman's sister, the children already called her "mother.")

This marriage practice can go the other way, too. When a husband dies, the widow may marry a brother or another man from her husband's family (another widespread practice that anthropologists call **levirate**). When Lassiter's wife's paternal grandfather died, two of his brothers came to the United States from Ireland to help rear and provide for his children. They stayed until the children left the home. For all intents and purposes, they acted as surrogate husbands and fathers during this time.

These practices (*levirate, sororate*) are found all over the world and are an indication of how seriously people take marriage, family, and kinship. To reiterate, marriage is especially important for *what it means to larger groups*; its significance extends way beyond our own ethnocentric assumptions of marriage being based on two people alone, who, once married, establish independent households (a practice that, in general terms, anthropologists call **neolocal residence**). Even with a divorce (which is also common in the ethnographic record), in many societies a break in the marriage does not always mean a break in family responsibilities. In societies like the !Kung or the Kiowa, a divorce does not mean that one parent is left to rear children alone. Because the children belong to a much larger kinship group, they are taken care of by both sides of the family, even after the divorce. It is an obligation set into motion by the original marriage. The kinship connections created by the marriage don't just disappear. Indeed, children belong to larger groups and hence are the responsibility of those larger groups, not just of one or two isolated individuals.

Marriage, then, is universal because of the larger groups it creates, re-creates, and maintains. Founded in the incest taboo, it forces people to build groups outside the narrow confines of their own family. Because humans depend on culture for survival and culture exists within a society (a system of interacting people), there is vastly more to marriage, ethnologically speaking. The practice of marriage forces people to transcend narrow notions of "us" and "them" and to create connections and alliances between and among larger groups. It's the cultural correlative of kinship; it requires that people think outside themselves and their immediate relatives. Consequently, it is at the very heart of the workings of traditional society the world over.[26]

Many anthropologists (although certainly not all) thus argue that the incest taboo and what it creates, marriage, is all about building what we know to be human society. The incest taboo, marriage, and the group alliances they created have engendered societies in which everyone was obligated to everyone else, in which everyone not only felt a responsibility to all those around them, but also knew it as their family duty on a profound level—a level that is hard for most of us to fully appreciate and understand today.[27]

MARRIAGE, FAMILY, AND KINSHIP: LESSONS FOR CONTEMPORARY FAMILIES

Today, families continue to change at a rapid pace. More and more of us live in small, portable, relatively confined, nuclear families—not necessarily because we want to but because we must. As members of a global market system, we are obliged to work within this system to survive. And one thing this system values highly is mobility; simply put, if we want to work, we must follow the jobs. Only modest nuclear families are small enough to move from job to job. As a result, we regularly make and remake our families from generation to generation as we move and split up and move again.

Lassiter's parents, for instance, left their respective family farms in the mid-twentieth century because small-family farming was no longer viable in a world increasingly dominated by larger and larger corporate-run farms. Both of his parents' families parted with the communities in which they had lived for generations to pursue jobs other than farming. The second and third generations of these families have since left the communities in which *they* had been raised and are now scattered all over the United States. His family scattered not because they wanted to live apart but because they had to follow the jobs in their respective fields. Like most Americans, we have come to define ourselves and our success primarily through the jobs we have, not by our connections to our families.

Over the past one hundred years or so, such experience with family and work has become commonplace. American families are becoming more and more alike: The small nuclear family is the ideal type for the larger market system. Nuclear families are the production grounds for future consumers and future workers who will consistently choose work, production, and consumption over family, because they have to.

Of course, depending on where you stand, you could point out lots of positive things about this new "family": We can *choose* not to have children and not be ostracized for it; we are not bound to family control or censure; and we are not obliged to live with or provide for our in-laws.

From many points of view, this is an ideal situation. But—and there's always a *but*—a price must be paid. From an anthropological point of view, we no longer live in the kinds of families that conceptualize responsibility to others in a broad way. Where once dozens of parents (e.g., the mom and dad and their brothers and sisters) reared children and saw them as their shared responsibility, today, one or two people raise children alone. Anthropologically speaking, this is brand-new; never have so many people the world over reared their children like this. We have yet to understand fully the consequences

The family farm of Luke Eric Lassiter's mother. Photos by Luke Eric Lassiter

of these changes. We often blame parents exclusively for the problems with children in our society without even considering the larger economic system that breaks up our communities, scatters our families, and dictates our lives.

So what do we do? What can we take from this anthropologically based discussion of marriage, family, and kinship and apply to our own families and our own lives? Several things come to mind. Importantly, we must recognize that as long as we live and work in a world capitalist economy, the structure of our lives has changed, and thus the very idea of family has changed; indeed, families will most likely never be as they once were. When we compare the modern nuclear family with other families, past and present, our sense of familial responsibility to others has narrowed considerably. Consequently, our overall outlook about responsibility to others—especially when compared to other societies more connected to larger ideals about family—has deteriorated remarkably.

ANTHROPOLOGY HERE AND NOW

MIGRATIONS OF THE MIDDLE CLASS

Anthropologists have closely studied the diverse changes experienced by families over the past several decades. Anthropologist Brian Hoey studies how many middle-class families have actively chosen to renegotiate their work lives (some at great expense) and relocate to places where they can have more control over their relationships with family and community. In his book *Opting for Elsewhere*, he suggests that the stories of these families are part of a public debate about what constitutes the good life in a time of economic uncertainty coupled with shifting social categories and cultural meanings.[1] Hoey's work documents how sweeping changes born of postindustrial economic restructuring impact both people and the places in which they live and work. You can learn more about his research on his website at brian hoey.com/research/research-lifestyle-migration.

Note
1. Brian Hoey, *Opting for Elsewhere: Lifestyle Migrations of the Middle Class* (Nashville, TN: Vanderbilt University Press, 2014).

This does not mean that people today have no conception of responsibility to others, for they clearly do. In large societies, people have always made social, political, and economic alliances outside the range of kinship (see chapter 4). They have adapted to changing circumstances in amazingly flexible ways. With this and our new understanding of family in mind, perhaps we should more consciously and explicitly recognize the importance and significance of making connections and crafting responsibilities to others outside the narrow frameworks of the human families we have left. To be sure, it is harder to do today, but it's not impossible. In America, for example, we are quick to point out that "my neighbor's kids are my neighbor's responsibility, not mine." In a world where family truly matters, my neighbor's kids will be my responsibility. And so will those of everyone else.

NOTES

1. Billy Evans Horse, conversation with author, July 1992.

2. We collapse kinship and family here for ease of reference. Admittedly, many anthropologists make a clear distinction between family and kinship. At the same time, there is little consensus on "family," and anthropologists continue to argue about how to define it as an analytical category. See George P. Murdock, *Social Structure* (New York: Macmillan, 1949); David Schneider, *American Kinship: A Cultural Account* (Englewood Cliffs, NJ: Prentice Hall, 1968); Barrie Thorne, ed., *Rethinking the Family*, 2nd ed. (Boston: Northeastern University Press, 1992); and Sylvia Yanagisako, "Family and Household: The Analysis of Domestic Groups," *Annual Review of Anthropology* 8 (1979): 161–205.

3. The following description is based on Lassiter's ongoing fieldwork in the Kiowa community from the early 1990s to the present (see, for example, Luke E. Lassiter, *The Power of Kiowa Song: A Collaborative Ethnography* [Tucson: University of Arizona Press, 1998]). Kiowa kinship is today reckoned in a diversity of ways among various families, and the historical patterns are much more complicated than those briefly (and only partially) presented here. When using Kiowa terminology exclusively, many more specific terms are also used; indeed, Kiowa linguist and historian Parker McKenzie once noted that at one time Kiowas used over thirty different relationship categories ("Kiowa Relationship Terms," Parker McKenzie Collection, Oklahoma Historical Society Research Center, Oklahoma City). For a historical description of Kiowa kinship, see, for example, Robert H. Lowie, "A Note on Kiowa Kinship Terms and Usages," *American Anthropologist* 25 (1923): 279–81.

4. Ralph Kotay, personal communication, March 2002. See also "Kiowa Relationship Terms," Parker McKenzie Collection.

5. Bernadine Herwona Toyebo Rhoades, "Keintaddle," in *Gifts of Pride and Love: Kiowa and Comanche Cradles*, ed. Barbara A. Hail (Bristol, RI: Haffenreffer Museum of Anthropology, Brown University, 2000), 89.

6. In earlier editions, to avoid confusion Lassiter did not qualify his presentation of Kiowa kinship thusly in the main text (though he did so briefly in the notes). After reviewing this chapter with Billy Evans Horse in June 2007, however, Horse felt strongly that he should clarify up front that the current practice of reckoning kin in the Kiowa community is a contemporary (and, at times, highly variable) expression of the older and more involved Kiowa way of reckoning kinship. See note 3.

7. Gus Palmer Jr., *Telling Stories the Kiowa Way* (Tucson: University of Arizona Press, 2003), xvi.

8. Adapted from Jane Richardson, *Law and Status among the Kiowa Indians* (Seattle: University of Washington Press, 1940), 65.

9. Palmer, *Telling Stories the Kiowa Way*, xv.

10. See, for example, Lassiter, *The Power of Kiowa Song*, 86–88, 167–69.

11. We limit our discussion here primarily to the incest taboo and its relation to cross-cousin and parallel-cousin marriage. Anthropologists usually engage in a much larger discussion about incest, exogamy, and endogamy. See, for example, William Arens, *The Original Sin: Incest and Its Meanings* (Oxford: Oxford University Press, 1986); Linda Stone, ed., *New Directions in Anthropological Kinship* (Lanham, MD: Rowman & Littlefield, 2001); and Claude Lévi-Strauss, *The Elementary Structures of Kinship* (Boston: Beacon Press, 1969).

12. See, for example, Edmund Leach, "Polyandry, Inheritance and the Definition of Marriage," *Man* 55 (1955): 182–86, and *Rethinking Anthropology* (London: Athlone Press, 1961); Rodney Needham, ed., *Rethinking Kinship and Marriage* (London: Tavistock, 1971), and *Remarks and Inventions: Skeptical Essays about Kinship* (London: Tavistock, 1974); W. H. R. Rivers, *Kinship and Social Organization* (New York: Humanities Press, 1968); Judith R. Shapiro, "Marriage Rules, Marriage Exchange, and the Definition of Marriage in Lowland South American Societies," in *Marriage Practices in Lowland South America*, ed. Kenneth M. Kensinger (Urbana: University of Illinois Press, 1984), 1–30; and Linda Stone, ed., *New Directions in Anthropological Kinship* (Lanham, MD: Rowman & Littlefield, 2001).

13. See Eileen Jensen Krige, "Woman-Marriage, with Special Reference to the Lovedu—Its Significance for the Definition of Marriage," *Africa* 44 (1974): 11–36, who writes that "marriage of a woman to a woman [is] found in many African societies" (11). See also Denise O'Brien, "Female Husbands in Southern Bantu Societies," in *Sexual Stratification: A Cross-Cultural View*, ed. Alice Schlegel (New York: Columbia University Press, 1977), 109–26, who writes that "the female husband may belong to any one of over 30 African populations, and she may have lived at any time from at least the eighteenth century to the present" (109).

14. See E. E. Evans-Pritchard, *Kinship and Marriage among the Nuer* (London: Oxford University Press, 1951); Regina Smith Oboler, "Is the Female Husband a Man? Woman/Woman Marriage among the Nandi of Kenya," *Ethnology* 19 (1980): 69–88; Ifi Amadiume, *Male Daughters, Female Husbands* (London: Zed Books, 1987); and M. Gluckman, "Kinship and Marriage among the Lozi of Northern Rhodesia and the Zulu of Natal," in *African Systems of Kinship and Marriage*, ed. A. R. Radcliffe-Brown and D. Forde (London: Oxford University Press, 1950), 166–206, respectively. See also Krige, "Woman-Marriage, with Special Reference to the Lovedu," and O'Brien, "Female Husbands in Southern Bantu Societies."

15. See Nancy Levine, *The Dynamics of Polyandry: Kinship, Domesticity, and Population in the Tibetan Border* (Chicago: University of Chicago Press, 1988).

16. William C. Young, *The Rashaayda Bedouin: Arab Pastoralists of Eastern Sudan* (Fort Worth, TX: Harcourt Brace, 1996), 65.

17. Ibid., 64–65.

18. Robert Lowie, *Indians of the Plains* (Washington, DC: American Museum of Natural History, 1954), 79–80.

19. Young, *The Rashaayda Bedouin*, 64.

20. See, for example, United Nations Population Fund, *The State of World Population 2000* (New York: United Nations Population Fund), especially chapter 6, "Women's Rights Are Human Rights."

21. Excerpted from Elizabeth Joseph, "Creating a Dialogue: Women Talking to Women" (paper presented to the Utah chapter of the National Organization of Women, May 1997).

22. Richard Lee, *The Dobe Ju/'hoansi*, 2nd ed. (Fort Worth, TX: Harcourt Brace, 1993), 80–82.

23. Cf. Jane Fishburne Collier, "Rank and Marriage: Or Why High-Ranking Brides Cost More," in *Gender and Kinship: Essays toward a Unified Analysis*, ed. Jane Fishburne Collier, Sylvia Junko Yanagisako, and Maurice Bloch (Stanford, CA: Stanford University Press, 1987), 197–220.

24. See Margery Wolf, *Women and the Family in Rural Taiwan* (Stanford, CA: Stanford University Press, 1972).

25. Cf. Margery Wolf, "Chinese Women: Old Skills in a New Context," in *Women, Culture, and Society*, ed. Michelle Zimbalist Rosaldo and Louise Lamphere (Stanford, CA: Stanford University Press, 1974), 157–72.

26. See Lévi-Strauss, *The Elementary Structures of Kinship*. But also see Arens, *The Original Sin*.

27. Ibid.

7

Beyond Universal Truth

Anthropological Approaches to Religion, Healing, and Knowledge

One major challenge for anthropologists in their ethnographic work is the encounter with knowledge or belief systems that run counter to the precepts of modern science. This kind of ethnographic research can touch upon some of the deepest and most unexplored ethnocentrisms of the anthropologist. Consider that contemporary anthropologists, like any graduate of a modern education system, have all been trained in the modern sciences, to a significant extent. It is not easy to leave this training behind, especially when one encounters alternative forms of knowledge during one's fieldwork. How should an anthropologist respond to a claim that a mountain is sentient; that a glacier will be angered if you cook near it with grease; that certain animals like peccaries or jaguars are human beings; that manioc, one of the most important staple crops for some Amazonian Indigenous people, can also suck human blood; that some men can transform themselves into a lion in order to kill an enemy; and so on?[1] How should the anthropologist present these findings in her or his ethnographic writing? Should he or she accept them as factual claims just because the people with whom we work insist that they are true? If the anthropologist instead presents them as the "beliefs" of a community, have the ethnographic "informants" been inadvertently portrayed as ignorant and superstitious?

In addition to these tricky philosophical questions about what counts as "fact" and "belief," anthropologists may also face professional constraints with regard to these issues. On the one hand, anthropologists have been accused of uncritically accepting the claims of one's ethnographic consultants and flouting the basic principles of modern science. On the other hand, anthropologists have been charged by fellow anthropologists as being ethnocentric for not giving sufficient credence to local, community-based claims of belief and experience.

These thorny issues continue to be hotly debated in anthropology today, but they actually go back to the origins of the modern discipline itself. If we recall Malinowski's presentation of Trobriand "magic" as a means to psychologically manage the stress of uncertainty, we can see that his ethnographic method introduced a profound epistemological challenge to anthropology. **Epistemology** is the philosophical term for questions related to knowledge. In trying to "grasp the native's point of view," Malinowski—and therefore, all anthropologists since him—have found themselves in the awkward position of sometimes having to judge whether the knowledge claims of their ethnographic consultants are true or not; or, in some cases, ignore them outright. Malinowski's solution was creative but ultimately left the dilemma unresolved. He sidestepped the issue by focusing on the "function" of magic, as he saw it, to satisfy important psychological and social needs. Whether magic was true was irrelevant to its social impacts, according to Malinowski.

This epistemological quandary continues to challenge anthropologists who are studying a range of cultural activities, from religion to healing. We can look more deeply at this issue by exploring, briefly, the Spiritist (not to be confused with "Spiritualist") religious tradition of Brazil. The history of Spiritism, or "Kardecism," is complicated. It was brought from Europe to Brazil in the late nineteenth century, and it combines Christian beliefs with a belief in the efficacy of spirits to affect the material world. Specifically, Spiritism centers on the belief that dead human spirits inhabit the spirit world apart from the living. These spirits may return to the material world through various incarnations, which allows them to advance morally and live in the spirit world indefinitely. If spirits have led a morally degenerate life, however, they may have to pass through numerous incarnations to learn the moral lessons necessary for immortality. Spiritists who live in the material world can aid these incarnations by allowing spirits to possess them and perform healings, which allows the spirits to advance morally through helping others who are in need.

One well-known spirit is Dr. Adolf Fritz, who, since around the midtwentieth century, has returned from the spirit world and performed such healings. According to Spiritists, Dr. Fritz was a surgeon during World War I who returns for moral advancement because of bad deeds he enacted in his last life. With the aid of other spirits, Dr. Fritz is most famous for possessing Spiritists and performing surgeries on those in need of medical help—without anesthetics or antiseptics.[2]

Compare this to the many Christian traditions that take seriously the incarnation of the Holy Spirit. Many Holiness and Pentecostal believers, for example, believe that "being filled" with the Holy Spirit is central to their experience and faith as Christians. Some Pentecostal congregations, however, take the incarnation of the Holy Spirit one step further: They explain that

Some Pentecostal Holiness believers handle live rattlesnakes in their services, as this gentleman is doing in a church in southeastern Kentucky. Photo by Keith Tidball

being filled with the Holy Spirit compels them to speak in tongues, take up serpents, and heal the sick in accordance with Mark 16:17–18, which reads,

> Faith will bring with it these miracles: believers will cast out devils in my name and speak in strange tongues; if they handle snakes or drink any deadly poison, they will come to no harm; and the sick on whom they lay their hands will recover.[3]

Hence, a small number of Pentecostal church services include the handling of snakes and the drinking of strychnine as the Holy Spirit moves the service.[4]

Compare this, further, with spirit possession in Malaysia. As in many societies, many Malaysians believe that angry spirits can inhabit and possess the body, causing harm. These spirits can sometimes be calmed or dispersed by religious practitioners, however. In modern Malaysian factories, spirit possession is a problem, especially among women who are pressured to work long hours, are underpaid, and are poorly treated. Easily susceptible to spirit possession, many women factory workers are possessed and enter into near madness. They, in turn, seek help from local religious practitioners to dispel the spirit, which may or may not be effective.[5]

These practices might sound bizarre to those of us who have no knowledge or experience of them. Part of our struggle to understand them is that they seem to involve the "supernatural," a realm that is thought to lie beyond what is "natural" or "everyday." This strict separation between the supernatural and natural worlds, however, is unique to the Western world and part of a philosophical tradition that can be traced back to the **Enlightenment**. This European movement of the seventeenth and eighteenth centuries pushed back against the intellectual and political domination of Christianity in Europe, celebrating the power of human reason over religious faith. The Enlightenment had a profoundly transformative effect on European society, leading to a growing faith in the ability of humans to acquire mastery over nature. The Enlightenment was the beginning of a series of important developments in Europe, including the development of modern science, the industrial revolution, and European colonization of the world, which ultimately led to the birth of modern secular society. An important legacy of the gradual secularization of European society has been the separation of the supernatural from the natural world.

Anthropologists have found that in many non-Western societies, there is rarely a rigid separation of the "supernatural" from the "natural." Anthropologist James Peacock recalls emphatically learning this lesson when he asked one of his Indonesian consultants if he believed in spirits. The consultant was puzzled. "Are you asking," the man replied, "do I believe what spirits tell me when they talk to me?" "For him," writes Peacock, "spirits were not a belief but an unquestionable relationship, part of the unity of his life."[6] The divide between the natural and supernatural is one of the ethnocentric assumptions that anthropologists must learn to think beyond if they are to take seriously the belief and knowledge systems of other peoples. In order to study sensitively practices such as "spirit possession," we must therefore begin with a critical examination of the terms "knowledge" and "belief" themselves.

KNOWLEDGE AND BELIEF

In the natural and social sciences, scholars have long tended to make a clear distinction between knowledge and belief—that is, between what we "know" (defined as true and factual) and what we "believe" (accepted on faith as true and real). Classically, we rank knowledge *over* belief, asserting that knowledge, which is assumed to be based on clear reasoning and scientific methods, is *more substantiated* than belief, which may not be based on "clear evidence" or "proof." To say "I believe that X is true" is assumed to be categorically different from "I *know* X to be true." But what does any one individual "know"? What, actually, is knowledge?

There has been a great deal of fascinating scholarship on this topic over the last half-century. Indeed, one of the most dynamic fields of contemporary scholarship, emerging in the last few decades, crossing a broad swath of traditional academic disciplines, is known as "science studies" or "science, technology, and society studies" (STS). Anthropologists have played a pivotal role in the development of this exciting new field of study. But before we get ahead of ourselves, it is important to consider the origins of the belief and knowledge divide.

Enlightenment scholars were eager to distinguish between knowledge acquired through reason and beliefs that were considered to be little more than flights of the human imagination. Thus, Thomas Hobbes, one of the early figures of the English Enlightenment, wrote in 1651 about what he considered to be the origins of religion:

[F]rom [an] ignorance of how to distinguish dreams from other strong Fancies, from Visions and Sense, [there arose] the greatest part of the Religion, of the Gentiles in time past, that worshipped Satyrs, Fauns, Nymphs and the like.[7]

Hobbes is saying that religious belief is rooted in ignorance and irrational thought, mistaking things like dreams or fantasies with reality. It is nothing more than the *assumption that* something is true.[8] Writing at the dawn of the Enlightenment, Hobbes implied that in order for us to break free of ignorance, we must embrace "truth" as evidenced by facts. If we fast-forward to the contemporary spirit-possession practices of the Spiritists, Pentecostal snake-handlers, and Malaysian factory workers, it is easy to assume that this Enlightenment vision of a rational, secular world has yet to be fully realized almost four centuries later.

Given the allure of the Enlightenment project to liberate humans from their misguided "fancies" and "illusions," it is not surprising that nineteenth-century anthropologists, the social evolutionists, were still guided by this framework in their investigations of what they called "primitive beliefs." They argued that religion, like other aspects of human society, evolved in stages, beginning with "primitive" belief in multiple spirits, beings, or gods (called **polytheism**), evolving to a more advanced belief in a single god (called **monotheism**), and culminating in the gradual disappearance of supernatural belief as it gave way to scientific knowledge of the world, in the final and most advanced expression of civilization.

James Frazer, among the most prominent proponents of this view, suggested that early primitive peoples sought to control their world through **magic**, invoking or manipulating the supernatural to bear on a desired outcome. But for Frazer, magic represented a savage state wherein people failed to recognize their own limitations, that their invocation of the supernatural to affect a certain outcome was mistaken. In Frazer's scheme, magic was a precursor to (and separate from) religion, which—with its more formalized rituals, distinctive specialists, and all-powerful gods—evolved as people began to recognize that their individual power to affect the natural world, compared to that of their gods, was actually much more limited. "The savage," wrote Frazer,

whether European or otherwise, fails to recognize those limitations to his power over nature which seems so obvious to us. In a society where every man is supposed to be endowed more or less with powers which we should call supernatural, it is plain that the distinction between gods and men is somewhat blurred, or rather has scarcely emerged. The conception of gods as supernatural beings entirely distinct from and superior to man, and wielding powers to which he possesses nothing comparable in degree and hardly even in kind, has been slowly evolved in the course of history.[9]

Simply put, religion was more "realistic" than magic and placed the supernatural beyond the reach of everyday believers. But by the same token, science, argued Frazer, was much more "realistic" than religion. Unlike magic and religion, science "worked" and was based on a clear understanding of *causation* (i.e., that one action causes another). As such, science would eventually replace religion as people developed a clearer understanding of their world—just as religion had replaced magic in the larger evolutionary story.

Contemporary anthropologists and other social scientists reject this view—that magic and religion are clearly distinct from one another, and that magic, religion, and science represent points along a continuum in the presumed progress of civilization. (In fact, science has not replaced religion in the modern world, and many contemporary people believe and find meaning in both magic/religion *and* science.) As discussed above, the ethnographic methods of Bronislaw Malinowski suggested new approaches to understanding the wide range of practices that fall under this umbrella of "magic, science, and religion." But the greatest contribution to this field came from a contemporary of Malinowski, another famous British ethnographer, E. E. Evans-Pritchard, and his classic ethnography, *Witchcraft, Oracles, and Magic among the Azande,* published in 1937. The Azande are a people found in today's South Sudan, the Central African Republic, and Democratic Republic of the Congo. As the title of this ethnography clearly states, Evans-Pritchard was exploring three closely entangled aspects of Azande cultural life. *Witchcraft* refers to the invisible means by which individuals cause harm to one another, sometimes resulting in death. *Oracles* are the mechanisms used to identify a witch. *Magic* concerns acquired powers, usually derived from medicinal plants; it can be used for good, such as to heal disease, ensure a fruitful harvest, or remedy the effects of witchcraft, or for ill, such as to attack an individual with malice.

Before discussing the enduring significance of Evans-Pritchard's ethnography, it is important to point out that it was not without its flaws. Evans-Pritchard was working in the British colonial sphere of Sudan, and there are moments of unmistakable colonial condescension in his writing. On multiple occasions, he refutes the reality of witchcraft, the predictive qualities of oracles, and the therapeutic actions of various herbal remedies. Despite these moments of clear bias, the bulk of the text is devoted to detailed, empirical descriptions of how these various practices work and make sense for the Azande.

Scholars have perhaps been most influenced by two conclusions from his discussions of witchcraft. First, he declares witchcraft to be entirely logical, once one accepts its most basic premises, and not in contradiction with a rational, empirical understanding of the world. He notes that after a short while living among the Azande, he "learnt the idiom of their thought and applied notions of witchcraft as spontaneously [as the Azande] . . . in situations where it was relevant."[10] Moreover, he points out that witchcraft has its "own logic, its own rule of thought. . . . Belief in witchcraft is quite consistent with human responsibility and a rational appreciation of nature."[11] This affirmation of the apparent rationality of witchcraft as a system of beliefs was shocking to a Western readership at the time, conditioned by their own biases toward colonized peoples. Evans-Pritchard's sincere and empirical style, even if occasionally obscured by his prejudices, opened a space for other anthropologists to start tackling Indigenous thought systems in a more rigorous matter.

Evans-Pritchard's second conclusion had perhaps an even greater impact. He argued that the root of Azande witchcraft was human jealousy toward one's neighbors. Indeed, any misfortune—sickness, death, a failed enterprise—could be attributed to witchcraft and the ill wishes of someone in the community. But he also showed that attributions of witchcraft are not in contradiction with an empirical understanding of cause and effect. In fact, the two complement each other. Azande can clearly recognize that an individual may have died of natural causes, but that does not mean witchcraft is not also involved. Evans-Pritchard explains the complementarity of the two viewpoints through a famous vignette on Azande granaries. He notes that all Azande enjoy sitting under their granaries, small structures elevated on wooden posts, to stay cool in the hot summer. They also recognize that termites will eventually eat through the posts over time, causing them to collapse. But for a granary to collapse at precisely the moment that someone is resting beneath it, thereby causing that individual's death, could only be explained by witchcraft. There is little that can be done about the physical cause of the collapsed granary, but the Azande give great attention to dealing with the socially relevant cause of witchcraft, which inevitably means confronting a jealous neighbor.

These two points—the logical rigor and sociological foundations of witchcraft discourse—were intriguing enough in their own right. But they became even more significant when Evans-Pritchard compared the Azande approach to misfortune with that of European society. He pointed out that in modern secular societies, we often lack a means to explain an individual's misfortune. A cancer diagnosis, a car accident, or a natural disaster can all be life-altering events. But the average Westerner lacks a meaningful explanation for them; typically, such events are considered to be simply bad luck or coincidence. By contrast, Azande witchcraft provides what Evans-Pritchard called the "missing link," connecting individual misfortune with social discord.[12] In other words, Azande witchcraft, although unfamiliar to Western readers, answered the so-called "Why me?" question that no doubt plagues all of us whenever we encounter personal misfortune.[13] Later generations of anthropologists found Evans-Pritchard's analysis of witchcraft particularly useful for developing critiques of modern, secular society and the limits of scientific discourse.

If we return to our examples from the beginning of the chapter, then we can better understand how Evans-Pritchard's work enabled a new kind of analysis of these phenomena. Take the Spiritist tradition in Brazil, which several medical and social scientists have studied since the 1960s and 1970s. They describe Dr. Fritz surgeries that are conducted by incarnates (Spiritists who have been possessed by Dr. Fritz) who have absolutely no medical training. Interestingly, in one study, almost 70 percent of surveyed patients reported a cure or an improvement in their condition as a result of Dr. Fritz surgeries. While Spiritists say that Dr. Fritz is directly responsible for the healings, many researchers have a different explanation. They argue that the "power of the mind" (or the placebo effect) to relieve the stress of illness is among the keys to understanding why Dr. Fritz surgeries and healings are so successful (and so popular).[14]

Or take the predominant explanations of snake-handling, to which researchers have directed a lot of scholarly attention. These researchers argue that (among other things) the snake-handling ritual is symbolic of the capitalist domination of Appalachia or other rural regions where snake-handling congregations are found. As poor and uneducated Americans, the argument goes, Pentecostal congregations take up serpents as a kind of "cultural critique" of the capitalist-based class system that dominates them (despite

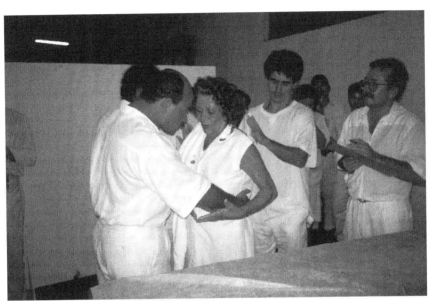

Dr. Fritz and Spiritists prepare a patient for surgery. Photo by Darrell Lynch

the fact that some serpent handlers today include middle-class and college-educated congregants).[15] This scholarly explanation is similar to explanations of spirit possession in Malaysia. While the women are adamant about being possessed by angry spirits, the scholarly explanation emphasizes that this is an unconscious resistance to exploitative work conditions.[16]

These kinds of scholarly explanations can be quite powerful and revealing in the same ways as Evans-Pritchard's. But as you may have noticed, they still do not address the truth of the spirit possession claims. Instead, they focus on the social context in which these events take place. We can therefore say they participate in what David Hufford calls a *tradition of disbelief*. Hufford argues:

> [The tradition of disbelief] takes a body of knowledge and considers it to be simply "the way things are" rather than a product of culture. It says over and over again: "What I know I *know*, what you know you only *believe*—to the extent that it conflicts with my knowledge."[17]

What Hufford means by this is that most of us proceed in our examinations, evaluations, or studies with an assumption that belief and knowledge are totally separate. The tradition of disbelief, which is based in the radical divide between knowledge and belief discussed above, forces us to choose between two diametrically opposed states. Either spirit possession truly happens or it is a mere belief.

In the following sections of the chapter, we will explore how anthropologists have tried to avoid the pitfalls of the tradition of disbelief. But first we want to show that careful ethnographic research itself can be important for at least moderating the epistemological quandary posed by the tradition of disbelief.

It turns out that in actual practice, so-called "believers" do not believe absolutely; likewise, figures who claim scientific authority may not "know" with certainty. If we turn to the work of Darrell Lynch on the Spiritists, we learn that their "belief" in Dr. Fritz is not simplistic, blind, or irrational. They are always critically examining their own "beliefs," examining the available evidence, and, in turn, often being extremely critical of Dr. Fritz surgeries:

> Many Spiritists openly question whether such and such a medium of Dr. Fritz is truly authentic, or is really faking it. . . . Little if anything of the communications from spirits is taken at face value. Each is generally weighed for its authenticity and logic within the belief system by each individual. And many communications are rejected as false or non-authentic. Belief among Spiritists is often a very critical process; more so, I would venture to say, than perhaps many of our mainstream beliefs, religious or academic.[18]

Lynch's description reminds Lassiter of an example from his own fieldwork in the Kiowa community. He once had a conversation about spirits with an elderly Kiowa man, a man who was often called on to drive spirits out of homes where they were not welcome. The man told Lassiter about several cases he had solved, but two are of particular interest here.

In the first, the elderly man was summoned to a home where the family asked him to examine a room from which strange noises had sporadically been heard. As he always did, he planned to stay with the family—for several days, if need be—to ascertain the nature of the problem. During the first night of his visit, he heard the noise but was not convinced that it was a ghost of any sort. Having been a carpenter in his younger days, he had a good idea what it might be. The next morning he wriggled under the house and retrieved a loose piece of PVC pipe. Case solved.

In the second story, the elderly Kiowa man told how he had been summoned to a home where a young boy had recently died. His ghost, the family said, had been visiting the house; they had seen him several times, walking the halls. The man stayed with the family for several days, until one evening he saw the ghost of the boy walk down the hallway and into the bathroom. He followed. There, before him, the boy stood in front of two towels on which his initials were embroidered. "You can't have these," the Kiowa elder said. "You need to leave

Photo by Danny Gawlowski

FredFroese / iStock

If our goal is to understand the complexities of religious experience, we must first and foremost be more critical of our own assumptions—whether rooted in traditions of belief or disbelief—and how we impose our ethnocentrism on others. Religious or sacred experiences may take many forms.

Eloi_Omella / iStock

ozgurdonmaz / iStock

them here with your parents." The boy's ghost disappeared, and after the family had destroyed the towels, the spirit was never seen again. Case solved.

What's the point here?

"Very few believers," writes Hufford, "ever categorically exclude material explanations from consideration, because their worldview includes both kinds of possibility."[19] Interestingly, disbelievers (engendered by a "tradition of disbelief") are not so quick to include both kinds of possibilities because they assume that there is a clear hierarchical division between knowledge and belief.

NEW HORIZONS IN THE STUDY OF ILLNESS

One important area of anthropology that was inspired by the work of Evans-Pritchard was the subfield of medical anthropology. Medical anthropology did not begin to take shape as a distinct subfield until the 1980s. One of the central areas of research in this subfield—emerging directly out of Evans-Pritchard's analysis of witchcraft—has been the social dimensions of illness. Like Evans-Pritchard's study of witchcraft, medical anthropologists have shown that all illnesses have a powerful social component. This conclusion challenges the perspective of biomedicine (the term anthropologists use for modern medicine), where doctors make diagnoses that are materially de-limited to the individual's physical body. While we generally do not expect (or want) our biomedical doctors to warn us about jealous neighbors, disappointed ancestors, or offended spirits, few of us experience disease as a medical textbook might describe it. Anthropologists have found that by asking sick individuals the "Why me?" question raised by Azande witchcraft, they can elicit fascinating experiences of illness that cannot be divorced from the pathological processes described by modern biomedicine.

John Janzen working among the Bakongo in Zaire (now the Democratic Republic of the Congo) in the 1960s and 1970s made a powerful demonstration of this point in his book, *The Quest for Therapy: Medical Pluralism in Lower Zaire*. He observed that the people he interviewed rarely made medical decisions on their own, at least for complicated ailments, but instead relied on a decision-making group that was usually composed of close kinspersons. Even more surprising, he discovered that when patients had access to modern medical care, they often turned to a variety of traditional therapies, particularly if they had complicated medical conditions. Janzen showed that one shared aspect of these traditional therapies is that they often sought to address social frictions, at work, between in-laws, within one's lineage group, or in one's village. The lesson that emerged again and again through the different cases that Janzen follows is that the physical symptoms of each patient were inseparable from the social tensions confronting the patient and his or her immediate social network.[20]

If the illness concerns of the Azande and Bakongo seem too remote to have much relevance for most contemporary societies, Angela Garcia's excellent ethnography on heroin addiction in northern New Mexico, *The Pastoral Clinic*, is a powerful demonstration to the contrary. Garcia was a student of Arthur Kleinman, one of the key figures who helped shaped the field of medical anthropology in its early days. Kleinman is famous for his interest in the problem of "social suffering" as it relates to illness.[21] Garcia's research builds on this approach to explore the heroin epidemic in the Hispano communities of northern New Mexico in the early 2000s. The Hispano are the descendants of the Spanish colonizers that first came to administer this northern outpost of the Spanish colony of Mexico in the sixteenth century, and are quite distinct from more recent Hispanic immigrant groups. In the early 2000s, the heroin epidemic in northern New Mexico was a harbinger of the opioid crisis that would subsequently devastate many areas of rural America.

Garcia followed numerous Hispano heroin addicts through the state of New Mexico's legal system, where she noticed that addiction was treated as an intractable biomedical condition. It was assumed that heroin use created pathological changes in the brain's neurological pathways that were extremely difficult to remedy. The harsh legal and therapeutic regimes that addicts were forced to endure was based on this narrow biomedical interpretation of heroin addiction. In her research, Garcia also noticed that most addicts felt there was "no escape" from their condition, but their hopelessness ramified through all aspects of their lives. The saw their problems to be "in their blood," in a way that was deeply tied to their families and the decline of the Hispano communities in which they grew up. For these Hispanos, heroin was not simply the cause of their troubles, it was also the only solace for the pain, both literal and figurative, of their fractured lives and communities.

Garcia helps to provide historical context to the laments of these Hispano addicts. She traces the decay of Hispano communities back to their "dispossession" from their land and livelihoods in the aftermath of the Mexican-American War (1846–1848). The United States annexed much of the American southwest from Mexico as a result of their victory in this war. Hispano communities, descendants of the Spanish colonizers of northern

Mexico, gradually lost many of their former lands under US law, which in turn eroded their traditional way of life.

Garcia's analysis shows that heroin addiction cannot effectively be treated as an individual disease and managed with court-mandated detoxification programs, at least when it reaches epidemic proportions, such as in northern New Mexico. Her research echoes the influential work of Victor Turner, a leading figure in the symbolic anthropology movement, whose research was particularly influential for John Janzen. Writing about a healing ritual of the Ndembu of central Africa, Turner argued that the suffering of the individual reveals that "'something is rotten' in the corporate group."[22]

In a similar vein, Garcia argues that heroin addiction requires a new kind of care that does not just treat the isolated physical body and its neurological dysfunctions through draconian legal and clinical measures. Rather, the "disease" of the heroin epidemic is ultimately a social problem. If healing is possible, then it will require attending to the fractured Hispano communities that she sees at the root of the epidemic.

TOWARD AN ANTHROPOLOGY OF KNOWLEDGE

The work of medical anthropologists like John Janzen, Angela Garcia, and many of their contemporaries has demonstrated the limitations of biomedical knowledge. These scholars do not dismiss the claims of modern medicine and science, but they show that other ways of knowing human suffering are also essential. Their work brings us back to the central point of this chapter and the potential contributions of anthropology to the study of knowledge and experience. Two things have traditionally kept all of us—that is, those raised in modern, secular societies (scientists, scholars, and laypersons alike)—from more deeply understanding the diverse ways of knowing the world. First, the "tradition of disbelief" lies at the heart of our ethnocentric bias toward other forms of knowing and is not easily overcome. The knowledge–belief divide which took shape in the Enlightenment and grounds much of contemporary Western thought makes it difficult for those of us raised in secular societies, including anthropologists, to fully appreciate so-called alternative ways of knowing the world. But in moving past our ethnocentrism, should we un-critically accept the claims on any non-Western knowledge or belief system merely because it seems to be the "native's point of view"? Do our attempts not to succumb to the "tradition of disbelief" doom us to an extreme epistemological relativism?

This brings us to our second obstacle to understanding alternative ways of knowing the world: the hard work of participant-observation. Once it becomes possible to put aside one's biases to learn about Dr. Fritz surgeries, Pentecostal snake-handlers, or Malaysian factory worker spirit possession, there is still the hard work of learning these alternative ways of knowing the world. These practices—indeed, all forms of knowing and experiencing the world—take place under specific social circumstances. The anthropologist must remain open to learning about these practices while also studying them critically. This kind of ethnographic research is admittedly difficult because it may require an apprenticeship or other form of training in order to learn the craft, techniques, and/or theoretical knowledge in question.

What we find is that when anthropologists take on this challenging work, taking the time and effort to learn these other forms of knowledge, the hierarchical divisions between "knowledge" and "belief" begin to dissipate, and new ways of experiencing the world become possible. Judith Farquhar's study of Chinese medicine provides an excellent example of this kind of ethnographic research. Although she does not explicitly frame her book in these terms, *Knowing Practice: The Clinical Encounter of Chinese Medicine* is a thoughtful and sophisticated meditation on how to navigate the epistemological quandary of the knowledge–belief divide.

Farquhar traveled to Guangzhou, China, in the early 1980s to conduct her research on Chinese medicine. Her timing was fortunate. From 1966 to 1976, China was essentially closed off to the rest of the world as the country was engaged in a deep, ideological struggle, known as the Cultural Revolution, about the future of China's communist revolution. The practice of Chinese medicine suffered during the Cultural Revolution, but the early 1980s was a moment of optimism both for China and the Chinese medicine profession. China was opening up to the world, although not yet integrated into the global economy. Chinese medicine was also enjoying a renaissance, having been freed from the ideological restrictions of the Cultural Revolution. Farquhar was able to spend eighteen months studying with some excellent teachers, who were enthusiastic to share their knowledge with foreign students for the first time.

Chinese medicine is based on philosophical concepts, such as yin and yang, the Five Phases, meridian channel theory, and other medical concepts that can be traced back to medical writings that are two thousand years old. In contrast to some forms of Indigenous healing, Chinese medicine does not

The Complexities of Traditional Healing

One of the lessons of medical anthropology is that healing is never a purely bodily event. For this reason, it is perhaps not surprising that many traditional healing systems weave together an elaborate array of rituals, prayers, medical theories, and therapeutic interventions. The work of medical anthropologist Duan Zhongyu, based at the Yunnan University of Chinese Medicine in Kunming, China, nicely captures this richness in her research on Dai medicine of southwest China.

The Dai people are closely related to the Thai people of Southeast Asia, and Dai medicine is an offshoot of what is now known in Thailand as traditional Thai medicine. Classically, Thai/Dai medicine was influenced by the medical theories of Ayurvedic medicine from India. Like Chinese medicine, Ayurvedic medicine has a long and rich literate tradition. Duan found, however, that a wide range of folk practices, not described in the classic medical texts, are essential to the everyday practice of Dai medicine. Almost all therapy sessions begin with a ritualist offering, in which

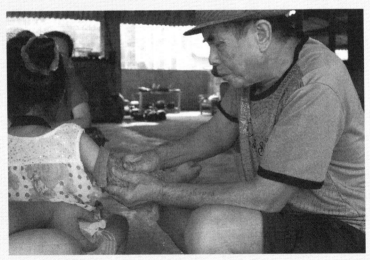

A Dai healer treats a young girl recovering from a bone fracture. He has just finished saying an incantation and is blowing on her arm, while he rubs it with a cloth that was soaked in an herbal decoction. Photo by Duan Zhongyu

the doctor prays to his or her teacher to provide the wisdom and skill to produce a cure. Many doctors also emphasize the centrality of various folk techniques, such as "blowing" on the patient's body. Blowing techniques include using the mouth to blow air, spray water, or blow across a small flaming torch held close to the patient's body. These techniques are accompanied by the soft whispering of secret incantations, unique to each doctor, to ensure the efficacy of the procedure.

Duan discovered that these incantations derive from a variety of sources, such as Buddhist scriptures, folk rituals, or even Mandarin Chinese. Regardless of the source, each doctor must develop his or her own repertoire of secret incantations, because they are considered key to achieving efficacious results. (To learn more like this, see *Traditional Thai Medicine: Buddhism, Animism, Ayurveda,* by C. Pierce Salguero [Hohm Press, 2007]).

conceptualize disease as originating from the spirit world or a dysfunctional human social world, as we might find in other medical anthropological accounts of illness. Nonetheless, it still presents a radical challenge to biomedical conceptions of disease and therapy. As Farquhar recognizes, there is no way to translate Chinese medicine pathological concepts such as hot, cold, dampness, or wind into biomedical categories, without misconstruing their meanings and diminishing their theoretical value in the process. The body in Chinese medicine is crisscrossed by meridian channels (used for acupuncture) through which qi and blood flow. The organs in Chinese medicine resonate with the seasons, the emotions, the flavors, the orifices (of the body), and much more.

What set Farquhar's research apart is that she did not debate the epistemological status of the unfamiliar concepts of Chinese. Instead, she looked closely at how they were mobilized in practice to achieve clinical results. Prior to Farquhar's research, scholars of Chinese medicine had rarely gone beyond the examination of classic Chinese medicine texts. But these textual studies often portrayed an overly idealized medical system or one that was plagued by contradictions. When Farquhar approached doctors about how they applied vague, contradictory, or idealized theoretical texts to their clinical cases, she was always told, "We take experience to be our guide." In other words, doctors worked out the nitty-gritty of these theoretical questions through practical applications in the clinic.

Drawing on the famous French anthropologist Pierre Bourdieu (see also chapter 4), who made the concept of "practice" central to his scholarship, Farquhar showed how the clinical work of Chinese medicine doctors transcends the dichotomy of knowledge and belief. The theoretical foundations of Chinese medicine are a given, in a sense, derived from the authority of ancient texts or perhaps passed on orally through a lineage of teachers. But these theoretical precepts are not a closed system. They continue to be debated and reinterpreted. There can be no rigid application of the knowledge they are thought to represent. Rather, as Farquhar found, it is only through practice, through the clinical experience of doctors, that this theoretical knowledge comes to life and is put to meaningful, sometimes lifesaving, uses.

Farquhar's ethnography and the work of Chinese medicine doctors can perhaps show us a way past Malinowski's epistemological quandary. When we allow ourselves to move beyond the "tradition of disbelief," and when we

ANTHROPOLOGY HERE AND NOW

Sorcery and Cancer

Trying to understand another belief system can be difficult, especially because it can extend far beyond just learning about beliefs and practices. And it can also take time—lots of time. Anthropologist Paul Stoller (West Chester University, Pennsylvania) began studying the religion of the Songhay people in West Africa over thirty years ago. Studying as an apprentice to a Songhay sorcerer, Stoller learned to appreciate the deeper complexities of things like magic and spirit possession and how these processes worked in the lives of Songhay people. But when he was diagnosed with cancer in 2001, he began to see all that he had learned in a new light. In his book, *Stranger in the Village of the Sick: A Memoir of Cancer, Sorcery, and Healing* (2004), he recounts how Songhay teachings transformed his own dread and fear of living with cancer and at the same time deepened his understanding of Songhay belief and practice. You can read the introduction to the book on the publisher's website at www.beacon.org/client/pdfs/7260_ch1.pdf.

are no longer constrained by the dichotomy of knowledge and belief, we can begin to appreciate the pragmatic ways that all of us engage with the world around us. While some of us may base our actions on the latest scientific studies, the majority of us operate in highly pragmatic ways that may be surprisingly similar to the doctors that Farquhar studied. We confront most problems in our individual and collective lives with partial information, contradictory theories, diverse experience, and a limited but known set of reliable interventions. There are rarely simple answers to the problems we confront, but through trial and error, through experience, reflection, and courage, we manage to arrive at workable, innovative, and sometimes highly effective solutions. As we confront what may feel like unprecedented and troubling times, we hope the lessons of anthropology can, as well, guide us toward building more just and flourishing futures.

NOTES

1. Paul Nadasdy, "How Many Worlds Are There? Ontology, Practice, and Indeterminacy," *American Ethnologist* 48, no. 4 (2021): 357–69; Eduardo Viveiros de Castro, "Cosmological Deixis and Amerindian Perspectivism," *Journal of the Royal Anthropological Institute* 4, no. 3 (1998): 469–88; Philippe Descola, *In the Society of Nature: A Native Ecology in Amazonia* (Cambridge, UK: University of Cambridge Press, 1994 [1986]); Harry West, *Ethnographic Sorcery* (Chicago: University of Chicago Press, 2007).

2. For a much more detailed discussion of Spiritism and the Dr. Fritz phenomenon, see Sidney M. Greenfield, "The Return of Dr. Fritz: Spiritist Healing and Patronage Networks in Urban, Industrial Brazil," *Social Science and Medicine* 24, no. 12 (1987): 1095–107; David Hess, *Samba in the Night: Spiritism in Brazil* (New York: Columbia University Press, 1994); *Spirits and Scientists: Ideology, Spiritism, and Brazilian Culture* (University Park: Pennsylvania State University Press, 1991); and Darrell William Lynch, "Patient Satisfaction with Spiritist Healing in Brazil," MA thesis, University of Tennessee, Knoxville, 1996.

3. *The New English Bible*, 1st ed. (New York: Oxford University Press, 1961).

4. As we mention in the text, many anthropologists and other scholars have taken up the study of snake-handling. See, for example, Thomas Burton, *Serpent-Handling Believers* (Knoxville: University of Tennessee Press, 1993); David Kimbrough, *Taking Up Serpents* (Chapel Hill: University of North Carolina Press, 1994); and Weston LaBarre, *They Shall Take Up Serpents* (Minneapolis: University of Minnesota Press, 1962).

5. Aihwa Ong, *Spirits of Resistance and Capitalist Discipline: Factory Women in Malaysia* (Albany: State University of New York Press, 1987).

6. James L. Peacock, *The Anthropological Lens: Harsh Light, Soft Focus* (Cambridge: Cambridge University Press, 1986), 18.

7. Excerpted from David Hufford, "Traditions of Disbelief," *New York Folklore Quarterly* 8 (1982): 47.

8. Hufford, "Traditions of Disbelief."

9. James G. Frazer, *The Golden Bough: The Roots of Religion and Folklore* (New York: Gramercy Books, 1981 [1890]), 30.

10. E. E. Evans-Pritchard, *Witchcraft, Oracles, and Magic among the Azande* (Oxford: Clarendon Press, 1976 [1937]), 19.

11. Ibid., 30.

12. Ibid., 23.

13. Michael Taussig, "Reification and the Consciousness of the Patient," *Social Science and Medicine* 14B (1980): 3–13.

14. See Greenfield, "The Return of Dr. Fritz"; Hess, *Samba in the Night* and *Spirits and Scientists*; and Lynch, "Patient Satisfaction with Spiritist Healing in Brazil."

15. A thorough survey of this and other themes in the literature on snake-handling can be found in Keith G. Tidball and Chris Toumey, "Serpent Handling in Appalachia and Ritual Theory in Anthropology," in *Signifying Serpents and Mardi Gras Runners: Representation and Identity in Selected Souths*, ed. Celeste Ray and Luke Eric Lassiter (Athens: University of Georgia Press, 2003).

16. See Ong, *Spirits of Resistance and Capitalist Discipline*.

17. Ibid., 47–48.

18. Adapted from Darrell Lynch, personal communication, March 13, 2002.

19. Hufford, "Traditions of Disbelief," 53.

20. John H. Janzen, *The Quest for Therapy: Medical Pluralism in Lower Zaire* (Berkeley: University of California Press, 1978).

21. Arthur Kleinman, *The Illness Narratives: Suffering, Healing, and the Human Condition* (New York: Basic Books, 1988).

22. Victor Turner, *The Forest of Symbols: Aspects of Ndembu Ritual* (Ithaca: Cornell University Press, 1967), 392.

Glossary

affinity: Kin relations engendered by marriage.

agriculture: The cultivation of crops for food, which, as it grows in intensity and scale, often becomes associated with several other subsidiary farming practices, including continuous land use, the use of fertilizers, irrigation, and/or livestock production.

alternate genders: The varied meanings and practices associated with differences in sexuality not easily ascribed to the conventional cultural definitions of "male" and "female" in any particular society, such as that expressed by homosexuals, transsexuals, or third/fourth genders.

ancient states: Clearly defined states that emerged five to six thousand years ago but were not modern nation-states. See also **states**.

Anthropocene: The current geological epoch in which human impacts (such as climate change) are considered a critical part of Earth's evolving systems.

anthropology: The study of human beings in all of their biological and cultural complexities, both past and present. The field is conventionally split into four subfields: biological anthropology, archaeology, linguistic anthropology, and cultural anthropology.

applied anthropology: The application of anthropology to human problems.

archaeology: The subfield of anthropology that deals with the study of material culture.

artifact: An object created by humans.

band: A type of social, political, and economic organization common among foragers who live in small, unsettled mobile groups that is characterized by strong kinship ties, loosely defined leadership roles, and a dependence on reciprocity.

bilateral kinship: A kind of kinship that reckons kin similarly through both male and female links, in which the children produced by a marriage assign relatedness to both parents' families.

binary gender system: Expectations for behavior that include fulfilling opposite or opposing roles in a two-gender (male and female) system.

biological anthropology: The subfield of anthropology that deals with the biological experience of humans.

biological sex: Differences in male and female biology, especially as it relates to biological reproduction.

bride service: The service (such as hunting) of a man to his wife's family after marriage.

bridewealth: A practice in which the husband's kin gives gifts to the wife's kin at marriage.

capitalism: An economic system having its roots in seventeenth- and eighteenth-century Europe and characterized by the production and distribution of goods and services for profit, the means for which are privately owned.

clans: The organization of several lineages into one collective unit.

class: The division of people into groups with differing access to resources.

clines: Gradations in phenotype or in another single characteristic within a species across its geographical range.

cognatic descent: The reckoning of descent more or less informally through both male and female links.

collaborative ethnography: A kind of ethnography that systematically engages consultants in the process of both practicing fieldwork *and* writing ethnography.

communication: In simple terms, the sending and receiving of information through sounds, gestures, and/or other indicators; in anthropological terms, the use of arbitrary symbols (including nonverbal and written signs) to impart meaning. See also **language**.

comparativism: The search for or study of similarities and differences between and among human beings in all of their biological and cultural complexities. See also **holism**.

consanguinity: Kin relations engendered by birth.

consultant: In ethnography, someone who informs and regularly consults on the ethnographer's understanding of a particular community's culture.

core: The so-called First World, the world's wealthiest and most powerful nation-states. See also **periphery** and **semi-periphery.**

cross-cousin marriage: The marriage of a woman or man to her or his "cross-cousin" (i.e., mother's brother's son/daughter or father's sister's son/daughter).

cultural anthropology: The subfield of anthropology that deals specifically with the study of culture in its many different forms, expressions, and practices.

cultural critique: The use of anthropological understandings gained through ethnography to critique the practices of one society or culture. Associated with Margaret Mead.

cultural evolution: The social, political, and economic changes that accompany the shift in human adaptive strategies, such as that illustrated in the shift from foraging to domestication.

cultural relativity: The idea that each society or culture must be understood on its own terms, not those of outsiders. Associated with Franz Boas.

cultural reproduction: The replication of cultural traits that enhance survival.

cultural selection: The influence of culture on biology—in particular, on biological reproduction.

culture: A shared and negotiated system of meaning informed by knowledge that people learn and put into practice by interpreting experience and generating behavior. Interdependent with society.

culture shock: The meeting of two or more systems of meaning in the body and in the psyche, expressed as anxiety, inappropriate behavior, or physical illness.

descent: The assignment of relatedness traced through common ancestry.

descent groups: Groups that claim a common ancestor or ancestors and like lineages can extend in time (past, present, and future) and space (across social, political, or geographical boundaries) and hold power above and beyond any one individual.

domestication: The modification and adaptation of wild plants and animals for use as food, which may take the form of horticulture, pastoralism, or agriculture.

dowry: A practice in which the wife's kin is expected to give the woman's inheritance to the husband's kin at marriage.

enculturation: The process of learning culture.

endogamy: Marriage within a certain group.

Enlightenment: Intellectual movement with roots in seventeenth-century Europe emphasizing reason, freedom of thought, and religious pluralism.

epistemology: The study of knowledge, including its origins, justifications, and limits.

essentialism: In anthropology, the mistaken idea that a particular behavior can reflect the essence of more complex cultural processes.

ethnocentrism: The tendency to view the world, sometimes exclusively, from the basis of one's own experience.

ethnographer: Someone who undertakes ethnography as an approach to studying culture.

ethnography: The study and description of culture, which specifically refers to both (1) a field method of studying culture in its social context; and (2) the approach to writing about culture.

ethnomusicology: The cross-cultural study of music.

ethnoscience: A kind of ethnography that focuses on recording the knowledge of culture as articulated through language.

eugenics: A popular movement that gained momentum in the late nineteenth and early twentieth centuries that, putting social Darwinism into practice, focused on the selective breeding, and elimination, of human populations. The movement climaxed with the end of World War II—although eugenics still has adherents today.

evolution: The process of biological change over time. See also **natural selection**.

evolutionism: See **social evolution**.

exogamy: Marriage outside a certain group.

experimental ethnography: An extension of Clifford Geertz's interpretive anthropology, which emphasized experimentation in translating the complexities of culture through ethnography.

extractive colonialism: One version of colonialism in which the colonial power occupies a territory primarily to extract natural and human resources (labor, land, minerals) to import for the benefit of the empire.

feminist anthropology: The branch of anthropology that first dealt with male bias in anthropology and questions concerning women's subordination but expanded to include the much larger study of gender and its relationship to culture and power.

field notes: The inscription of observations that emerge from direct participation and observation in the process of ethnographic fieldwork.

fieldwork: A research approach that combines participant observation, interviews, and other field methods that, in cultural anthropology, often yields ethnographic texts.

foraging: A kind of human subsistence strategy characterized by the gathering of plants and/or hunting of animals for food.

functionalism: A theory of culture that posits that various human behaviors or practices function to serve basic human needs, especially but not limited to those psychological needs.

fundamentalism: In the study of religion, belief in and adherence to absolute religious tenets and principles, such as the literal interpretation of religious texts.

gender: The wide range of meanings assigned to biological sexed individuals.

gender-based inequality: Unequal access to resources and other cultural assets based on gender.

gender roles: The attitudes, identities, practices, and meanings deemed appropriate to one's specific gender. See also **sexual division of labor.**

genocide: The extermination of one group of people by another.

globalization: A worldwide process of socioeconomic interdependence.

Great Chain of Being: A belief about the order of the natural world as created by the Judeo-Christian God having currency into the eighteenth and nineteenth centuries that posited the Earth was only a few thousand years old, that its fundamental and hierarchical design had always existed as God had created it, and that it had changed little since creation.

historical particularism: An approach to understanding cultural diversity that postulates that each society or culture is the outgrowth of its past. Associated with Franz Boas.

holism: A perspective emphasizing the whole rather than just the parts. See also **comparativism.**

horticulture: A kind of human subsistence strategy characterized by the small-scale, nonindustrial cultivation of plants for food.

human genome: The DNA sequence for human beings.

incest taboo: A rule or rules regulating sex and/or marriage between people considered to be kin.

industrialism: The intensive and large-scale production of manufactured goods having its roots in the industrial revolution, which first emerged in Europe in the eighteenth century with the shift from handcrafted to factory-produced goods.

internal differentiation: The relationship of differences within a system.

interpretive anthropology: Ushered in primarily by Clifford Geertz, this form of symbolic anthropology focused on understanding and studying culture as a form of text, dialogue, and interpretation. See also **experimental ethnography.**

intersectionality: A perspective (drawn from feminist theory) on the dynamics of negotiating many and overlapping social identities at once, including those of race, ethnicity, sex, gender, age, dis/ability, nationality, language, or otherwise.

interviews: In anthropology, the use of fieldwork-based conversation for developing local understandings of cultural practices.

kinship: Networks of relatives based on affinity and consanguinity.

Kula: An extensive network consisting of trading partners scattered throughout several western Pacific islands. Associated with Bronislaw Malinowski, who described the Trobriand trade of arm shells and shell necklaces, each of which moved on this larger trading network in opposite directions.

language: A system of communication, verbal and/or nonverbal, that among humans depends on the cultural assignment of meaning to symbols, the arrangement of which depends on grammatical rules.

levirate: A practice in which a widow marries the brother or another man from the family of her deceased husband.

lineages: Large descent groups that extend in time (past, present, and future) and space (across social, political, or geographical boundaries) and that hold power above and beyond any one individual.

linguistic anthropology: The subfield of anthropology that deals specifically with the study of language and its relationship to culture.

linguistics: See **linguistic anthropology**.

Linnaean hierarchy: The classification of the natural world into kingdoms, phyla, classes, orders, families, genera, and species. Associated with Carolus Linnaeus.

magic: The invocation or manipulation of the supernatural to bear on a desired outcome.

maladaptive practices: Cultural habits or customs that threaten human survival (e.g., pollution).

market exchange: The exchange of goods and services through the use of money.

marriage: In the study of kinship, the broadly diverse, socially sanctioned union of two or more individuals, which, being based largely on the incest taboo, exogamy, and endogamy, widens any given network of kin.

material culture: Materials that human beings purposefully create either as tools to adapt to their environment or as meaningful expressions of their experience.

matrilineal descent: A kind of kinship that reckons descent through female links, in which the children produced by a marriage trace their descent through the mother's side of the family.

matrilocal residence: A marriage practice that establishes residence with the wife's family after marriage; though at times associated with matrilineal societies exclusively, it is often used synonymously with uxorilocal residence.

monotheism: Belief in a single deity.

nation-states: Modern states characterized by a centralized political authority that consolidates power, minimizes dissension through force and other means, maintains rigid geographical and territorial boundaries, and governs a population who embrace expressed socially, politically, and/or economically based principles via a "national identity." The prestate Cahokia, for example, was not a nation-state (e.g., its boundaries were fluid). The United States, however, is a nation-state (e.g., its boundaries are clearly and rigidly defined).

natural selection: The complex process of adaptation to change in the physical environment, which depends, on its most basic level, on reproduction and variability. Associated with Charles Darwin and his original theory of how biological change, or evolution, worked.

neolocal residence: A marriage practice that establishes a separate household from that of a married couple's parents and/or parents' kin.

nonbinary gender: Gender-neutral identification rejecting expectations for behavior that include fulfilling opposite or opposing roles of a two-gender, male-or-female status.

parallel-cousin marriage: The marriage of a woman or man to her or his "parallel-cousin" (i.e., mother's sister's son/daughter or father's brother's son/daughter).

participant observation: An approach to doing fieldwork involving long-term participation and systematic documentation (such as taking field notes and conducting interviews) within a particular society, community, or group. Often it engages four stages: making entrée, culture shock, establishing rapport, and understanding the culture.

pastoralism: A kind of human subsistence strategy characterized by the domestication, control, and breeding of a specific herd of animals.

patriarchal traditions: Kinship or societal structures emphasizing male authority and control.

patrilineal descent: A kind of kinship that reckons descent through male links, in which the children produced by a marriage trace their descent through the father's side of the family.

patrilocal residence: A marriage practice that establishes residence with the husband's family after marriage. Though at times associated with patrilineal societies exclusively, it is often used synonymously with virilocal residence.

periphery: The world's poorest nation-states. See also **core** and **semi-periphery**.

physical anthropology: See **biological anthropology**.

political economy: The large-scale integration and interdependence of political and economic systems, especially as it relates to industrialism, capitalism, and the development of modern nation-states.

polyandry: The marriage of one woman to more than one man.

polygamy: The marriage of one person to two or more spouses at the same time, it takes the form of either polygyny or polyandry.

polygyny: The marriage of one man to more than one woman.

polytheism: Belief in multiple spirits, beings, or gods.

population: In biology, an interbreeding group.

power: The far-reaching process of influence that can be expressed directly or indirectly, implicitly or explicitly.

prestates: A type of social, political, and economic organization characterized by mounting social integration (which is often kinship-based), centralized political leadership, and market exchange. Also called chiefdoms and kingdoms. See also **states**.

public anthropology: Public-facing work of anthropologists meant to address a particular social problem or issue.

race: A powerful social and cultural category that, while having no actual counterpart in human biology, differentiates groups of people based on observable physical characteristics and their presumed relationships to behavioral differences.

reciprocity: The exchange of goods and services between two or more people without the use of money.

redistribution: The flow of resources into a centralized locale and/or political authority, which is in turn reallocated to support the wealth, power, prestige, and/or logistics of that political authority.

reflexivity: In anthropology, the recognition that one's experiences (including personal and cultural dimensions) can influence current anthropological research and its outcomes.

relativity: See **cultural relativity**.

religion: The belief in and engagement with the supernatural.

ritual: In the study of religion, patterned group practice meant to engage the supernatural.

semi-periphery: Nation-states that mediate the flow of economic resources between the world's core and its periphery.

settler colonialism: A form of colonialism in which the colonists come to stay in the colonized territory, displacing the original inhabitants/Indigenous populations through occupation of land; not an event but a process and structure.

sexual division of labor: The division of labor and assignment of specific tasks based on gender. See also **gender roles**

social Darwinism: A form of social evolution popular in the late nineteenth and early twentieth centuries, surmised from Charles Darwin's theory of natural selection, which posited that first, "inferior" groups of people remained inferior because of their biological differences, or, more simply, because of their race, and second, that "favored races" would inevitably supplant the unfavorable ones through the process of "survival of the fittest." Associated with Herbert Spencer. See also **eugenics**.

social evolution: A theory of cultural change popular in nineteenth-century anthropology that posited that all human societies passed through a progressive sequence of development from savages to barbarians and, finally, to civilization. Also called evolutionism or unilineal evolution.

society: A group of interacting individuals, which, among humans, is interdependent with culture.

sociocultural anthropology: See **cultural anthropology**.

sororate: A practice in which a widower marries the sister or another woman from the family of his deceased wife.

states: A type of social, political, and economic organization characterized by large-scale social integration (which may or may not be kinship-based); centralized, hierarchical, and bureaucratized political systems; and market exchange.

symbolic anthropology: The ethnographic study of symbolic forms and their negotiation within and between human groups.

taxonomy: In biology, the classification of the natural world. See **Linnaean hierarchy**.

third gender: A status and role that often emerges in binary gender systems where individuals who do not meet the expectations for male or female behavior inhabit another, or "third" (or "fourth") gender identity.

tribe: A type of social, political, and economic organization whereby different settled or nomadic communities are united through descent groups or common organizations (like warrior or religious societies).

unilineal descent: A kind of kinship that reckons descent through either male or female links, in which the children produced by a marriage trace their descent through either the father's or the mother's side of the family. See also **matrilineal descent** and **patrilineal descent**.

unilineal evolution: See **social evolution**.

uxorilocal residence: A marriage practice that establishes residence with the wife's family after marriage (often used synonymously with matrilocal residence).

virilocal residence: A marriage practice that establishes residence with the husband's family after marriage (often used synonymously with patrilocal residence).

woman marriage: The practice in many historic and some contemporary African societies in which women enter into nonsexual marriages with other women, whereby one woman is socially recognized as male (i.e., as a "female husband") and thus could, for example, pass property from "father" to son.

world system: The global integration of the world's people into a single economic system based on capitalism. Associated with Immanuel Wallerstein, who argued that the world's political economy is split into a core, periphery, and semi-periphery.

Index